Happy Trails

A DICTIONARY OF WESTERN EXPRESSIONS

Robert Hendrickson

Volume II:
Facts On File
Dictionary of
American Regionalisms

 Facts On File®

AN INFOBASE HOLDINGS COMPANY

Happy Trails: A Dictionary of Western Expressions

Copyright © 1994   by Robert Hendrickson

Facts On File, Inc.
460 Park Avenue South
New York NY 10016
USA

Library of Congress Cataloging-in-Publication Data
Hendrickson, Robert, 1933–
    Happy trails : a dictionary of western expressions / Robert Hendrickson.
        p.   cm.—(Facts on File dictionary of American regionalisms ; v. 2)
        ISBN 0-8160-2112-0
1. English language—Dialects—West (U.S.)—Dictionaries.   2. West (U.S.)—Social life and customs—Dictionaries.   3. Americanisms—West (U.S.)—Dictionaries.   4. Figures of speech—Dictionaries.   I. Title.   II. Series: Facts on File dictionary of American regional expressions ; v. 2.
    PE2970.W4H46   1994   93-42888
    427'.978—dc20

Facts On File books are available at special discounts when purchased in bulk quantities for businesses, associations, institutions or sales promotions. Please call our Special Sales Department in New York at 212/683-2244 or 800/322-8755.

Text and Jacket design by Catherine Hyman
Printed in the United States of America

VC MP 10 9 8 7 6 5 4 3 2 1

This book is printed on acid-free paper.

For my grandson Adam.

"Who are you indeed who would talk or sing to America?
Have you studied out the land, its idioms and men?

—Walt Whitman, "By Blue Ontario's Shore"

Acknowledgments _____

It would be impossible to make a complete dictionary of any language; as Walt Whitman wrote, "Every existence has its idiom, every thing has an idiom and tongue." So a writer does his best, in this case he tries for a good representative selection. Many others, some far better scholars, have helped me in this endeavor, especially the numerous people who have over the years generously supplied me with words, phrases and stories recorded in these pages. These include, besides the numerous sources noted in the book, Karen Kafeiti, Lauren Walsh, Bill Fenton, Charlie Jay, wherever you are, and, going back 10 years or so, Heidi Rosenbaum. My heartfelt thanks to all of you. I should also thank for their friendly cooperation the many people with whom I talked in my travels through the Western states, especially Bob and Becky Hendrickson, whose Western hospitality I enjoyed when I stayed at their Austin, Texas home. Special thanks are in order too for my editor, Texas-born Susan Schwartz, who suggested the happy title for this book, and for my copy editor, Texan Joan Atwood, who not only coped with a handwriting dreaded by copy editors the country over but whose important contributions to the book were substantial. Most important to me, of course, has been my wife, Marilyn, whose constant help over the years deserves a perfect poem, not a mere mention in an acknowledgment.

Introduction _____

Ⅰn *Roughing It* (1872), Mark Twain wrote, ". . . all the peoples of the earth had representative adventurers in the Silverland, and as each adventurer had brought the slang of his nation or locality with him, the combinations made the slang of Nevada the richest and the most infinitely varied and copious that had ever existed anywhere in the world, perhaps, except in the mines of California in the 'early days.' "

Twain might have substituted "West" for "Nevada" or "California," as he did indeed elsewhere in *Roughing It,* when he spoke of "the vigorous new vernacular of the occidental plains and mountains." For of all American regional talk, the Western idiom is certainly the youngest and most lively, dating back (apart from some Spanish terms) only a little over a century, by most expert estimates, and only 150 years or so, according to other historians. And thanks to dime novels, border tales and excellent Western novels and movies, not to mention "spaghetti Westerns" and television series, I would guess that it is the "foreign" regional vernacular best known by Americans from other regions (more so even than Southern speech), that is, the idiom Americans are most familiar with aside from their own. After all, only in this century have the star athlete and entertainer come to equal the cowboy as the ideal hero in the popular imagination, where the brave lone ranger still ranks high.

Happy Trails represents a lone writer's attempt over many years to corral a good representative selection of Western speech from earliest to recent times, using the numerous sources from which this river of regionalisms was and is fed. My aim is an entertaining book for the general reader, a "reader's book" full of stories and interesting fact and fable about the West and its lingo, yet as accurate as possible and perhaps making a few scholarly contributions as well. Most of these 3,500 or so expressions, ranging from *airin' the lungs* to *yippie ki yi yay,* are still used, some have certainly become widely known throughout the United States and the world, while others are now mainly historical terms, no less interesting and all still "living" at least in the sense that they are frequently used in Western story, song and film. The book necessarily *swings a wide loop,* including fascinating expressions coined or inspired by explorers, mountain men, cowboys, cowgirls, ranchers, miners, loggers, lawmen, badmen, politicians, sheep herders, farmers, the oil rich and dirt poor and even dudes who came West, among many other groups. American Indian, Spanish, Mexican, French, German,

Chinese, Japanese, Scandinavian and African-American language gifts are treated, some more extensively than others, as are the contributions of religious groups like the Mormons. Regarding Spanish loans alone, Edna Ferber wrote in *Giant* (1952): ". . . you can't talk to anyone . . . in Texas five minutes without using words borrowed from the Spanish . . . How about *Reata. Retana. Remuda. Corral. Ranch. Stampede. Mesa. Canyon. Rodeo. Sombrero. Pinto. Bronco.* Thousands of words." (Four more that immediately come to mind are *bandanna, buckaroo, chaps* and *lariat;* this book records hundreds.)

In the words of Mark Twain again, *Happy Trails* is "a record of several years of variegated vagabondage" in the Western states, not to mention a lifetime of reading. Among the thousand-plus books used, hundreds of which are noted in these pages, I have consulted ground-breaking scholarly works such as J. Frank Dobie's and Ramon Adams'; Andy Adams' *The Log of a Cowboy;* John Russell Bartlett's *Dictionary of Americanisms;* Mitford M. Mathews' *The American Dialect Dictionary* and *A Dictionary of Americanisms on Historical Principles;* John Farmer's *Americanisms;* H. L. Mencken's *The American Language; The Oxford English Dictionary;* Webster's *Third New International Dictionary; The Random House Dictionary of the English Language;* newspapers and magazines, such as *Dialect Notes* and *American Speech;* and the behemoth *Dictionary of American Regional English* edited by Frederic Cassidy (two volumes of an estimated six published so far). Western correspondents have also kindly supplied material, and I have not ignored Western movies and television dramas, either. But the bulk of the material is from the hundreds of diaries, biographies, histories, essays, poems, songs, short stories and novels consulted, many of which are cited here.

Western fiction alone has been a great pleasure to read. These works are not by any means all "Westerns"; many are stories set in the West, ranging from the works of classic American authors such as Mark Twain, Bret Harte, Stephen Crane, Willa Cather and John Steinbeck to those of modern-day masters like Walter Van Tilburg Clark, A. B. Guthrie, Jr., Wallace Stegner, Cormac McCarthy, Thomas McGuane and Larry McMurtry. But the genre "Western" has proved an invaluable source. Authors of these tales—including geniuses of the genre Zane Grey, Luke Short, Max Brand and Louis L'Amour—have been extraordinarily prolific and often recorded Western speech with keen ears. The amazing Max Brand (one of the pen names of Frederick Faust), who created Dr. Kildare and Destry of *Destry Rides Again,* himself wrote some *30 million* words over a 20-year career, the equivalent of about 530 books—he clearly could write faster than any Billy the Kid could draw! Some of these Westerns are better than others, but all at the very least have their redeeming features. For the reader's information, and pleasure, below is a list of the books selected by the Western Writers of America as the 25 best Western novels ever written, all of which have proved invaluable:

The Virginian by Owen Wister
The Ox-Bow Incident by Walter Van Tilburg Clark
Shane by Jack Schaefer
The Big Sky by A. B. Guthrie Jr.
The Searchers by Alan LeMay
Riders of the Purple Sage by Zane Grey
Paso por Aqui by Eugene M. Rhodes
Bugles in the Afternoon by Ernest Haycox
The Long Rifle by Stewart E. White
Vengeance Valley by Luke Short
The Hell Bent Kid by Charles O. Locke
Cheyenne Autumn by Mari Sandoz

Destry Rides Again by Max Brand
Hondo by Louis L'Amour
The Sea of Grass by Conrad Richter
Ride the Man Down by Luke Short
The Day the Cowboys Quit by Elmer Kelton
Stay Away, Joe by Dan Cushman
The Time It Never Rained by Elmer Kelton
True Grit by Charles Portis
Monte Walsh by Jack Schaefer
Flint by Louis L'Amour
From Where the Sun Now Stands by Will Henry
Hombre by Elmore Leonard
The Wonderful Country by Tom Lea

To this distinguished list, I would certainly add, among others, Willa Cather's *Death Comes for the Archbishop*, John Steinbeck's *The Red Pony* and *Of Mice and Men*, Cormac McCarthy's *Blood Meridian* and *All the Pretty Horses*, Edna Ferber's *Giant* and Larry McMurtry's *Lonesome Dove*. Mention should also be made of wonderful films like *Stagecoach, The Covered Wagon, Red River, Cheyenne Autumn, The Searchers, Shane, The Ox-Bow Incident, Cimarron, The Alamo, Giant, McCabe and Mrs. Miller, A Man Called Horse, Monte Walsh* and *The Unforgiven*. The Western is hardly the impoverished form some critics make it out to be, and I count Cormac McCarthy among the two or three best American novelists writing today.

Though this is possibly the most varied and among the largest collections of Western expressions, I doubt that anyone could possibly put together a *complete* dictionary of Westernisms, even if one lived a lifetime in the West working everything from cows and sheep to dude ranches, read everyone from Black Bart, the PO-8 to Molly Ivins and watched every fine film and spaghetti Western as well. For Western speech is constantly changing, migration to the area continuing at the highest rate in the country even though the unfenced life of the West is finished. Even cowboy lingo continues to grow. Said cowboy poet, or "poet lariat," Paul Zarzski at the 1993 Cowboy Poetry Gathering in Elko, Nevada: "Cowboys have always used this wonderful fresh language, and they'll make up a word when they need one. A guy'll tell you something like, 'There's a high-class buck out there jumpin' garden hoses.' These people are surrounded by this language and powerful physical experiences [that inspire new language]."

Many distinctive Western expressions are used throughout the West, including terms like *canyon, corral, bull-snake, civit cat* (for a skunk), *mush* (for cooked cereal), *catch colt* (for an illegitimate child), *lug* (for a fruit crate), *jerky, sourdough* and *raising Cain.* But there are numerous differences. The West can be divided into three main speech regions: the Southwest, the Northwest and the Central West. These, in turn, are further divided by experts who *know their cans* into many subregions, including the California Southwest, West Texas, Central Texas, South Texas, Utah West, Colorado West and Northern California. Each of these regions and subregions has its own peculiar words but shares the use of many expressions with other Western regions as well. In the Northwest, for example, including the states of Washington, northern Idaho and northern Oregon, what is generally called the ring-necked pheasant is called the *Chinese pheasant,* and the Scandinavian-derived word *snoose* is used for snuff or a snuff user. In the Southwest, because of its proximity to Mexico, Spanish words like *taco, enchilada* and *frijole* were widely used long before these dishes became popular in other areas of the West and the United States as a whole. Here were born to American talk the Spanish-derived terms to which Edna Ferber referred, quoted above.

Texas, a part of the Southwest, serves as a good example of a Western subregion and contains three subregions itself: West Texas, South Texas (sometimes called East Texas) and Central Texas. Central Texas is noted for the use of such words as *smearcase* for cottage cheese (the term brought there by the many German settlers in the area), the use of *grass sack* for burlap bag and the use of *tool house* for tool shed, among other differences.

West Texas speech, featuring the Western drawl, is, like other Southwestern and Far Western speech, more strongly influenced by General American dialect. The West Texas drawl extends the slight *uh* glide of General American speech (where *uh* is added before *l* and *r* in a stressed syllable, as in *shOO-UHr,* sure) to many more sounds. *School,* for example, is *skool* in the Middle West but pronounced *SkOOuuhl* in the Western drawl. This same *uh* drawl is added after, among other letters, *a, ow,* and *eh,* examples being *Auhlbert* (Albert), *fowahl* (fowl), and *Elauhlmer* (Elmer). The Western drawl of West Texas is more restrained and not so musical as the more Southern drawl of South Texas. While it is an unhurried speech, the Western drawl doesn't suggest "relaxed laziness;" it suggests cogitation, or weighing one's words, rather than mere indolence. Many ranching terms enrich this dialect, and one hears colorful remarks like "It's such a fur piece you've got to ride a pregnant mare to get back" and "If you ain't the lead horse the scenery never changes."

Technically, the dialect of South Texas is of both the twangy lilting South Midland variety of Northeast Texas and the Southern plantation variety heard in Southeast Texas. Of course these two dialects and that of West Texas mingle throughout the state, but the South Texas dialect is more influenced by Southern and Mountain speech and to a much smaller extent by General American. Nowhere in the United States is there a more effortless speech, one more relaxed in delivery. South Texian is distinctly nasalized with a slow tempo and is intoned almost monotonously. Its vowels are held long, and the first syllables of words are often accented, especially in short words. Speakers are apt to speak rather too loud, for aliens, throughout the great breadth of the Lone Star State.

"There is something good and something bad of every land" in Texas, as an old saying puts it, for the state was settled by immigrants from many lands, including Mexicans, Germans, Czechs, and Northerners, as well as people from the Southern states; recently there has been a massive invasion of Yankees. Spanish ways and words are common in a state founded by Spaniards; even something as basic as the famous *10-gallon hat* that Texas cowboys wore in days past has its roots in the Spanish word for braid, *galón*—because the wide-brimmed hats worn by cowboys were originally decorated with a number of braids at the base of the crown. The nearest thing in Texas today to a 10-gallon hat is called a *Stetson,* every red-blooded male Texan owning at least one of these. This basic Texan hat shows Yankee influence. The *Stetson* was invented by Philadelphian John Batterson Stetson, who had to travel west because of poor health at the time of the Civil War. While out West it occurred to this dude that no one was manufacturing hats suited to the cowboy, and on his return to Philadelphia in 1865, he went into the hat business, specializing in Western-style headgear. The wide-brimmed, 10-gallon felt hats he manufactured immediately became popular with cowboys. They have been called *Stetsons* or *John B.'s* ever since, and the John B. Stetson Company remains today one of the world's largest hat manufacturers.

In more recent times Spanglish, a lively combination of Spanish and English, has become so prominent a way of speech throughout Texas that it is also known as *Tex-Mex* and *Texican.* From one end of the state to the other there are so many slight variations in ways of speaking that Texans can't even agree on the pronunciation of *Texas*—the leading contenders are *Tex-siz* and *Tex-sis,* with the Yankee *Tex-shus* a distant third. Dyed-in-the-wool Texans hold stubbornly to their pronunciations, too. A visiting Britisher told one rancher: "The Hereford bull, who comes originally from my own part of the world, does not pronounce himself Hearford, as you seem to suppose, but Herreford." "Is that right?" the rancher replied. "Wal, he pronounces himself Hearford on my ranch."

Hospitable Texans *do* still say *Y'all all come!* Stetson tipped over his eyes, the typical Texan will say things like *Kin ah carry you home?* for "Can I give you a ride (or lift)?"; *Ah need to visit with you,* when he means he wants to chat with you on the phone; and *Kin ah hep you* for "Can I help you?" One woman who worked for Air France in *Dallas* and was taught to say *France* like a Frenchwoman habitually answered the phone, "Air Frawnce, kin ah hep you?"

Texans particularly like to pronounce the *en* sound their own way. They don't cotton to it being pronounced *en*, so when they talk about the *awl bidness* they might mention the *innerjy crunch* or the *free interprise system*. By the same system *ten* becomes *tin*, *Twenty* is *twinny*, *cent* is *cint*, *went* is *wint*, *friendship* becomes *frinship*, *tennis* becomes *tinnis*, *temperatures* are *timperatures*, *entertainment* is *innertainment*, *Wednesday* is *Winsday* and—to put an *indin* to this—Kennedy Airport is *Kinnidy Airport*.

The rule in Texas is to say *heidi* (howdy) to anyone who says *heidi* to you. *Thank you* is pronounced *thang cue*. Other *wards* with pronunciation unique to the *airs* (ears) of most *Markins* (Americans) include *hem* for *him*, *blond* for *blind*, *aint* for *aunt*, *main* for *mean*, *day-ins* for *dance*, *rum* for *room*, *drouth* for *drought*, *suede* for *sweet*, *bob wahr* for *barbed wire*, *prod* for *proud* and *small* for *smile*. The *Lard* only knows how many more such specimens there are from Hico (pronounced *Hy-co*) to Houston.

Many common words with the *ay* vowel sound are pronounced with *eh* in Texian, including *nehkid* (naked) and *eht* (ate). The *aw* sound is heard in words like *dawg* (dog) and *cawst* (cost); the long *i* is generally pronounced as *ah,* as in *fahuh* (fire) and *hahuh* (hire); and many Texans pronounce the *oo* sound as *oh,* as in *poh* (poor) and *shoh* (sure). Among consonant changes from General American, the *d* is often dropped after *n,* as in *wonner* (wonder); the participal *ing* is generally pronounced *in,* as in *sittin* (sitting); and the *n* is often dropped completely, as in *kawfuhdis* (confidence), being replaced with a distinctly nasalized *aw,* which one speech teacher calls among "the main reasons for the extreme nasality in Texas speech."

The Southern *yawl* of *you-all* is almost as popular in Texian as in Southern speech. *All,* in fact, is also used after the interrogative pronoun *what* ("What-all did you do yesterday?") and *who* ("Who-all is coming?"). *Is all,* a short form of *that's all,* is commonly added to the end of sentences, as in "He just wants some meat, is all." Sometimes unheard questions are replied to in Texian with *Says which?,* a practice similar to the African-American English *Say what?* Other typical Texian usages are indicated in these sentences:

■ She's the hell-raisin'est woman I know.
■ I'm about to rustle up some grub (prepare some food or a meal).
■ I reckon he's went (gone) to El Paso.
■ He bought some blinky (sour) milk.
■ I might would (I may) do it.
■ She put a big pot in a little one (outdid herself entertaining).
■ He done went there.
■ Did you seed (see) that?

- She give him the gate (divorced him).
- I'll wait on (wait for) you.
- He wouldn't go 'thout (contraction of *without* used in place of "unless") they took the train.
- Don't pay him no nevermind (attention).
- She's about to law (sue) him.
- Ain't nary a one (nobody) coming.
- I might could do that.

Sadly, a lot of Texans feel as embarrassed about their dialect as New Yorkers do about Brooklynese. An article by *New York Times* Houston bureau chief Robert Reinhold, to which I owe several of these examples of Texian, reports Fred Tarpley, a language and literature professor at East Texas State University, as saying, "Unfortunately, Texans have a great inferiority complex about their language [though] this is an honorable dialect that we speak for historical reasons; I feel we need to extend the Texas pride to speech." As British travel writer Jan Morris has noted, "One feels the pull of metropolitan life in Texas, as one does all over the horizon." While the rural areas are fighting a strong holding action, the big *innernational cities* in Texas are increasingly becoming merely international, losing a lot of their Texian flavor. Observers have reported that Houstonians in particular, a breed of archetypal doers, are beginning to sound like everybody else, in both pronunciation and vocabulary, even eliminating such historic Texas redundancies as *cashmoney*. Few people shout *Yahoo!* in the Big H anymore, but elsewhere in the land where seldom is heard a discouraging word, there are still nice euphemisms, like *winter Texans* for senior citizens wintering in the state, places with names like *The Crazy Woman Hotel* at Mineral Wells, statues like the one to the cow called Moola at Stephenville and local football teams with names like the *Itasca Wampus Cats,* the *Mesquite Skeeters* and the *Hutto Hippos.* Far from the great city's rattle, the rural rearguard and others proud of their heritage are holding the Alamo, and it will be a long time before they surrender, if ever.

One could go on at great length about expressions and quirks peculiar to other regions of the West, often only *two whoops and a holler* away from Texas. In the Rocky Mountain area, for example, we find *battens* used for clapboard shingling, a *bar pit* means a ditch alongside a road, and a newly weaned calf is a *weaner.* In Northern California, natives almost exclusively among Westerners use the old term *chesterfield* for a sofa, *rustic siding* for clapboard and *coast* as a synonym for beach ("Let's go to the coast today"). Suffice it to say that much of what has been rounded up from Texas for an example here could *sure as shootin'* be said about other Western regions and the West as a whole, from the use of the ubiquitous drawl to the changes taking place through modern-day migration. Allowing for some change, it seems certain that Western speech similar to that which we have known for over a century will be with us for a long time to come, if only because of the memorable expressions, often *wild, wooly and full of fleas,* the dialect has contributed to and continues to contribute to the language. And that, being what *Happy Trails* is all about, seems as good a place as any to end this lengthy introduction. As old cowboys once said, and no doubt still say, I reckon it's time to *mosey on, vamoose, light a rag, drag it, hit the grit, get out of here like a kerosened cat* and *ride that beast with the bellyfull of bedsprings—it's time to whistle up the dogs and piss on the fire and get down to the main bidness. Hope you'll side me, pardners, browsing along till the last dog is hung.*

R. H.
Peconic, New York

A

a Perhaps only UGH! has been deemed by dime novels and Hollywood to be more representative of American Indian speech than the omission of *a* as an article. Willa Cather made an interesting observation on this American Indian habit (and there is no telling how widespread the habit really was) in *Death Comes for the Archbishop* (1927): " 'Have you a son?' 'One. Baby. Not very long born.' Jacinto usually dropped the article in speaking Spanish, just as he did in speaking English, though the Bishop had noticed that when he did give a noun its article, he used the right one. The customary omission, therefore, seemed a matter of taste, not ignorance. In the Indian conception of language, such attachments were superfluous and unpleasing, perhaps."

Abert's towhee A Southwestern desert bird named for soldier-naturalist Lt. J. W. Abert (1820–87), who has several other Southwestern birds and animals, including *Abert's squirrel,* named after him.

abogado The Spanish word for lawyer; still used in the Southwest and recorded there as early as 1803. "Why did you send for the abogado Poindexter when my brother called?" [Bret Harte, *On The Frontier,* 1884]

above his (her) bend Above his or her ability. "Shooting like that's above his bend."

above snakes Tall; distant from the ground. "He's a lean, rangy cowpoke, about six and a half feet above snakes."

abra A narrow mountain pass; from the Spanish *abra* meaning the same.

acequia The Spanish word for a wide irrigation ditch; used mainly in the Southwest and first recorded there in 1844.

aces and eights See DEADMAN'S HAND.

acid test This expression dates back to Western frontier days, when peddlers determined the gold content of objects by scratching them and applying nitric acid. Since gold, which is chemically inactive, resists acids that corrode other metals, the (nitric) acid test distinguished it from copper, iron, or similar substances someone might be trying to palm off on the peddlers. People were so dishonest, or peddlers so paranoid, that the term quickly became part of the language, coming to mean a severe test of reliability, and is now used throughout the United States.

1

Acoma An Indian tribe of New Mexico and Arizona, the name meaning "people of the white rock" in their language, in reference to the pueblos in which they lived. Acoma is also the name of a central New Mexico pueblo that has been called "the oldest continuously inhabited city in the United States." The name is pronounced either *eh-ko-ma* or *ah-ko-ma*.

acorn calf A runt or weak calf; sometimes used to describe a physically weak person. It was once believed that cows that ate too many acorns gave birth to such calves.

adder's tongue A Western name for the wildflower better known as the dogtooth violet *(Erytheronium americanum)*, probably because the plant's first leaf, which points pushing up from the ground in early spring, suggested a snake tongue to some settlers.

adios Introduced in the Southwest in about 1830, this Spanish word meaning goodbye (literally, "to God") is now widely used throughout the country. In Texas it can also mean get going, vamoose: "You better adios before the law comes."

admirable bolete A colorful, edible mushroom *(Boletus mirabilis)* of Rocky Mountain forests and the Pacific Northwest.

admiring A term used in Texas for casting an evil eye on someone. "Her admiring of his arm made him break it."

adobada sauce A sauce for meats. "He sat at the table and she [a Mexican woman] made a plate for him of roast mutton with adobada sauce . . ." [Cormac McCarthy, *All the Pretty Horses*, 1992]

adobe (1) A house made of *adobe*, the Spanish for sun-dried clay or mud bricks; the term is first recorded in the Southwest in 1759. (2) Things of Mexican origin, as in the slang expression *adobe dollar*, a Mexican peso. (3) Military personnel. See also DOUGHBOY.

adobe-maker A derogatory slang term in the Southwest for a person of Mexican descent.

afoot Someone walking, someone without a horse. "A man afoot is no man at all," instructs an old Western saying.

agarita A Spanish word sometimes used in Texas for the barberry *(Berberis trifoliata)*; excellent jellies and wines are made from the barberry's red, acid berries. Also called the *agrillo* and the *agrito*.

agave Any of several Southwestern plants with tough, spiny sword-shaped leaves. Named for Agave, daughter of the legendary Cadmus, who introduced the Greek alphabet, the large *Agave* genus includes the remarkable century plant *(Agave americana)*, which blooms once and dies (though anytime after fifteen years, not after one hundred years, as was once believed). Introduced to Europe from America in the 16th century, this big agave is often used there for fences. It is regarded as a religious charm by pilgrims to Mecca, who hang a leaf of it over their doors to ward off evil spirits and indicate that they have made a pilgrimage.

agricultural ant The Western harvester ant *(Pogonomyrmex barbatus)* and several related species, because they were once believed to plant, cultivate and harvest food; they do eat seeds, clearing the area around their nests and storing the seeds there.

agrillo See AGARITA.

agrito See AGARITA.

aguardiente This Spanish word for a strong alcoholic drink has long been used in the Southwest for any potent liquor. *Aguardiente* translates literally as "fiery or burning water"; the many minor variations on the word include *argadent* and *aguadiente*. A major variation is *Taos lightning*.

ah A pronunciation of *I,* as in, "Ah speak Ainglish."

ahorseback On a horse. " 'Besides,' she heard him say. 'I looked around [for tracks] when I first came. Nobody has been out of here ahorseback since the rain.' " [Louis L'Amour, *Hondo,* 1953]

aim Intend. " 'Aimin' to make quite a stay in Osage?' " [Edna Ferber, *Cimarron,* 1930]

ain't on it An old term meaning to decline an offer. "I ain't on it—I don't like the idea one bit."

ain't that a dinger Isn't that something great. "Now, by God, ain't that a dinger. In a way I was already a foreman. Life sure enough looked good." [Max Evans, *The Great Wedding,* 1963]

airin' the lungs Cursing. "Ain't much of a shame, a man airin' his lungs once in a while."

air the paunch (belly) To vomit. "He drank a lot too much and aired his paunch." It can also mean "to boast."

airtights Sealed, airtight cans of food. "The old cowboys ate a lot out of airtights." See also KNOW ONE'S CANS.

ajo The Spanish word for garlic but often incorrectly applied to the white desert lily *(Hesperocallis undulata)* in Western desert regions.

à la Comanche To ride a horse by hanging onto one side, as the Comanches used to do to protect themselves in battle while they fired arrows from under the horse's neck, as has been depicted in scores of Western movies.

alameda A road or promenade lined with trees, especially poplar trees (also known as alamo trees) on each side; the word is an American borrowing in the Southwest of a Spanish word meaning the same.

alamo (1) The name of several poplar trees, including the cottonwood; from the Spanish *alamo* meaning the same. (2) A Franciscan mission in San Antonio, Texas besieged by 6,000 Mexican troops in 1836 during the Texan war for independence. The siege lasted 13 days and ended with all 187 of the men defending the Alamo being killed—but only after they had inflicted casualties of over 1,500 on the Mexican army. "Remember the Alamo!" became the Texan battle cry of the war. (3) The most recent use of the Alamo's name is San Antonio's *Alamodome* sports stadium constructed in 1992 at a cost of $130 million.

albondigas A type of meatball or meatball soup of Spanish origin often served in the Southwest.

albur A card game of Spanish origin played in the Southwest.

alcalde A Spanish word for a local official such as a mayor or judge that was often used in the early Southwest and is recorded as early as 1803; it was also applied to early justices of the peace in the area and to any important or influential person.

alegria A synonym for the amaranth *(Amaranthus paniculatus)*, the bright-red leaf juice that Mexican women used as a cosmetic in the early Southwest.

alforja Spanish for a leather or canvas saddlebag, the word once frequently used by cowboys in the Southwest and often corrupted into

such pronunciations as *alforkas* and *alfarkys*.

alfresco Now widely used in the United States, *alfresco,* meaning outdoors (as in "We dined alfresco"), was originally confined in use to the West. It is first recorded in 1853 as a borrowing of the Spanish *al fresco* meaning the same.

algaroba The mesquite *(Prosopis glandulosa);* this Spanish name is often used in the Southwest for the mesquite but is actually a misnomer, for the conquistadores named the mesquite *algaroba* thinking it was related to their carob tree *(algaroba),* which it is not.

alibi out of To make a spurious excuse, to shift the blame. "He alibied out of it, but no one believed a word he said."

alight (light) and look at your saddle An invitation to a rider to get off his horse and visit a while and come inside for a drink or a meal. "It's a hot day. Light and look at your saddle, pardner."

alkali (1) A word used in the West to indicate a poor soil unsuited for farmland because of the soil's high percentage of soluble salts. (2) The Western alkali plains themselves. (3) A person, such as a prospector, who lived on the alkali plains. The word alkali itself is Arabic in origin. Arab chemists in medieval times extracted sodium carbonate from the marine saltwort plant, calling the substance *al-galiy* (ashes of salt wort). Later chemists applied the term *alkali,* a transliteration of the Arab word, to all salts with properties similar to sodium carbonate. "Sunrise found the white stage lurching eternally on across the alkali, a driver and bottle on the box, and a pale girl staring out at the plain, and knotting in her handkerchief some utterly dead flower." [Owen Wister, *The Virginian,* 1902] See also ALKALIED.

alkali dust Dust of the alkaline deserts of the Southwest. ". . . his coal-black eyebrows and mustache white with alkali dust . . ." [Conrad Richter, *The Sea of Grass,* 1936]

alkalied (1) Poisoned by alkaline water. Cowboys believed that cattle so poisoned could be cured by feeding them a plug of tobacco wrapped in slices of bacon; cuts caused by alkali dust were said to be healed by applying canned tomatoes, which are acidic. It is now known, however, that toxic alcohol found in certain plains plants cause so-called "alkali poisoning." (2) Someone seasoned in the ways of the West, an old hand, a veteran, especially a veteran of what was called "the big dry country," the alkali plains.

alkali grass A perennial salt grass of the *Distichlis* species growing in the alkaline soils of the West.

all Often used in Western speech after "who" and "what," as in "What all did you do yesterday?"

all bally-which-way Twisted in every direction, highly confused. " 'I

got to warn you about that country, boy . . . Just when you think you know it, somehow it's twisted all bally-which-way.' " [Louis L'Amour, *The Haunted Mesa,* 1987]

all his bullet holes is in the front of him He's brave, not a coward. " 'He led us into an ambush. But I ain't ashamed of him, nohow. All his bullet holes is in the front of him.' " [Louis L'Amour, *Hondo,* 1953]

all horns and rattles Having a terrible temper, always ready to strike out like a rattlesnake or bull.

alligator (1) A name used in the plains region of western Texas for the large tiger salamander. (2) A sled used in logging.

alligator juniper A native Southwestern tree (*Juniperus deppeana)* with bark similar to an alligator's skin.

alligator weed An aquatic plant (*Alternanthera philozeroidas)* that clogs waterways in coastal Texas and other areas.

all I know is what I read in the papers This saying has become a popular American expression since Oklahoman Will Rogers used it in his 1927 *The Letters of a Self-Made Diplomat to His President.* It has various shades of meaning but is commonly used to mean "I'm not an expert, I'm just an ordinary person and what I've told you is true to the best of my knowledge." It implies one may be wrong because one's sources are nothing exceptional.

all leather An old Western term, not heard much anymore, for someone very genuine and reliable. "He's sure been all leather all his days."

all man A man of superior strength, skill, endurance. "You've got to be all man to hold down a ranch that big."

all oak and iron-bound In the best of condition, of high quality; perhaps like a well-made oak cask. "I'm feeling all oak and iron-bound."

allocochick Though they spoke several different languages, northern California Indians in the 19th century all gave the name *allocochick* to their shell money, called *wampum* by Eastern tribes.

alpine A term attached to many plants found in the Rocky Mountain area, including the *alpine fir, alpine hemlock* and *alpine columbine,* Colorado's state flower.

all-spine A multi-branched, leafless, thorny plant *(Koeberlinia spinosa)* of the Southwest, also called *all-thorn* and *crucifixion thorn* because Christ's crown is said to have been made from it.

all-thorn See ALL-SPINE.

all wool and no shoddy Something or someone genuine, trustworthy, pure; *shoddy* was a cheap material manufactured during the Civil War.

amargosa A Spanish name common in Texas for the goat bush *(Castala erecta); amargosa* is Spanish meaning "bitter," in reference here to the bush's bitter-tasting bark, which is used for making certain medicines.

ambulance A synonym for a prairie wagon; also called a dougherty wagon. "At Birkenshaw's an ambulance met us, and off got a respectable person who shook hands . . ." [Owen Wister, *Out West,* 1893]

American A term Westerners used for a horse bred in the East and brought West by emigrants, as opposed to the smaller and inferior horses found in the region. "He rode an American horse while I had to be content with a Spanish pony." The term was also applied to Eastern-bred cows.

amigo Friend, from the Spanish word meaning the same, often heard in the Southwest; *por amigo* means "for friendship." "*Por amigo,* I tell you how to get it. Dig here and you will find a burro load of gold money." [J. Frank Dobie, *Coronado's Children,* 1930]

amole A Spanish word used for any of several Western wildflowers, especially the soap plant and soap weed, whose roots are used to make a soap substitute.

anaqua The sugarberry *(Ehretia anacua),* an evergreen tree with edible fruit. The Spanish word *anaqua* has yielded American pronunciations like *knockaway* that have also become Western names for the tree.

ándale A Mexican term used in the Southwest for hurry up, get going, get a move on it, pronto. "Come on, man, ándale, ándale!"

Angeleno Anyone residing in Los Angeles, California; this Spanish term dates back to the mid-19th century.

angels (angelenos) on horseback A dish of oysters wrapped with bacon, broiled and served on triangles of buttered toast that apparently originated in California early in the 20th century, though some say the name is a translation of the earlier French *anges à cheval.*

angle in To enter. "He angled into the room real easy-like."

Anglo A term for an English-speaking white person, an Anglo-American, that originated among Spanish speakers in the Southwest in the early 19th century and is now common throughout the United States. Unlike GRINGO, it is not always a derogatory term. *Anglo* can also mean the English language. "He doesn't speak Anglo."

angoras Fur chaps made from goat hides without the hair removed that were worn by early cowboys and often dyed green and pink, among other colors! *Woolies,* similarly, were chaps made from sheepskin without the wool removed.

angry acacia See ANGRY TREE.

angry tree A Southwestern tree *(Alcacea gregii)* that, when disturbed, shakes violently, its leaves ruffling like the hair on an angry cat, and emits a very unpleasant odor, its "bad temper" lasting an hour or so. It is also called the *cat's claw* and *angry acacia.*

animal Often used as a euphemism in the West, and other regions, for a bull and sometimes for a stallion. "When the high-toned ladies were present, we called a bull an *animal.*"

animule A joking term for any animal; formed from the combination of *animal* and *mule* and in use since the early 19th century.

ankle express To walk, go by foot. "It was fifty miles away, but I went by ankle express."

ankle over To walk over. "How about you ankle over to my place this afternoon?"

Annie Oakley The stage name of Phoebe Annie Oakley Mozee (1860–1926), star rifle shot with Buffalo Bill's Wild West Show. Married at 16, Annie joined Buffalo Bill at 25 and amazed audiences for more than 40 years with her expert marksmanship and trick shooting. Annie once broke 942 glass balls thrown into the air with only 1,000 shots. Her most famous trick was to toss a playing card, usually a five of hearts, into the air and shoot holes through all its pips. The riddled card reminded circus performers of their punched meal tickets, which they began to call *Annie Oakleys,* and the name was soon transferred to free railroad and press passes, both of which were customarily punched with a hole in the center. Today all complimentary passes, punched or not, are called *Annie Oakleys,* and the expression is also used in yacht-racing for a ventilated spinnaker or headsail.

answer the last call (roll call)   Long used as a Western euphemism for "to die." "I'm over ninety now, getting ready to answer the last call."

antelope   The pronghorn *(Antiloca-pra americana)* of the Western plains. It is of a separate family that differs widely from the Old World antelope; nevertheless, it has been called the *antelope* ever since it was so named in the journals of the Lewis and Clark expedition in 1804.

antelope brush   A Southwestern shrub *(Purshia tridentata)* that is an important browse plant for cattle and sheep.

antelope chipmunk   This Southwestern ground squirrel *(Citellus leucurus)* with a white-lined tail like an antelope's is also called the *antelope ground squirrel,* the *whitetail antelope squirrel,* and the *white-tail chipmunk.*

antelope horns   A Southwestern milkweed plant. *(Asclepias asperula),* so named for the shape of its erect green pods.

antelope jackrabbit   A white-sided jackrabbit *(Lepus alleni)* common to the Southwest.

antigodlin; antigoglin   Still used, despite being old-fashioned, in the West and South for something askew, at an angle, out of line. "Fix your slip, it's all antigodlin."

anvil   (1) A Texan term for rude fireworks made by pouring gunpowder into a hole in an anvil and exploding it by lighting a fuse. (2) A verb describing a galloping horse "making sparks" by striking its hind feet against its forefeet.

anymore   Nowadays, as in "We use a dishwasher anymore."

Apache   (1) The Apache Indians were so named from a Zuni word meaning "enemy," which was actually applied to many nomadic bands of Indians roaming the Southwestern United States. Among their greatest leaders were Cochise and Geronimo. The Apaches called themselves *dene,* an Athabascan word meaning "human being." (2) An *apache* is a Parisian criminal or ruffian, and an *apache dance* is a violent dance originated by the Parisian *apaches.* The word in its gangster sense was coined by French newspaper reporter Emile Darsy, who is said to have read of bloodthirsty Apache Indians in the works of American author James Fenimore Cooper and thought that their name would aptly fit denizens of the underworld. (3) A word used mostly in the Northwest for what is often called a *Mohawk haircut* elsewhere.

Apache plume A Southwestern shrub *(Fallucia paradoxa)*, so named because of the supposed resemblance of its red feathery seed clusters to Apache Indian war bonnets.

Apache State A nickname for the state of Arizona because of the great numbers of Apache Indians once residing in the territory.

apache tears A poetic name for the round translucent glassy pebbles found in Western obsidian formations. This volcanic glass is highly valued by collectors.

aparejo A packsaddle made of stuffed leather or canvas and used on mules and other animals, a borrowing of a Spanish word meaning the same.

aparejo grass A grass of the Southwest *(Sporobolus depauperatus)* used to stuff APAREJOS.

a-plenty Plenty. "I got a-plenty of friends who've taken all they could get and were honest in figurin' they had it comin' to them." [Elmer Kelton, *The Time It Never Rained,* 1973]

Appaloosa A hardy breed of white horses with dark spots and white-rimmed eyes developed by the Nez Percé Indians and probably named after the Palouse River of western Idaho; the breed has been called the "Dalmatian of horses." The designation *appaloosa,* first recorded in 1849, is also applied to the spotted *appaloosa catfish.*

apple A derogatory name given to certain American Indians by other American Indians, who believe their values are too much like those of whites; that is, they are, like an apple, red on the outside and white on the inside. " 'Goddamit,' one Indian yelled at another as the argument began. 'You ain't shit, you fucking apple.' " [Sherman Alexie, "Every Little Hurricane," 1993]

apple bird A woodpecker *(Asyndesmus lewisi)* that often feeds on the fruit of Western apple orchards.

appleknocker In the Pacific Northwest, a person unskilled in logging work, a neophyte, a farmer. The word has wide U.S. slang currency for an ignorant person, a hick.

apron-faced horse A horse with a large white streak resembling a white apron on the forehead.

Arapaho A name of uncertain origin for an Indian of a Western plains tribe of the Algonquian family. The name may derive from a Pawnee word for trader or from a Spanish word meaning "the ragged ones."

arbuckle So popular was Arbuckle's coffee in the late 19th-century West that it became a generic name for coffee. The word also meant a tenderfoot, that is, a cowboy the boss got free for Arbuckle Coffee premium stamps.

arched his back (1) Bucked, said of a horse. "The mustang arched his back and threw her." (2) Said of a person about to become angry.

are A pronunciation of *hour*. "Ah'm hongry an it's a whole are till lunch."

are you quits? Do you give up? " 'I said are you quits?' 'Quits?' 'Quits. Cause if you want some more of me you sure as hell goin' to get it.' " [Cormac McCarthy, *Blood Meridian, or, The Evening Redness in the West*, 1985]

argonaut A historical name for the men who went to prospect for gold in California during the gold rush of 1849, because many of them traveled there by ship.

ariviper A San Carlos Indian word used in the Southwest for a stream of water running a few feet under the desert sands.

Arizona The 48th state, which entered the Union in 1912, takes its name from the Papago Indian *Arizonac,* "place of the few or little springs." A nickname is Apache State.

Arizona cloudburst A facetious term for a desert sandstorm.

Arizona fever An expression commonly used in the late 19th century to describe a person's great desire to migrate to Arizona.

Arizona nightingale A humorous term for a braying burro or mule.

Arizona paint job A weather-beaten unpainted wooden building.

Arizona ruby A garnet gem found in the Southwest and also called the *Navajo ruby.*

Arizona strawberries American cowboys and lumberjacks used this term as a humorous synonym for beans, also employing the variations *Arkansas strawberries, Mexican strawberries* and *prairie strawberries.* Dried beans *were* pink in color like strawberries. One wit noted that the only way these beans could be digested was for the consumer to break wild horses.

Arizona tenor A person suffering from tuberculosis and the coughing that accompanies it; many people with the illness were drawn to the dry Arizona climate.

Arkansas toothpick See BOWIE KNIFE.

Arkansas travels A humorous term used in the West for diarrhea.

Arkansas wedding cake A jocular Pacific Northwest term for corn bread.

armadillo A burrowing mammal of the family *Dasypodidae* with strong claws and a protective covering of bony plates. It has come to be associated with Texas, where it was first reported along the Rio Grande in 1854; its name means "little armored one" in Spanish.

armas Large leather flaps hanging from a saddle that serve as a kind of chaps to protect a rider's legs in the brush.

arn A frequent Western pronunciation of *iron*.

around the horn! A cry used by loggers in the Pacific Northwest meaning "Watch out—a log is swinging through the air to be loaded!"

arrowbush Indians in the Southwest used to make arrows from the straight branches of *Pluchea sericea,* accounting for its common name *arrowbush*.

arroyo A Spanish word used in the Southwest for a brook or creek, a small watercourse with steep sides that is often dry except during heavy rains. Used in the Southwest since the early 19th century, *arroyo* can also mean a channel, gully, dry wash, stream bed or valley.

arroz con pollo A Mexican chicken and rice dish seasoned with garlic, saffron, paprika and other spices that was first introduced to the United States in the Southwest but is now known throughout the country. The Spanish name strictly translates as "rice with chicken."

artillery A term for personal firearms that arose in the West at the turn of the century and spread throughout the country. "He's packing heavy artillery."

arty-facts A pronunciation of *artifacts*. " 'If you're down in New Mex-ico, buy us some arty-facts,' the old woman said." [Larry McMurtry, *Cadillac Jack,* 1982]

as long as grass grows and water runs A promise, meaning "forever," often made to Indian tribes in the West regarding their rights to their lands and their freedom. "The invaders [settlers] pleaded for Statehood, and Statehood forever laid aside the promise to the red man that he should have freedom 'as long as grass grows and water runs.' " [*Colliers,* November 30, 1907]

aspen poplar A variety of poplar, also called the *quaking poplar,* common in the West on dry open ridges.

as pretty a hand Said of a skilled worker. "He's about as pretty a hand with rough stock ever come out of these parts." [Thomas McGuane, *Keep the Change,* 1989]

as pretty as a bald-faced heifer Descriptive of a very pretty, wholesome, angelic-looking woman.

assessment work A Western mining term meaning the work that needed to be done annually on a claim in order to hold it.

assin' around Fooling around. " 'Get on the goddamned horse,' said John Grady, 'and quit assin' around.' " [Cormac McCarthy, *All the Pretty Horses,* 1992]

association saddle The official saddle required in all rodeo contests, one that "favors the horse," cowboys say.

as stylish as a spotted dog under a redwagon An old expression meaning very stylish, up to the minute in fashion.

atago A Spanish word for a train of pack animals often used in mountainous areas of the Southwest.

atall At all. " 'Go ahead and jaw!' Barton cut in . . . "Don't mind me atall." [William Hopson, *The Last Shoot-out,* 1958]

attle A term for waste rock used in Western mines. "A huge pile of attle blocked the entrance to the old mine."

augerino A humorous old term for an imaginary evil creature whose greatest joy is to empty irrigation ditches by boring holes in them.

augur Probably deriving from "argue," *augur* can mean to talk or to argue, while *auguring* means talking, and an *augur* is a big-mouthed bore. *Auguring contests* were talking contests held in the early West in which two men commenced talking at a rapid rate, often babbling senseless sentences for hours, until one of them quit.

avalanche A corruption of the French word *ambulance* (a wagon), *avalanche* was commonly used to mean a wagon in the old West.

Avenging Angel The name given to the 1862 Colt revolver when part of its barrel was sawed off. Avenging Angels were used by Brigham Young's Mormon followers, one of whom was said to have killed hundreds with his.

awl A common Western pronunciation of *oil*. "I'm in the awl bidness."

ax handle A humorous measure of length among loggers of the Northwest; Paul Bunyan was said to be 24 ax handles high.

ax-handle party An expression used for a brawl by loggers of the Pacific Northwest.

ay, chihuahua! A mild expletive sometimes heard in the Southwest. This was a frequent oath of the Cisco Kid's sidekick on *The Cisco Kid* radio program in the 1940s.

B

baa-baa This Southwestern name for a sheep probably originated as a contemptuous cowboy expression and can still be derisive, but it has lost some of its sting today and is even used by sheep herders.

Babe Ruth of rodeo Casey Tibbs (1928–90), rodeo's all-around-champion nationally in 1951 and 1955 and saddlebronc champion six times.

baby blue eyes The Western wildflower *Nemophila menziesii*, which has small blue flowers that suggest baby blue eyes to some.

baby buggy The usual Western name for a baby carriage; sometimes used in other regions as well.

baby in the bushes A euphemism for a child born to an unwed mother.

baby morning glory An expression used in Texas for a dwarf variety of the morning glory flower.

bachelor's lantern A lantern made from a candle and an open tin can with holes punched in it.

bachelor's wife An old term for a tin plunger with a wooden handle used for washing clothes.

backbreaker A low tree stump, hard to cut because it is so close to the ground.

back East A term used by Westerners referring to the eastern United States. Easterners, in turn, say *out West* in referring to the western United States. *East* in the expression means anywhere east of the Mississippi River or in the general direction of the East Coast.

the back forty A term used in the West for a large piece of cultivated land, or as a joking name for out-of-the-way waste land.

back in the saddle again (1) Back at work, back in one's regular routine. (2) A humorous term for menstruation sometimes used by women in the West and South.

back one's play Loggers in the Northwest use this phrase to mean standing behind a person, backing up someone. "I'll back his play this time, but this is his last chance."

back the breeze To talk too much; used by loggers in the Northwest. "Quit backing the breeze and get to work."

bad Very ill. "He is awful bad, and I don't know if he'll ever get better." *Bad sick* is also used.

badger fight See PULLING THE BADGER.

Badlands A barren, severely eroded region in southwest South Dakota and northwest Nebraska. According to the *Century Magazine* (1882, XXIV), "The term Bad Lands does not apply to the quality of the soil. The Indian name was accurately rendered by the early French voyageurs as *Mauvaises Terres pour traverser*— bad lands to cross. The ground between the buttes is fertile, and the whole region is an excellent cattle-range, the rock formation affording the best possible winter protection." *Badlands National Park* is in South Dakota.

bad man, badman A Western historical term for an outlaw or professional gunfighter who had killed people; many were brutes, bullies and psychopaths, but several who carried the title were men who had killed others in arguments or in self-defense. In *The Great American Outlaw* (1993), Frank Richard Prassel has this to say about the compound word *badman*, as opposed to *bad man:* "Indirectly [John] Wayne gave popular language the very word. His film *The Angel and the Badman* (1946) fixed the compound in ver-nacular English with a contradictory meaning. A badman is not necessarily bad; *goodman* has no meaning. Films issued before 1946 consistently divided the term; those made later routinely adopted the compound. For the original it was of no significance; whenever John Wayne played a badman, as he did with some frequency, something was clearly wrong with the law. His mere appearance in the role of a criminal made justification for illegality pointless; it could be assumed."

bad medicine Among the Indians, *bad medicine* meant a person's bad luck, his spirits working against him. Cowboys used the term *bad medicine* to describe any very dangerous person, such as a feared gunfighter. See also MEDICINE.

bad place in the road A small, out-of-the-way town or place of little consequence, a bend or spot in the road.

bad sick See BAD.

bait A light meal; the expression probably doesn't derive from "a bite" but from an old meaning of *bait* for a meal. "I'll get me a bait before we leave."

bajada A Spanish term used in the Southwest for a steep trail or road or any steep, severe descent. "We made our way down the rocky bajada."

baker's bread Commercially made store-bought bread as opposed to homemade bread; heard throughout the United States but most commonly in the West and North.

baldface (1) A horse or cow (such as a Hereford) with a long white mark on its face; "Baldface" is thus frequently a nickname for a horse. (2) A logging term meaning to push a collection of loaded log cars with an engine.

bald-faced shirt A cowboy's name for a man's stiff dress shirt that may derive from the use of *baldface* for a cow with a long white marking down the center of its face. *Boiled shirt* is also used.

baldhead The rounded top of a Southwestern plateau, mesa or mountain, which are often bare of vegetation. Also called a *whaleback*.

baldheaded An expression used mainly in the West and North for a hurried action taken without caution or much thinking: "He really went at it baldheaded." As Maximilian Schele de Vere put it in *Americanisms* (1871), the expression probably derives from "the eagerness with which men rush to do a thing without covering the head."

bald-headed prairie Barren prairieland with little or nothing growing on it. " 'Nothing but bugs and blood last season. Nothing but baldheaded prairie,' the boss told Cecil." [Edward Hoagland, *Seven Rivers West*, 1986]

baldies Desert, barren country. " 'You're right—it's the money, not the killing,' Wesley Hardin said. 'They don't care who gets killed, out here in the baldies.' " [Larry McMurtry, *Streets of Laredo*, 1993]

baldy (1) A BALDFACE horse or cow. (2) Any mountain peak covered with snow; also called *Old Baldy*.

balled up A euphemism for constipated. "I'm all balled up."

ball of snakes See WATERMILLION.

balloon bread A puffed-up bread that looks as heavy as a standard 1½-pound loaf but is about a pound lighter.

balm tree A common name in the Northwest for the balsam poplar.

banana A name given in the Southwest to the sweet, fleshy fruit of the yucca. *(Yucca aloifolia)*, which is shaped like the banana.

banana slug The slug *Ariolimax columvianus*. William Least Heat Moon in *Blue Highways* (1982) wrote of an Oregon area: "I poked about the woods and turned up a piece of crawling yellow jelly nearly the length of my hand. It was a banana slug, so named because the mollusk looks like a wet, squirming banana."

banco A piece or large tract of land detached from its position when a river changes its course, often leaving it on the other side of the river.

band (1) A Western term for a large flock of sheep (2,500 or so). (2) A large herd of cattle or horses. (3) To herd animals together.

bandido A Mexican outlaw; the word is seldom applied to American bandits. *Bandido* is Spanish meaning "outlaw."

bandit (1) A robber or desperado; from the Spanish *bandido* (outlaw). (2) A raccoon, which is so called in Texas because of its mask-like face.

bankrupt worm The little parasite roundworm of the genus *Trichostrongylus* is called the *bankrupt worm* because it often infects cattle herds, sometimes bankrupting those cattlemen whose stock it attacks.

bar A straight horizontal line used in cattle brands that resulted in the word becoming part of many ranch names, such as the famous Bar X.

barbed wire When in the 1850s farmers began fencing in their land with barbed wire—twisted strands of wire fence with sharp barbs at regular intervals—ranchers tore the fences down so their herds could pass. This led to *barbed wire fence wars* in the West, notably one that broke out in Texas in 1884, and helped end the reign of the cowboy by the close of the century.

barbed wire deal A term used in the Northwest among loggers meaning any situation that is very difficult or thorny to handle.

barbed wire fence war See BARBED WIRE.

bar ditch A common pronunciation in Texas and Oklahoma for a *barrow ditch*. It is commonly thought to be called a bar ditch because it prevents (bars) herds of animals from getting on the roadway. But the *bar* in *bar ditch* is probably a shortening of *barrow*. Also called a *bar pit*. See also BARROW PIT.

bardog A humorous term for a bartender. " 'Sure! Get a bardog to save ya! You're too yella t'save yourself.' " [Richard Matheson, *The Gun Fight*, 1993]

bardogging Tending bar, being a BARDOG.

barefoot Cowboy talk for coffee served black, without milk or cream.

barefoot An old descriptive term for an unshod horse. "Them Indians moved mighty silent on their barefoot ponies."

barf To vomit; a term with wide currency, but chiefly used in the West and North.

bark A historical expression once used to mean a scalp; *to take the bark off someone* was to scalp someone.

barking squirrel Another name for the PRAIRIE DOG.

barking wolf A synonym for the COYOTE.

barleycorn sprints An expression used among loggers in the Northwest for dysentery suffered after a long bout of drinking.

barnyard pipe A corncob pipe.

barometer bush The silverleaf *Leucophyllum texanum*, so called in Texas because after heavy rains this wildflower changes color overnight, turning hills and fields a soft lavender.

bar pit See BAR DITCH.

barrio A Spanish word common in the Southwest, and many other areas of the country, for a Spanish-speaking, usually poor, section of a city.

barrow See BAR DITCH.

barrow pit A ditch next to a graded road; so named because the soil taken from it is "borrowed" for landfill. Also called a *bar pit* and a *barrow ditch*.

Basin State A nickname for the state of Utah. "The Judge has friends goin' to arrive from New Yawk for a trip across the Basin." [Owen Wister, *The Virginian*, 1902] See also GREAT BASIN.

basket makers American Indians who were among the oldest inhabitants of the Southwest, living in the region from about 100 to 500 A.D., before the making of pottery there.

bathin' one's countenance Washing one's face, in cowboy talk.

a Bat Masterson A fabled gunfighter; after William Barclay "Bat" Masterson (1853–1921), a Western lawman who never lost a gun battle. Masterson is one of the few gunfighters who didn't die a violent death. He became a sports writer in New York City and is said to have "died at his desk gripping his pen with the tenacity with which he formerly clung to his six-shooter." Masterson got the nickname "Bat" because when a sheriff in Kansas he often batted down lawbreakers with his cane instead of shooting them.

battens The term preferred in California and the Pacific Northwest for wooden siding used to cover houses.

battery A historical word for a revolver. In 1906 Mark Twain wrote in the magazine *Horses Tale*, "There's no telling how much he does weigh when he's out on the war-path and has his batteries belted on."

Battle-born State A nickname for Nevada, the 36th state, because it was admitted to the Union in 1864 while the Civil War was still being fought.

batwings Very wide leather chaps that were popularized in early Western films but aren't seen much anymore; they were widely used in the early West.

bawling The loud noises made by a cow in some kind of distress.

Bay Bridge Another name for GOLDEN GATE BRIDGE over San

Francisco Bay. ". . . in the unsmogged breezy clarity we could see the bridges—Dumbarton, San Mateo, even the Bay bridge . . ." [Wallace Stegner, *All the Little Live Things,* 1967]

Bay City A nickname for San Francisco since the mid-19th century.

bayo A dun horse, often with a black line running down its back or with other black markings. Also called a *bayo coyote.*

bayo coyote See BAYO.

Bayou Salade French trappers probably gave this name to South Park, Colorado, because of the salt springs there.

bay steer A reddish-brown steer noted for its spirit.

be after someone with a sharp stick To be determined to have satisfaction or revenge. Bartlett called this phrase a Westernism in 1848. "He's after those politicians with a very sharp stick."

bean Slang for penis. " 'A cold clime will perk a boy up and make him want to wriggle his bean.' " [Larry McMurtry, *Lonesome Dove,* 1985]

beaner A derogatory term in the Southwest for a Mexican, someone of Mexican ancestry; a Mexican migrant worker. Other such names include *bear* and *beano.*

bean master A humorous term used on the trail for a cook; patterned on the analogy of *wagon master.*

beans Bullets. See also NO BEANS IN THE WHEEL.

bearberry honeysuckle The most common Western honeysuckle shrub *(Lonicera involucrata),* which yields paired black berries that bears are said to favor.

bear cabbage A Western wildflower *(Hydrophyllum capitatum)* that is neither eaten by bears nor a cabbage, though both Indians and settlers once ate the strong-tasting plant. Also called *cat's breeches, waterleaf* and *pussyleaf,* among other names.

bear cat Something extraordinary. "That's a bear cat of a mountain to climb!"

bear claw See BEAR PAW.

bear flag The white flag with a star and grizzly bear upon it that was adopted by Americans in California in 1846 when they defied Spanish authorities and proclaimed the California Republic. It has since become the California state flag.

bear grass A Southwestern plant of the Nolina genus that also goes by the names *basket grass, threadgrass* and *devil's shoestring.* The abundant red-plumed plant is sometimes fed to livestock in emergencies and is used for weaving, and its husks are burned in campfires by cowboys on the range.

bear paw A popular Western pastry made with nuts and raisins that roughly suggests a bear's paw in shape; also called a *bear claw*. It appears to have originated in California in about 1940.

bear story Any exaggerated story or tall tale, the term having originated among Western hunters with tales of their exploits hunting bears.

bear trap saddle A deep small saddle enclosed with a cantle, making it very difficult for even a tenderfoot to fall out.

beast with a belly full of bedsprings A colorful cowboy term for a bucking horse. "It was my turn out of the chutes—on a beast with a belly full of bedsprings."

beat out Worn out, tired. " 'Now don't you go getting yourself beat out,' Luz said, smiling . . ." [Edna Ferber, *Giant,* 1952]

the Beautiful Bodacious Babylon of the West A colorful old name for Dodge City, Kansas, once a wild and rowdy cowtown on the Santa Fe Trail.

became shot Killed by being shot. ". . . a cowboy would ride up and warn you not to trespass on his watering rights, and if you persisted . . . one day you became shot. That was the phrase they used: 'Poor Waddington. Running his cattle north toward Skunk Hollow. He became shot.' " [James Michener, *Centennial,* 1974]

bedded Cowboy talk for a roped animal that has been thrown so hard that it lies still.

bedding ground A place where a herd of cows can sleep at night. "Our herd now amounted to some six-hundred head, and it was a pretty sight of an evening to see them streaming from various quarters toward the bedding ground." [Reginald Aldridge, *Life on a Ranch,* 1884]

bed down (1) To kill. "He bed him down with one shot." (2) Teddy Roosevelt wrote in the *Century Magazine* (April 1888) that to *bed down* cattle "simply consists in hemming them into as small a space as possible, and then riding round them until they lie down and fall asleep."

bedfast Bedridden. "He's been bedfast since he got hurt."

bed-ground (1) A place selected on a drive where sheep are bedded down for the night. (2) A place where a cowboy spreads his blankets.

bed-slat An emaciated animal, such as a cow with protruding ribs that resemble bed-slats.

bed wagon A wagon that carries bedrolls and supplies for cowboys on the job; food is carried in the *chuck wagon.*

beef (1) An adult cow, bull or steer, especially one raised for its meat. (2) To kill a cow, bull or steer for meat. "I reckon we'll beef the yearling tomorrow."

beefalo See CATTLO.

beef driver A synonym for a cowboy, first recorded in 1834. "The saloon was filled with beef drivers, gamblers and women."

beef drover A synonym for a cowboy, first recorded in 1855.

beef-head An old nickname for a Texan, common in the late 19th century and referring of course to the many cattle in the state.

beefsteak See GIMLET.

beefsteaked Descriptive of a horse with sores caused by a saddle that doesn't fit right.

beehive cactus Another name for the barrel cactus (*Echinocactus Johnsonii octocentrus*) of the Southwest deserts.

beeves Cattle; the plural of *beef*, an adult cow, steer or bull raised for its meat.

belled snake A rattlesnake, whose rattle warns of its presence the way a bell does on a collared cat.

bell horse The lead horse or mule in a pack train of horses or mules, so named for the large bell customarily attached to its neck.

bellota An oak (*Quercus arizonica*) found in the Southwest; its acorns were used as food by the Indians.

belly cheater; belly robber; belly burglar *Belly cheater* is an old American cowboy term for a cook that may date back to the 19th century but is first recorded as U.S. Navy slang in the form of *belly robber*, specifically referring to a commissary steward. The term has also been used for an Army mess sergeant. Another, later variant is *belly burglar*.

belly up Dead. "They found him belly up in the desert."

benighted An old term for being overtaken by nightfall. "She was benighted before she could get home."

a Ben Thompson Any legendary gunfighter. The real Ben Thompson (1842–84) was a professional gambler who was said by some to be the fastest shot in the West and several times shot the gun out of an opponent's hand. He died in an ambush in which he was greatly outnumbered.

bentonite A soft clay used as a fuller's earth that is found chiefly near Fort Benton, Montana.

best Better. "You'd best go home."

the best thing out The best story. " 'Jest heard the best thing out, boys . . . Jim was just tellin' the richest yarn . . .'" [Bret Harte, "How Santa Claus Came to Simpson's Bar," 1863]

be the whole herd To be the most important person. "He was the whole herd, all right, no one else came close."

between a rock and a hard place In days past if one was badly in need of money, almost bankrupt, he or she was said to be between a rock and a hard place. This expression was probably born in Arizona during a financial panic early in this century, but over the years, its meaning changed. It came to mean being in a very tight spot, on the horns of a dilemma in making a hard decision. The words do lend themselves to this last definition, for wherever one turns in making the decision, there is something as hard as or harder than rock to face.

between grass and hay The period between childhood or adolescence and becoming an adult.

between two suns See quote. "And I went, too, between two suns, as my uncle used to say of any man who disappeared." [Conrad Richter, *The Sea of Grass*, 1936]

beyond sundown See SUNDOWN.

big-balled for a shoat With a lot of nerve for a young or small person. " 'If,' said Marcus, 'you figure on coming back here for your job, forget it. You can't work for me again. You are big-balled for a shoat [a young pig].' " [Charles O. Locke, *The Hell Bent Kid*, 1957]

Big Bellies A name given by white settlers to the Gros Ventre Indians of Montana; also called the *Great Bellies.*

big bend Land adjoining a large bend in a river. As a proper name, the term is usually applied to a region in Oregon and Washington near the Columbia River and to a region in southwestern Texas on the Rio Grande.

Big D A common nickname for Dallas, Texas.

big dry country See ALKALIED.

Big Foot A huge, hairy, humanoid creature said to inhabit the Pacific Northwest forests, so named because of the size of its alleged footprints, said to be 16 to 17 inches long and 7 inches wide. This abominable snowman of the California mountains is also called *Bigfoot* and *Sasquatch,* the name Sasquatch recorded in 1925, some 35 years before the name Bigfoot.

Big H A nickname for Houston, Texas. " 'Houston,' Dub said. 'I can tell you one thing, we don't put it out to pasture near as quick down in Big H as they do out here in Vegas.' " [Larry McMurtry, *The Desert Rose*, 1983]

bigheaded Conceited, too self-confident. "They [easily] led him into the ambush because he was bigheaded." [Louis L'Amour, *Hondo*, 1953] *He's (she's) got the bighead* means "he (she) is conceited."

bighole To suddenly stop a train or a truck; the expression, a longer variant of which is *bighole the air,* refers to the air escaping from the air brake valve when a train's brakes are sharply applied. "He saw the cows on the track and bigholed the train."

big jaw See LUMPY JAW.

Big Muddy A nickname for the Missouri River.

big pasture A joking name sometimes used for any state prison.

Big Sky; Big Sky State A nickname for Montana. "It was going fast, the Big Sky was. . . . All sorts of famous people—celebrities—were vacationing there." [Rick Bass, "Days of Heaven," 1991]

big swimmin' A river at flood stage. "He took 'em across the big swimmin'."

bilk To cheat.

bilker A cheap cheater, one who "never misses a meal and never pays a cent."

bill-show An old term for any wild west show, probably deriving from the shows of Buffalo Bill Cody.

billy-be-damned An old euphemistic curse. "He was so billy-be-damned thorough with it . . ." [Jack Schaefer, *The Kean Land,* 1953]

a Billy the Kid A fabled gunman, after Henry McCarty (1859–1881), who took the name William H. Bonney and was dubbed "Billy the Kid" for his youth and small size

after he killed his first man when barely 18. He was perhaps the fastest draw in the West, and his shots often hit their mark before his gun was seen to leave his holster. He was killed by sheriff Pat Garrett, who caught him off guard.

bindle A bedroll, blanket roll; *bindle* here probably derives from *bundle.*

bindlestiff A tramp or hobo, one who carried a BINDLE. "Before he knew it he was a bindlestiff himself." [John Steinbeck, *East of Eden,* 1952] Also called a *blanket stiff.*

bing cherry The popular dark red, nearly black firm fruit of the Bigarreau group. The tree was developed in 1875 by a Chinese farmer named Bing in Oregon, where over a quarter of the United States' sweet cherry crop is grown. Other cherry varieties named after their developers include the Luelling, for the man who founded Oregon's cherry industry in 1847.

bird-egg pea The milkvetch, *Astragalus ceramicus,* also called *painted pod,* whose striking spotted pods somewhat resemble a bird's eggs.

Bird Woman A name given to the Shoshoni Indian woman Sacagawea (pronounced *Sa-cuh-juh-we-uh*), famous guide for the Lewis and Clark expedition in 1805.

biscuit shooter A derogatory term for a ranch cook; used jokingly by cowboys.

bisnaga A plumb, spiny cactus whose juicy pulp and water have often quenched the thirst of travelers in the desert.

bit Twelve and one-half cents; a Spanish coin of that value. See also BIT HOUSE.

bitch See POSSUM BELLY.

bitch light See quote. "In her day, they had no wicking to make candles, so they melted bear grease or fish oil in a tin pan and lighted a twisted strip of rag in it, and it was always a devilish mess, even before the children slatted it over—a bitch light." [Annie Dillard, *The Living*, 1992]

bites See quote. "Most of the men carried home-made fifty-caliber cartridges empty of powder and filled with cyanide. 'Bites,' they called them. A man would no more be without them than without his extra keg of water. When Indians attacked and there was no escape or defense, a hunter could always bite the bullet." [Lucia St. Clair Robson, *Ride The Wind*, 1982]

bite the dust Everytime we hear of still another desperado *biting the dust* in Western films, we are hearing an almost literal translation of a line found in Homer's *Iliad*, written thousands of years ago. American poet William Cullen Bryant translated the words in 1870: ". . . his fellow warriors, many a one, Fall round him to the earth and bite the dust." Earlier, Alexander Pope had eloquently translated the phrase as "bite the bloody sand" and English poet William Cowper had it, literally, as "bite the ground." The idea remains the same in any case: a man falling dead in combat, *biting the dust* in his last hostile, futile act.

bit house A historical expression for a Western saloon that served all drinks, food, cigars and so forth for one price—one bit, or 12½ cents.

bitterbrush *Purshia tridentata,* also known as *antelope brush* and *buckbrush;* among the most widely distributed of Western shrubs.

bizzing A term common in Utah and Colorado for the dangerous game children play hanging onto the back of a car and skiing on one's shoes when the road is icy or otherwise slippery.

blab A board attached to a calf's nose and mouth to prevent it from suckling anymore; also called a *blab board* and a *blab-board weaner.*

Black Bart, the PO-8 The *nom de plume* of Charles E. Boles, the daring robber who held up stagecoaches in the 1870s and did it alone on foot (he had no use for horses) with an unloaded shotgun (he had no use for violence)! A consummate artist at his chosen work, Black Bart wasn't a bad poet, either. He wrote many poems for his victims, the following sample certainly his rationalizations for his crimes:

I've labored long and hard for bred
For honor and for riches
But on my corns too long you've tred
You fine-haired Sons of Bitches.

Unfortunately, little is known of Black Bart. The man who signed his poems PO-8 appears to have disappeared after being released from jail in 1888.

black blizzard A term for a severe dust storm; the expression originated with the dust storms of the Great Depression that ravaged the farms of Oklahoma and Kansas in the 1930s. Also called a *black roller* and *black snow*.

blackbrush A small Southwestern desert shrub (*Coleogyne ramosissima*) with a blackish appearance when grouped together. The desert tar bush *Flourensia cernula* also goes by this name.

black-eyed Susan An old joking name for not a flower but a revolver.

black grama Any of several popular species of Southwestern grasses, including the dark purple grama grass *Bouteloua eriopoda,* the gallita grass *Hilaria jamesii* and the muhly grass *Muhlenbergia porteri.*

black hawk A dark-colored, red-tailed hawk (*Buteo calurus*) native to the West. The name is also given to the *Mexican black hawk, Swainson's hawk* and *Harris's hawk.*

blackland A dark soil that can be heavy and sticky, though the term is also used to mean a dark, loose soil.

black persimmon The persimmon tree (*Diospyros texana*) of southwest Texas, so named because of its dark-fleshed fruit. Its other names include the *mustang persimmon, possum plum, chapote* and *Mexican persimmon.*

Black Robe A historical name given to Jesuit missionaries working among Indians in the West, the name originating with the Indians themselves and referring to the robes the Jesuits wore. They were also called *Black Gowns.*

black roller See BLACK BLIZZARD.

black sage The sagebrush *Artemisea arbuscula* or *Artemisea tridentata,* so named because of its dark-colored stem; this plant is also called *black sagebrush.*

black snow See BLACK BLIZZARD.

black water Weak black coffee; or, sometimes, any coffee, weak or not.

black wax Another word for gumbo (sticky, heavy soil); used in Texas and other Western states.

bladebones Large shoulder bones of an animal. "The men turned out in the early morning darkness to dig their graves with bladebones of antelopes . . ." [Cormac McCarthy, *Blood Meridian, or, The Evening Redness in the West,* 1985]

blanco An Indian name for white men in the Southwest; from the Spanish *blanco* (white). "He seldom wound the watch . . . because he knew where the sun stood and when the moon rose, unlike the puzzling *blancos*, who were to be pitied because they seemed not to know and had to depend on this ticking thing." [Fred Grove, *Phantom Warrior*, 1981]

blanket Indian A derogatory term commonly used in the 19th century for an Indian thought to be docile and of a low cultural level because he or she wore a blanket instead of dressing like white people. *To wear the blanket* meant that an Indian was "half-civilized."

blanket stiff See BINDLESTIFF.

blatting The noise a sheep makes; sometimes applied to humans. "That's just Shorty blattin' cause he's lost a hand." [Jack Schaefer, *Monte Walsh*, 1958]

blazer (1) An old Westernism meaning a superlative person. "T'other gal is likely enough, but the mother's a blazer!" [Mrs. Kirkland, *Western Clearings*, 1845] (2) A bluff or a lie.

blazing star Slang for a stampede. "The herd . . . burst like a bombshell into the most disastrous of all plains mishaps—'a blazing star'. The solid herd streamed suddenly in all directions, scattered in knots and bunches, and two and threes, and vanished into the storm and dark-

ness." [*Munsey's Magazine*, XXV, 1901]

bless the meat and damn the skin Part of an old grace said before a meal: "Bless the meat an' damn the skin,/ Throw back your 'eads an' all pitch in."

blind as a one-eyed mule in a root cellar Completely blind, unable to see or understand. "You know the law. The law is blind as a one-eyed mule in a root cellar." [Elmer Kelton, *The Time It Never Rained*, 1973]

blind the trail To cover over one's tracks, to make them appear to be heading another way. "We tried to blind the trail, but he never stayed more than an hour behind us."

blind trail A trail, with markings, blazes or signs that are difficult to make out or follow.

blinky milk Milk that has turned sour. "He sold us some blinky milk."

blister bug A small grayish beetle *(Lytta cinerea)*, found mostly in Texas, that causes blisters on the skin if touched.

bloat A reaction in cows to drinking ALKALI water. "Every last cow except three that died of bloat. Alkalie water." [Jack Schaefer, *Monte Walsh*, 1958]

blobbermouth A term heard in Texas for a talkative person, a variation on *blabbermouth*.

blocker A long loop used to rope cattle by the feet, named after its inventor, South Texas roper and cattleman John Blocker.

blonde bound An expression used among loggers for someone who blames his being late to work on being delayed by a woman.

blonde Swede A logger's term for an old man.

blooddrops A tiny red wildflower, a wild poppy, that looks like drops of blood among the grass.

blossom rock Quartz rock that has oxide stains, indicating that minerals such as gold or silver are nearby.

blowed A term applied to a gusher in the oil fields but used generally in Oklahoma to mean "became immensely big or profitable." As Sam Walton said of his Wal-Mart chain: "It was the retail equivalent of an oil gusher: as they say in Oklahoma, the whole thing just sort of blowed." [Sam Walton, *Made in America,* 1992]

blow his stirrup An expression used in rodeo competitions for what happens when a broncobuster loses his foothold on the stirrup, resulting in his disqualification in the event.

blowing Talking. " 'Blowing like this before breakfast,' he said, 'is bad for the digestion.' " [Jack Schaefer, *First Blood,* 1953]

blow out his lamp To kill someone. "Billy the Kid blew out his lamp."

blow snake A name given in the West to the long, harmless snake *Heterodon contortrix,* known as the *hognose snake* in other parts.

blowhard A braggart. The term can be traced back to the American West in about 1855. To *blow your own horn,* or to promote yourself, derives from a much older expression, *to blow your own trumpet,* which goes as far back as 1576. Such "hornblowing" may have its origins in medieval times, when heralds blew their trumpets to announce the arrival of royalty but commoners such as street vendors had to blow their own horns.

bluebonnet The blue-flowered lupine *Lupinus texenis,* the official state flower of Texas. Due to extensive seeding, great masses of them bloom along the roadsides in the spring. Also once known as *buffalo clover.*

blue devil A historical term that was applied to the fence-cutting cowboys during the Texas "fence war" in the 1880s, when farmers fenced in the open ranges.

blue lightning A humorous name for a revolver or six-shooter.

blue meat An old term for the meat of an unweaned calf.

blue-mouthed alligator A colorful curse. "You yaller-skinned, rat-eyed, long-drawn-out blue-mouthed alligator!" [Max Brand, *The Black Signal,* 1925]

Bluemouths An Indian tribe residing west of the Choctaws. Not much is known about them, but the Choctaws told travelers that there was a large city where these blue-mouthed or blue-lipped people lived and that if a person tried to kill one of these people he would become insane.

blue norther A strong, icy north wind, so cold it could turn your nose or hands blue; mostly used in Texas cattle country. Also called a *blue whistler* and a *blue Texas norther*. See also NORTHER.

blue racer The quick, bluish green snake *Coluber constrictor mormon* found west of the Rockies.

bluestem A name given to both prairie beardgrass *(Andropagon)* and bluestem wheatgrass *(Agropyron smithii)*, among the most common of Western wheatgrasses.

blue whistler See BLUE NORTHER.

bluewood The native Texas shrub or tree *Condalia hookeri*, also called *chaparral, purple haw basil* and *logwood;* it has bluish black fruit, and its wood yields a blue dye.

boardwalk A sidewalk made of boards, common in many early Western towns though seen only in historical replicas today. "The east side of Main boasted a boardwalk. The West side had only a dusty path." [Lewis B. Patten, *Pursuit,* 1957]

boar's nest Any small camp for male workers only, usually cowboys, and consisting of a few small buildings.

bob ruly American pioneers called a burned out area a *bob ruly,* which leads some to think that the term might have been named after a notorious firebug of old. But *bob ruly,* first recorded in 1848, though older, is just how the French words *bois brûlé* (burned woods) sounded to American ears.

bobtailed flush or straight A bobtailed flush or straight in poker is a three-card flush or straight, one that is worthless because poker rules require five-card flushes or straights. The term apparently originated in the West in the mid-19th century, the word modeled on the short-cut tails of bobtailed horses.

bob-wire A common pronunciation of *barbed wire*. "Chaos demanded order, and the means of order were to be barbed wire—'bob-wire', most people used to call it." [James Frank Dobie, *A Vaquero of the Brush Country,* 1929]

bodark; bodock The Osage orange tree *(Maclura pomifers)*. It is so called because the Indians used its wood for making bows, and the French thus called it the *bois d'arc* (bow-wood) tree, which became corrupted in English to *bodark* and *bodock*. It is called the *Osage orange* because it grew in Osage Indian country and has large, rough-skinned, greenish fruits somewhat suggestive of an orange, but inedible. The spiny-branched tree is often used for hedges and called the *Osage thorn*. It is first recorded in 1804 by the Lewis and Clark expedition as the *Osage Apple*.

boggy-top pie A pie with a sweet, gooey topping. "Harpe said, 'You better try a slice of this boggy-top pie, Charlie. It's mighty good.'" [Elmer Kelton, *The Time It Never Rained*, 1973]

bog rider An old term for a cowboy responsible for freeing cows that get stuck in mud holes on the trail.

bohind A humorous expression used by Texans for the buttocks; probably from BOHUNKUS and *behind*.

bohunkus A humorous term for the buttocks. It may derive from *bohunk*, a derogatory term for any eastern European, which in turn comes from *Boh*emian and *hunk* for Hungarian.

boiled shirt; biled shirt (1) A miner's name for a snob. ". . . if a man wanted a fight on his hands . . . all he had to do was appear in public in a white shirt . . . For those people [Western miners] hated aristocrats. They had a particular and malignant animosity toward what they called a 'biled shirt.'" [Mark Twain, *Roughing It*, 1872] (2) A cowboy's name for a man's stiff dress shirt.

boil over Said of a horse when it starts to buck. "He boiled over and began bucking."

bois d'arc See BODARK.

bois de vache Buffalo chips, which were often used as fuel for fires in the early West.

boll-weevil A term used among Western oil workers for either a novice or a worthless person, after, of course, the insect that ruins cotton plants.

bologna bull An inferior quality animal fit only to make bologna when slaughtered.

bolson Any low-lying area surrounded by mountains; named after the Bolson Desert in Mexico.

bonanza Rich gold mines in the early West were called bonanzas, from the Spanish word for "smooth sea" (hence good luck or success). When miners discovered a rich mine or vein of ore, this was said to be a *bonanza,* and the word came to mean sudden good luck. The expression is first recorded in 1844.

bone orchard A cemetery. "'The town's empty as a bone orchard.'" [William Dale Jennings, *The Cowboys*, 1971]

boneyard An emaciated animal, especially a horse or cow, or an emaciated person. "That old boneyard's good fer nothin'."

bonnet string The chin strap on a cowboy hat. "He pulled his bonnet string tight."

boof An old word meaning a scare or fright. "He got some boof when I come up behind him."

booger To become excited and act nervously. "Something boogered the herd."

boogers Things that excite or frighten horses or cattle; probably derives from *boogerman* for a ghost. " 'Do you reckon a man could drive a herd from there' . . . 'It's in my mind. If you'd come along to keep the boogers off.' " [Louis L'Amour, *Bendigo Shafter,* 1979]

books School, schooltime. "Has books begun yet?"

boomer An itinerant worker, one who comes to work in an area where there is plenty of work due to boom times.

boondoggle One source says that early cowboys used the term *boondoggle* to mean making saddle trappings out of odds and ends of leather to wile away their idle hours, *boondoggling* soon coming to mean to do any work of no practical value, merely to keep or look busy. But there are several stories concerning the word's origins. The old yarn about *boondoggle* being suggested by Daniel Boone idly whittling sticks to throw to his dog does convey the sense of the word but is just another spurious tale.

booshway Deriving from the French *bourgeois,* for the leader of an expedition in the West or the head trader, *booshway* came to mean any big boss and then became a joking name for a pretentious person or a self-styled big shot.

boot A receptacle for a horseman's rifle. "Coy had slipped the Winchester back into its boot once he cleared town." [Sam Brown, *The Crime of Coy Bell,* 1992]

Boot Hill Now a joking name for any cemetery, the term was first applied to any small cemetery in the West where men who died in gunfights, who died with their boots on, were buried. The first such is said to have been in Deadwood, South Dakota; the Mount Moriah cemetery there is now a big tourist attraction. "On a knoll, peopled with stone and wooden monuments, stood Boot Hill, the final resting place of the loved and the unloved, the killer and the saint." [James Wesley, *Showdown in Mesa Bend,* 1972]

boot pack A roomy rubber boot higher than a shoe, although the term once meant a high moccasin.

boots and saddles! Most Americans are familiar with the old Western song "Give Me My Boots and My Saddle," but this familiar cavalry call has nothing to do with boots and saddles, as one might suspect. It derives from the old French cavalry command *Boute selle* (Put saddle!), which the British corrupted to *boot and saddle!* and which American cavalrymen further corrupted to *boots and saddles!*

border tale A Western story. "I am sorry to have to lie so outrageously in this yarn. My hero has killed more Indians on one war trail than I have killed in all my life. But I understand this is what is expected of border tales. If you think the revolver and Bowie knife are used too freely, you may cut out a fatal shot or stab wherever you think wise." [William F. (Buffalo Bill) Cody in a letter to his editor, 1875, quoted in Loren D. Estleman, *This Old Bill,* 1984]

born a-horseback An old expression for a cowboy or anyone who rode a great deal. "He was born a-horseback."

born in a hurricane Descriptive of someone who can handle the most extreme situations, do the hardest, most difficult work. ". . . this man, Otis claimed, would go out by himself for weeks at a time with his bedroll and lariat and would single-handedly rope, brand, vaccinate, and castrate hundreds of calves . . . 'He was born in a damn hurricane, this feller was—" [Thomas McGuane, *Keep The Change,* 1989]

born with a burr up his butt Said of an extremely cranky person. "He's irritable all the time—he was born with a burr up his butt."

borracho Drunk: a drunk person; from the borrowing of a Spanish word meaning the same. "He's muy borracho."

borrasca See quote. "A borrasca was a mine that showed no ore, or one in which the good ore had petered out." [Jack Cummings, *The Rough Rider,* 1988]

borrego A Spanish word used in the Southwest for both a male sheep and a fleecy cloud.

borrowed A euphemism for stolen.

boss dice A dice game with special rules played at bars, mainly in California.

boss of the Plains An old name for the big STETSON hat.

Boston A historical term once used by Indians of the Northwest for any white American, as opposed to the English, French and so forth. These *Bostons* were also called *Bostonians* by the Indians and were so named because so many settlers came from New England or had connections with that great hub of commerce.

Boston dollar A humorous old term for a penny, reflecting the cowboy's disdain for what he regarded as Eastern stinginess.

bottom Descriptive of a horse with great stamina or staying power. "That horse has real bottom."

boudin A dish made from the intestines of buffalo, which was considered a great delicacy by hunters and trappers. It is from a French word meaning "sausage."

Bowie knife One writer defines the *bowie* (pronounced *boo-ie*) *knife* as "the principal instrument of nonsurgical phlebotomy in the American Southwest." This lethal instrument was not invented by the legendary Colonel James Bowie (1799–1836), friend of Davy Crockett and hero at the Alamo. According to testimony by a daughter of Rezin Pleasant Bowie, the colonel's older brother, it was her father who invented the knife in about 1827, though Jim Bowie did make it famous in a duel that year at Natchez, Mississippi in which six men were killed and 15 wounded. The common long-bladed hunting knife was originally made at Rezin Bowie's direction by Arkansas blacksmith James Black, who ground a large file to razor sharpness and attached a guard between the blade and handle to protect the user's hand. After Jim Bowie killed one man with it in the Natchez duel, he is said to have sent his knife to a Philadelphia blacksmith, who marketed copies of it under Bowie's name. Its double-edged blade was 10 to 15 inches long and curved to a point. Also called an *Arkansas toothpick* and a *California toothpick,* it was even carried by some congressmen.

bowleg country The West, country where cowboys ride herd. "Out in Bow Leg country Lin McLean had met a woman . . . and made her his lawful wife." [Owen Wister, "A Journey in Search of Christmas," 1897]

bow your back To work hard. "Why, if I had your youth and my brains, I could walk on the backs of my cattle to Omaha. Go on out there, Joe, and bow your damn back." [Thomas McGuane, *Keep The Change,* 1989]

box Can. See usage example at TIN.

box canyon A narrow or blind canyon with steep sides that ends at a rock wall.

bozo A word of Southwest origin with Spanish antecedents that means fellow or man but has come to have a derogatory connotation. It possibly derives from the Spanish *mozo* (young man). Wrote Alfred H. Holt in *Phrases and Word Origins* (1936): "With the word *'bo* (for hobo) in mind, and a cold in the head, what more simple than to change *mozo* (pronounced with the Mexican *s,* not the Spanish *th*) into *bozo?*"

bracero Any Mexican laborer in the Southwest; formerly a Mexican migrant picker legally admitted to the United States, the word derives from the Spanish *bracero,* (someone with strong arms).

braggin' ranch A big Texas ranch. " 'Course it's kind of wildish up there, not like here, and we only got a small place—couple hundred thousand acres—it ain't what you'd call a braggin' ranch . . .' " [Edna Ferber, *Giant,* 1952]

brag on To brag about. "You ought to heard him brag on his dog."

Brahma A famous Western cattle breed first imported from India, its place of origin, by South Carolinian Dr. James Bolton Davis in 1849.

brake See BREAK.

brand (1) *Brand,* though long commonly used in the West, is not a word of Western American origin. Related to the word *burn,* it is Old English meaning "torch." The ancient Egyptians marked their cows with brands thousands of years ago. (2) Outfit; organization. "I work for this brand, ma'am." [Jack Cummings, *The Rough Rider,* 1988]

brand artist A rustler or rustler's accomplice who could deftly alter the brands on stolen cattle, creating a different design from the existing one and often doing so with the most rudimentary tools over a campfire.

brand blotter; brand blotcher; brand burner More names for someone who illegally alters a brand on cattle.

branded-in-the-hide Someone true-blue and uncompromising in his or her beliefs, a dyed-in-the-wool believer. "He was a branded-in-the-hide conservative."

brasero A charcoal-holding container used in Southern Texas homes for cooking and sometimes for heating.

brassy See quote. "There are days in our Southwestern country that people call *brassy* but should be called steel. The sun beats down with a merciless white fire until the cloudless sky is scarcely blue but rather like the blade of a knife that for days has been ground to stone. And all day it cuts open the breathing body of the prairie and lays its bones dead and bare in the pitiless glare before you." [Conrad Richter, *The Sea of Grass,* 1936]

brave around A term used in the early West to describe a man swaggering about like an Indian brave. "There he was bravin' around as usual—that man could strut sittin' down."

breachy (1) Descriptive of a cow given to breaking out of enclosures, a cow that breaches barriers. (2) By extension, a person without sexual restraints, one who leaps the fence of propriety.

bread-and-with-it An old perhaps obsolete expression for a meal featuring food other than just bread, though it would not be a grand meal. "You're welcome to come on in and have bread-and-with-it."

breadroot See INDIAN BREADROOT

break; brake Rough ground; a gulch.

break for the tall timber Depart hastily with no good-byes; also *pull* (or *put, strike) for the tall timber.* "He broke for the tall timber, knowing the Rangers weren't far behind."

break in two In the Southwest, when a horse tries to throw a rider by suddenly changing from running to bucking, or vice versa, he is said to *break in two.* Similar expressions are *to boil over* and *to wrinkle his spine.*

break one's pick To quit, to be fired; an expression used especially among Western miners.

break trail To forge a path through obstructions. "There he was, head low, breaking trail through the deep snow."

Break-up; Breaking Up A late 19th century term in the Southwest for the Civil War.

breed Short for *half-breed*. " 'You're a damn fool, Wright. But what can you expect from a breed?' 'That's a lie!' shouted Ernie. 'My mother wasn't no Indian!' " [Jack Schaefer, *Shane,* 1949]

breed a scab on one's nose; breed a scab A warning to someone that he or she is raising or stirring up trouble, is looking for a punch on the nose. "Keep talking like that you're breeding a scab on your nose."

breeding ranch; breeding range Terms used in the past for a ranch or range where ranchers bred horses from their stock.

breedy Descriptive of a worthwhile horse, one worth using for breeding purposes. "I wouldn't trade this breedy horse for three of yours."

Bremmer cattle A common pronunciation of *Brahma* cattle, a variety of large silver-gray cattle that originated in India. "Watch out for that Bremmer bull."

bresh A common Western pronunciation of *brush.*

Brevoortia Ida-Maia The *floral firecracker,* as this plant is popularly called, shows how oddly things sometimes get their names. Ida May, the daughter of a 19th-century California stagecoach driver, had noticed the bulbous plant many times in her travels and pointed it out to Alphonso Wood, a naturalist always interested in collecting botanical specimens. Wood named the single plant, a member of the lily family, *Brevoortia Ida-Maia, Brevoortia* in honor of his fellow American naturalist J. C. Brevoort and *Ida-Maia* in gratitude to the observant little girl who had brought the scarlet-flowered perennial to his attention.

Brewer's blackbird A Western blackbird named after American ornithologist T. M. Brewer (1814–1880).

brides of the multitude A euphemism for prostitutes. "Here, along three city blocks [in Denver], the 'brides of the multitude' practiced the oldest profession." [Matt Braun, *The Brannocks,* 1986]

bridlewise (1) A well-trained horse, one that responds to reins and bridle. (2) Any obedient person. "She'll soon enough make him bridlewise."

Brigham's Destroying Angels. See quote. "[Porter] Rockwell was said to be the leader of [Brigham Young's] Destroying Angels. It was whispered that these were the men who eliminated those troublesome to the church . . ." [Louis L'Amour, *Bendigo Shafter,* 1979]

Brigham Young cocktail Any potent whiskey; so called, according to an old joke, "because after one sip, you're a confirmed polygamist."

Brigham Young weed A plant of the *Ephedra* genus found in Utah and throughout the West and named for Mormon leader Brigham Young. It also goes by the names *Mormon tea, Brigham tea, teamster's tea, clapweed* and *canatillo.*

bristlecone pine *Pinus aristada,* an upland tree common to the Western states, one specimen of which, Methuselah, growing at 10,000 feet in California's White Mountains, is thought to be the world's oldest living tree at over 4,700 years of age.

brittlebush; brittlebrush A low-growing Southwestern shrub *(Encelia farinosa)* whose flowering stems turn dry and brittle when its seeds mature; also called *golden hills* because of its yellow flowers glowing golden on the desert.

broadhorn An ark or flatboat used to transport freight on Western rivers; so named for the two long oars projecting like horns from its sides.

brockle-face A cow with a blotched, mottled or pied face.

Broken Arrows A name given to a hunting band of the Sioux Indians

residing on the Platte River in Nebraska in the 19th century.

broken-mouths Old sheep, which generally lose some of their teeth and appear broken-mouthed.

bronc See BRONCO.

bronco (1) A name from the Spanish for rough and wild, given to a small half-wild horse of the West, probably descended from horses that escaped from early Spanish settlements. (2) Any wild, unbroken horse. Also called a *bronc.* (3) Sometimes used as an adjective meaning wild and unruly. "He gets real bronco when he's had too much to drink."

bronco-buster A cowboy who breaks wild horses to the saddle; also called a *bronc-buster, bronc-peeler, bronc-rider, bronc-twister, bronc-fighter, bronc-snapper, bronc-scratcher,* and *bronc-stomper.*

bronco busting Breaking horses for the saddle. "He had a lot of pain, I guess; his insides were all shot from staying at broncho [sic] busting too long." [Walter Van Tilburg Clark, *The Ox-Bow Incident,* 1940]

bronco grass The grass *Bromus secalinus,* also called *devil's darning needle* because of its inch-long needle, which gets snarled in clothing.

bronze gas A term used in Oklahoma, Colorado and other areas for the unleaded gasoline sold at gas pumps.

broomtail (1) A mare with a long, broom-like tail. (2) Any small, inferior wild horse.

brush breaking Breaking brush by riding through it. " 'Brush breaking' derives its name from the peculiar brittleness of the timber in the high dry altitude of the Southwest. One can ride full speed into a piñon tree and the chances are that the momentum will knock off even good-sized branches." [*Reader's Digest,* October 1941]

brush hand A cowboy who works in the brush country of the Southwest.

brush lodge: brush hut; brush house Lodgings made of brush that were used by some Western Indians, often as temporary quarters.

brush popper A cowboy who works cattle in the brush country of the Southwest. "Walton knew that I was a brush popper and that I hankered for ranger service . . ." [James Frank Dobie, *A Vaquero of the Brush Country,* 1929] Also called a *brush buster, brush thumper, brush whacker* and *brush hand.* The term can also be an insult: "It will be the biggest mistake you ever made, you Texas brush-popper." [Charles Portis, *True Grit,* 1968]

brush rabbit The cottontail rabbit (*Sylvilagus bachmani*) found throughout the West.

brush splitters A name once used for wild brush cattle, the old Texas longhorns.

a bubble off plumb   See HALF A BUBBLE OFF.

buck (1) A derogatory term for an Indian man that dates back to the early 19th century. *Buck warrior* and *buck aborigine* were synonymous, though they are rarely, if ever, used anymore. (2) When said of horses, to leap up, arching the back and landing with head low and forelegs rigid. (3) *Buck* for a dollar may have its origins in animal skins that were classified as "bucks" and "does." The bucks, larger and more valuable (some 500,000 of them were traded every year in 18th-century America), could have become a part of early American business terminology (ca. 1800) and later become slang for a dollar. But *buck*'s origin could just as well be poker. A marker called a *buck* was placed next to a poker player in the game's heyday, in the West during the late 19th century, to remind him that it was his turn to deal next. When silver dollars were used as the markers, they could have taken the name *buck* for their own.

buck a game To bet on a gambling game; to lose money gambling. "If you're going to buck a game, be sure you know it first."

buckaroo A cowboy, often one who breaks horses. It is probably a corruption of the Spanish *vaquero,* meaning the same. The first recorded quotation using the word, in a letter from Texas, shows the mispronunciation of *vaquero* by Americans: "These rancheros are surrounded by peons and *bakharas* or herdsmen." The mispronunciation "bakhara" was further corrupted to *buckhara*, *buckayro* and finally *buckaroo*. *Buckaroo* has probably lasted because it is a good descriptive word, suggesting a cowboy on a bucking horse. It inspired well over 50 other American slang words ending in "-aroo" or "-eroo." *Stinkaroo*, a bad play or movie, still has wide currency, as does *the old switcheroo*, the act of substituting one thing for another. Others not so familiar anymore are *antsaroo*, ants in his pants; *jugaroo*, a jail; and *ziparoo*, energy.

buckarooing Working as a cowboy. " 'I've got a place fer you in my plans.' 'Buckarooin', I hope.' " [Jack Cummings, *The Rough Rider*, 1988]

buckbrush A word used for any shrubby plants or browse plants that animals feed on. See also BIT-TER-BRUSH.

bucket man Rustlers and other unlawful elements gave this name to any cowboy loyal to his employer; the expression refers to the buckets of sheep disinfectant loyal hands had to carry to pour into sheep dip vats. *Bucket men* were also called *sheep dippers*.

buck fence A rail fence made of whole or split logs nailed to a sawbuck (a sawhorse).

bucking on a dime When a horse does all his bucking more or less in one spot, he is said to be *bucking on a dime*.

bucking season The season when sheep breed, generally in late December or January, so that lambs are born in the gentler weather of spring.

bucking straight away A horse that makes long straight-ahead jumps with no twisting is said to be *bucking straight away*.

bucking the tiger See quote. "All betting was against the house, known in Western parlance as 'bucking the tiger.' " [Matt Braun, *The Brannocks*, 1986] See BUCK THE TIGER.

buck-kneed Knock-kneed; the word is applied to both horses and people.

buck nun An old cowboy term for a single, celibate man or recluse who lives by himself without a woman, often in winter camps.

buckle bunnies A cowboy term for rodeo groupies.

buck out To give up entirely, to stop resisting and die—all the bucking gone out of you like a horse that has finally been broken.

buckskin See DUN.

buckskins Clothes or shoes made from the strong soft yellowish or grayish leather prepared from the skin of a buck or deer. "He had discarded his buckskins and was wearing a full-dress uniform." [G. Clifton Wisler, *My Brother, the Wind,* 1979]

buck the tiger A historical term meaning to play against the bank in faro. Faro was called *the tiger* because professional gamblers carried their faro outfits in boxes with a Royal Bengal tiger painted on them, and tigers were also painted on the chips.

buffalo Most people believe that *buffalo* is a misnomer, a name applied with zoological inexactitude to the American bison. Cortés described the creature as "a rare Mexican bull, with crooked shoulders, a hump on its back like a camel and with hair like a lion," but later explorers thought it was the Asian or African water buffalo and called it after the Spanish *bufalo,* already used in Europe as the name for those animals. Actually, the water buffalo and the American buffalo both belong to the bison family, so the real mistake of early explorers was in calling the native American animal simply *buffalo* and not qualifying it with a name such as *prairie buffalo. Buffalo* is first recorded by de Soto's expedition in 1541 as a name for the bison.

Buffalo Bill Colonel William Frederick Cody (1846–1917), the peerless horseman and sharpshooter who became the original *Buffalo Bill,* earned his nickname as a market hunter for buffalo (bison) hides and as a contractor supplying buffalo meat to workers building the Union Pacific Railroad in 1867. To his glory then, and shame now, he killed 4,280 buffalo in one year, mostly for their hides and tongues. It is hard to separate truth from fiction in Cody's life, his fame owing much to the dime novels that made him a celebrity in the late 19th century. Buffalo Bill was a herder, a pony express rider, a scout and cavalryman for the U.S. Army during the Civil War and an Indian fighter who is said to have killed the Cheyenne chief Yellowhand single-handedly. He was a member of the Nebraska state legislature in 1878. His Wild West Show, which he organized in 1883, toured the United States and Europe, bringing him great personal fame, yet financial problems caused this legendary American hero to die in poverty and relative obscurity. Today his name conjures up visions of "sportsmen" picking off buffalo from the platforms of moving trains, abundant buffalo meat rotting on the plains, and the destruction of the great herds. Thanks to early conservationists, some 20,000 American bison survive today, protected on government ranges.

buffalo boat A boat made by stretching buffalo hides over a frame of poles or an empty wagon body; often used by Westering caravans to cross swamps and rivers.

buffalo chips Dried buffalo dung. "There was a space wagon-tongue lashed there and a sheet of canvas . . . 'What's that for?' 'Buffalo chips,' a bystander said. 'The womenfolks walk behind the wagon and pick up buffalo chips and toss them onto that canvas. They're the only fuel you are likely to find.' " [Louis L'Amour, *Comstock Lode,* 1981] Also called *buffalo wood.*

buffalo cider See quote. "Buffalo cider is the ludicrous name given to the liquid in the stomach of a buffalo, which the thirsty hunter drinks when he has killed his game at a great distance from water." [Maximilian Schele De Vere, *Americanisms,* 1871]

buffalo clover See quote. "Yet the hills could hardly be so lush with buffalo-clover—as we used to call the bluebonnet—and red bunch grass, so soft and lovely, as they are in the eyes of memory." [Frank Dobie, *Coronado's Children,* 1930] See also BLUE BONNET.

buffalo eaters A name given by other Indian tribes to the Northern and Middle Commanches, who subsisted mainly on buffalo meat.

buffalo fever An obsolete term for the excitement men felt at the prospect of going on a buffalo hunt.

buffalo gnat A small black fly with a humped body like a buffalo; they were a scourge of buffalo in the summer.

buffalo grass A short low-growing grass *(Buchloe dactyloides)* common on the dry plains near the Rocky Mountains. "And it was good grass: buffalo grass and some bluestem."

[Thomas McGuane, *Nothing but Blue Skies,* 1992]

buffalo horns An old name for Western mountain ranges whose summits appear serrated, like the teeth of a saw.

buffalo soldier An Indian name for black U.S. soldiers stationed in the West. One explanation of the name: "The officers say the negroes make good soldiers and fight like fiends . . . The Indians call them 'buffalo soldiers,' because their wooly heads are so much like the matted cushion that is between the horns of the buffalo." [F. M. A. Roe, *Army Letters,* 1872]

buffalo stamp See quote. "The rock lies . . . but a few inches below the surface, which is largely dotted with 'buffalo stamps.' These are said to have been caused by buffaloes crowding together, stamping and licking the ground, led there by a saline element in the soil." [Anonymous, *Western Wilds,* 1878]

buffalo wallow A natural depression in the earth that fills with water and mud; here buffalo wallow in the spring of the year, rubbing themselves on the ground to rid themselves of shedding hair.

buffalo wolf A gray wolf *(Canis lupus nubilus),* so named because it preyed upon the buffalo.

bug-eater (1) Any worthless person; the derogatory term is also used in humorous expressions like *son of a* *bug-eater.* (2) A humorous, derisive nickname for a Nebraskan. The name derives either from the impoverished appearance of Nebraskans in various parts of the state in times past or from the state being overrun in part by locusts; there were even suggestions made at one time to make food of the locusts, one farmer writing a book with the theme "If you can't beat 'em, eat 'em." According to *Notes and Queries,* June 15, 1883: "Several Nebraskan entomologists and journalists actually got up a dinner at which locusts were served in various styles."

bug juice An old slang term for the bad liquor so common on the frontier.

build a smoke Roll a cigarette. "Hondo shoved his hat back and began to build a smoke." [Louis L'Amour, *Hondo,* 1953]

bullberry The buffalo berry *(Lepargyraea argentea).*

bullboat A historical expression for a light boat made of a willow frame and covered with the hide of a bull elk or other animal skins; it was used by Indians and traders in the early West. See also UP SHIT CREEK WITH-OUT A BULLBOAT.

bull bucker A term used by loggers for the man bossing the gang that fells and bucks (cuts into logs) the fallen trees.

bull-built Descriptive of a husky barrel-chested man.

bullcorn An expression of mild disgust meaning "nonsense." "That's a lot of bullcorn."

bulldog (1) A short haircut like a crewcut, the hair standing up an inch or so tall. (2) A hooded stirrup often worn by cowboys in the past.

bulldogging "One of the men . . . reached well over the animal's back to get a slack of the loose hide next to the belly, lifted strongly, and tripped. This was called 'bulldogging'." So did an early writer describe the way cowboys wrestled steers to the ground in the West. They often, however, leaped from their horses and twisted the cow's neck, flipping it over. Neither method suggests the way bulldogs fought bulls when such cruel contests were held in England—for the bulldog seized the bull's nose in its mouth. Esse F. O'Brien's *The First Bulldogger* (1961) therefore suggests that a black cowboy named Bill Pickett would sink his teeth into a bull's nose while wrestling it to the ground, his method being responsible for the name of the more conventional method!

bull drunk Belligerently drunk. " 'He was bull drunk . . . pulled his Colt.' " [Larry McMurtry, *Lonesome Dove,* 1985]

Bull Durham Long the most popular brand of tobacco rolled into cigarettes or smoked in pipes by cowboys.

bull fuck A term used for a creamy gravy, especially among loggers. Also called *bull gravy*.

bull of the woods The boss or foreman, a tough guy, the term used especially in logging camps.

bullpen Any level area surrounded by tall mountain peaks in the Rocky Mountains.

bull-snake See quote. " 'The big yellow and brown ones won't hurt you; they're bull-snakes and help to keep the gophers down.' " [Willa Cather, *My Ántonia,* 1918]

bulltongue cactus A Nevada cactus *(Opuntia linguiformis)* with pads shaped something like a bull's tongue.

bull train A term used in the early West for the reliable wagon trains pulled by oxen. A bull train driver was called a *bullwhacker,* so named for the "whack" of his whip.

bull wagon boss See quote. "The wagon-master, in the language of the plains, was called the 'bull-wagon boss' . . . and the whole train was denominated a 'bull-outfit.' " [Buffalo Bill Cody, *Story of the Wild West,* 1888]

bullwhacker See BULL TRAIN.

bum; bummer Sheepherders give this name to a lamb that has lost its mother, or whose mother has deserted it, and which has to be raised by humans or by another ewe tricked into believing the lamb is her own. Also called a *bummie* and a *leppie.* "Bummies were the motherless lambs, orphaned for one reason or another." [Giles A. Lutz, *The Feud,* 1982] See also BUTTERMILK.

bum-rub A humorous term recorded in Utah for sitting on folded laundry and rubbing back and forth to save the wear and tear of ironing.

bunch To herd together cattle or other range animals. "We bunched some 4,000 head out on the prairie."

bunch grass See quote. " 'Bunch grass' *[Sporobolus airboides]* grows on the bleak mountain sides of Nevada and neighboring territories, and offers excellent feed for stock, even in the dead of winter, wherever the snow is blown aside and exposes it; notwithstanding its unpromising home, bunch-grass is a better and more nutritious diet for cattle and horses than almost any other hay or grass that is known—so stock-men say." [Mark Twain, *Roughing It,* 1872]

bunch quitter A horse that breaks from the herd and goes its own way.

bunkhouse A building separate from the main ranch house where hands have sleeping and living quarters.

bunko Any swindler or cheat, from the Spanish *banca* (a game of chance at cards). The term originated in the

West, Herbert Asbury advising in *Sucker's Progress* (1938): "Eight-Dice Cloth was introduced into San Francisco by a crooked gambler who made various changes in the method of play and christened it Banco. After a few years this was corrupted into Bunco, sometimes spelled Bunko, and in time Bunco came to be a general term applied to all swindling and confidence games."

Buntline Special   The heroes in Western writer Ned Buntline's stories used special long-barreled Colt revolvers that were soon called *Buntline Specials* after the prolific author.

Buntlinism   Ned Buntline, the pen name of Edward Z. C. Judson (1823–86), was an adventurer, trapper and soldier in the Far West whose life pales those of the heroes of the over 400 dime novels he wrote. This founder of the Know-Nothing party, rioter and accused murderer gave William Cody the name Buffalo Bill and featured him in a series of dime novels. His rowdy, jingoistic political doctrine inspired the term *Buntlinism*.

Bunyan camp A logging camp in the Northwest that doesn't provide bedding for workers, who must live primitively like the legendary Paul Bunyan.

burn (1) To brand cattle and other livestock; also used to describe the rustler's practice of altering cattle brands. (2) An area where the vegetation has been burned, either intentionally, for cultivation, or accidentally.

the burning drink   A Sioux Indian name for whiskey. ". . . many were poisoned by the white man's whiskey (what Bone Hand always called 'the burning drink')." [Jean Rikhoff, *The Sweetwater,* 1976]

burnt cattle Cattle whose brands have been changed by rustlers. "He spotted close to fifty burnt cattle in the herd."

burn the breeze To ride a horse fast. "He was really burning the breeze on that old paint." Also *burn the wind.*

burn the earth To ride at full speed. "I was half a mile in the lead, burning the earth like a canned dog." [Andy Adams, *The Log of a Cowboy,* 1903] Also *burn the prairie.*

burn the wind See   BURN   THE   BREEZE.

burrito A tortilla wrapped around meat, beans, cheese or other fillings. *Burrito* is Spanish for "little burro," and the word was originally confined to the Southwest but is used nationwide now with the spreading popularity of the food.

burro A donkey, from the Spanish meaning the same; used mostly in the Southwest.

burro deer See MULE DEER.

burro grass The popular name for the perennial tough range grass *Scleropogon brevifolius* of the Southwest, apparently because it is commonly thought to be fit only for burros to eat.

bush rabbit See BRUSH RABBIT.

bushtail; brushtail A name commonly used by Western loggers for a horse.

bushwacker An old term for an outlaw who bushwacked (ambushed) somebody.

bushwah; booshwa Buffalo chips; also has general usage in the United States as a euphemism for bullshit, nonsense.

buster See BRONCO-BUSTER.

busthead Any cheap, strong, inferior whiskey. "That busthead gave me some hangover."

a Butch Cassidy A fabled gunfighter, after *Butch Cassidy,* an alias of George LeRoy Parker (1866–1909?), who once worked as a cattle butcher and later led a gang called the Wild Bunch, one of whose members was the Sundance Kid (Harry Longabaugh). Legend holds that he was killed in a gunfight with Bolivian troops, but his sister claimed that he visited her long after his alleged death.

butte A French word, adopted by early explorers in the West, meaning an isolated hill or mountain rising abruptly above the surrounding land.

butter-churn horse See quote. " 'Butter-churn horse? I know a little about horses, but that's new to me.' 'If you put a can of milk on his back, he'd churn it into butter.' " [Wayne Barton, *Return to Phantom Hill,* 1983]

buttermilk A name given to a motherless calf, apparently because orphaned calves are fed the skim milk remaining after butter is churned. See also BUM.

button Any kid, child or inexperienced teenager trying to become a cowboy. "They had worked together when Charlie was a big button and Page a cowboy in his twenties." [Elmer Kelton, *The Time It Never Rained,* 1973]

buzzard (1) A New World vulture of the family Cathartidae, especially the turkey vulture. "The pile of bodies was about three feet high. A dozen buzzards were flapping and fighting on it, tearing at the fresh meat." [John Cunningham, *The Rainbow Runner* (1992).] (2) A cantankerous or contemptible person, usually in the form *old buzzard.* "The old buzzard swore he'd stay alive just to annoy them."

buzzard bait A worthless man or animal, good only as food for the buzzards.

by doggies A mild exclamation. " 'You got any varnish?' 'Sure have, by doggies, a whole gallon of it.' " [Max Evans, *The Great Wedding*, 1963]

by Godfrey! A euphemism for "by God!" " 'No, by Godfrey! we're pay-ing. Me and Shane.' " [Jack Schaefer, *Shane*, 1949]

C

caballero Deriving from the Spanish meaning "a man on horseback," *caballero* came to signify a gentleman as well. It also meant, in the words of a Texas cowboy early in this century, "a hardened but gay cowboy who can jump on his horse any minute and tell the world to go to hell."

caboodle An old expression for a lot, an amount. "I'll take the whole caboodle of them." Also heard as *the whole kit and caboodle* in many areas of the country.

caboose See POSSUM BELLY.

cabrito This Spanish word for a kid or young suckling goat has come to refer more specifically to the Texas specialty of barbecued suckling goat, which is said to be the most delicious of barbecued meats.

cabrón Meaning "a cuckold" in Spanish, *cabrón* has long been a strong curse in the Southwest among Mexicans and Mexican-Americans, though some use it humorously.

cack A poor-fitting saddle that irritates a horse; the word, used mostly in Texas and Montana, may derive from the prickly cactus.

cackleberry A Western logger's humorous designation for eggs.

cacomestle *Bassaris astuta,* a close relative of the raccoon, takes its common name *cocomestle,* from a Nahuatl word meaning the same.

cactus apple; cactus berry Names for the fruit of the yucca.

cactus boomers A name once common for wild brush cattle, the old Texas longhorns.

cactus candy Candy made in the Southwest from cactus pulp and sugar.

cactus mouse; cactus rat Common names for the Southwestern white-footed mouse *(Peromyscus eremicus)*.

cain't A common pronunciation of *can't.*

cake See quote. " 'Cake, Yankee, is feed . . . 'Concentrated cow-feed . . .' " [Edna Ferber, *Giant,* 1952]

calaboose Any jail, but usually a small one in a small town; it derives from the Spanish *calaboza* (dungeon).

44

Calamity Jane Those who tried to outshoot Calamity Jane (Martha Jane Canary Burke, 1852–1903) brought calamity upon themselves. The legendary Western markswoman's *nom de guerre* came to mean a woman who predicts or suffers calamity as well as the queen of spades (associated with death) in poker.

calcified fact A hard, sure fact. " 'I just saw a lot of injustice in the court system and I saw people my own age in positions of authority that I had grown up with and know for a calcified fact didn't have one damn lick of sense.' " [Cormac McCarthy, *All the Pretty Horses*, 1992]

calf fries A Southwestern dish of fried calf testicles. (See also PRAIRIE OYSTER.)

calf-kneed Knock-kneed, like an awkward calf.

calf-slobbers The meringue of meringue pies, because it resembles the white, stiff salivation of a sucking calf; used in the Southwest.

caliche A calcium carbonate soil formation in arid parts of the Southwest.

calico fever An old humorous term for an infatuation with a woman or women in general; someone "woman crazy" is said to have "a bad case of calico fever."

calico pony; calico mustang Any spotted or piebald horse.

calico salmon The dog salmon *(Oncorhynchus keta),* so named in the West because of its mottled color in summer.

California (1) Lexicographers aren't positive about the origin of the word *California,* but the 31st state, which entered the Union in 1850, may be named after a woman named Calafia in an old Spanish romance, this Calafia ruling over an island called California. On the other hand, other etymologists insist that *California* is a Catalan word meaning "hot oven"—a story that's not good for the tourist trade. (2) The word *california,* uncapitalized, is a term used by cowboys for throwing a calf by holding its neck and tripping it.

California banknote (1) An animal hide, such hides often used as a medium of exchange during the 1849 gold rush. (2) Silver used as a medium of exchange.

California blanket Hobo language for newspapers used as blankets.

California breakfast A derogatory expression that, according to a January 1962 *Western Folklore* article, means "a cigarette and an orange."

California collar A joking term given to the hangman's noose when vigilante justice ruled in early California.

California fever The desire to go to California, the term first recorded not when gold was discovered but after explorer J. C. Frémont journeyed there in 1844.

California lion   The tawny mountain lion *(Felix concolor)*, also called the *catamount*, COUGAR and *mountain cat.*

California pants   Strongly made riding pants, often reinforced with buckskin, prized among cowboys in the early West.

California prayer book   A joking term for playing cards, popular in gold rush days.

California socks   Socks made out of flour sacks slipped into and tied to the legs. Cowboys pulled their boots over these "socks," which were warmer than conventional hose.

California toothpick   See BOWIE KNIFE.

Californio   An old name California residents called themselves. "They don't consider themselves Spanish, nor do they think of themselves as Mexicans . . . They call themselves Californios . . ." [Louis L'Amour, *The Lonesome Gods,* 1983]

calling the brands   A cowboy adept at deciphering or reading the often complicated brands on cattle was said to be good at *calling the brands.*

calm as a horse trough   Very calm, smooth waters.

camas   *Camassia esculenta,* also called the *quamash* flower, the sweet bulbs of which Northwestern Indians used for food; from a Nootka Indian word meaning "sweet."

camas eater   This was a nickname given to the first settlers of Oregon, who depended on the camas bulb for food.

camino real   A term from Spanish meaning "royal road" and once used in the Southwest for a main public highway built by the state. It also referred to several specific roads leading from Mexico into California and New Mexico.

camisa   A shirt, blouse or chemise; a borrowing of the Spanish word meaning the same. "She wore a cotton camisa and a long skirt."

camp bird   The Rocky Mountain jay. See also CAMP ROBBER.

camp on one's trail   To trail, follow someone persistently. "The sheriff camped on his trail until he caught him."

campoodie   An old Spanish term used in the Southwest for an Indian village, a rude collection of huts. Wrote Mark Twain in an 1869 piece: "It is worse than an Indian campoodie."

camp robber   A nickname given to the Canada jay *(Perisoreus canadensis)* and various other birds that filch food and small ornaments from campsites.

camp swamper A historical term for a worker who did all the odd jobs in camp—from providing food to caring for the horses and cooking—while the trappers went after beaver pelts.

campyard A camp roughly similar to the motels of today, where a cowboy's horse could be put up and there was a cabin for him to stay in as well.

can See TIN.

canada Spanish for a small, narrow canyon. ". . . the faint bawling of a calf for its mother in some dim, starlit canada." [Conrad Richter, *The Sea of Grass*, 1936]

canal Any large irrigation ditch in the Southwest.

canatillo See MORMON TEA.

candelabrum cactus Another name for the majestic Cholla cactus *(Opuntia arborescens)*, which resembles a candelabra.

cane cholla The prickly pear *(Opuntia* species) of the Southwestern desert; also called the *cane cactus* and *walking-stick cholla* because its straight stems are sometimes used for making canes.

cane grass A name given to tall grasses in general.

can I carry you home? May I give you a ride or a lift? "Kin ah carry you home?"

canned dog A dog with empty tin cans tied to his tail; to can a dog and set him loose was once thought great fun to some.

canned milk Condensed milk in a can. "When canned milk had come out, some cowpuncher galoot had written in praise of it:

'No tits to pull.
No hay to pitch.
Just punch a hole
In the son of a bitch.' "

[A. B. Guthrie Jr., *Arfive*, 1970]

can openers Cowboy slang for spurs.

cantina A Spanish term for a bar or saloon in Texas and other Southwestern states, where cantinas with colorful names like "The Spring of Golden Dreams" were once common.

can't pour piss out of a boot Can't do the simplest things. "When it comes to ranchin', he can't poor piss out of a boot."

canyon Used mostly in the West for a very deep valley or gorge with steep sides, sometimes with water flowing through the plain; the word derives from the Spanish *canôn* (a large tube or funnel).

canyoned Enclosed in a canyon. "We were canyoned and had to travel two miles to reach a crossing."

capador See quote. " 'He's the capador. He castrates the males and that makes them steers. And [as an additional duty] he nicks a piece off the end of the left ear of male and female and sticks it in his pocket, and he marks the right ear with a hole and a slit, for identification. At the end of the day he adds up, and the number of pieces of ear in his pocket shows the number of calves we've branded . . . [As for] the testicles of the castrated calves, the tumbadores roast them on the coals, they burst open and they eat them as you'd eat a roast oyster . . . very tasty . . . the vaqueros think they make you potent and strong as a bull.' " [Edna Ferber, *Giant,* 1952] See also TUMBADORE.

capon egg A joking expression used to tease a tenderfoot, no such thing as a capon egg existing, of course. "Before you clean out the stall, go down to the coop and collect all the capon eggs."

caporal The boss, manager or foreman of a ranch, one who directs the workers but doesn't pay them; a borrowing of the Spanish word for the name.

capper A shill or lure in gambling establishments or at medicine shows and auctions. "There were always two or three cappers he used to boost the price at his auctions."

caracara A Southwestern vulture-like hawk *(Polyborus cheriway auduboni);* the name derives from an Indian word for the predatory bird.

carajo A term describing any base person, often applied to rough mule skinners and ox drivers in the past, perhaps because they often used the word as an exclamation. *Carajo* means "penis" in Spanish.

carajo pole Southwestern term for the long stem of a maguey plant used as a goad for animals or even men.

caramba! A Spanish exclamation of admiration or annoyance. "Caramba! Look at that girl!"

carcel A prison or jail; a borrowing from the Spanish.

card A pronunciation of *coward.* "Texas chili ain't for cards."

carnival Any horse that bucks in a spectacular manner is said to *carnival.*

Carson county See quote. "Originally, Nevada was a part of Utah and was called Carson county . . ." [Mark Twain, *Roughing It,* 1872]

carve To separate or cut out cattle from a herd. "We're gonna do some carving today."

casa House; the Spanish word has been used in the Southwest since the early 19th century.

casa grande A large house.

case; caser An old term for a dollar bill. "He handed him a five-case note [five-dollar bill]."

cash down To pay or settle up. "Cash down now or get off the train."

cash in Short for "to cash in one's chips or checks," to die. "He cashed in up in Colorado."

cashmoney A Texan redundancy for "cash."

cast-iron dog An humorous term once used in the Southwest for the hairless dog known as a *pelon* to Mexicans.

catawampus cat An ill-tempered, scolding woman, a shrew; an expression heard in Texas.

catch-rope A lariat or lasso.

catch colt A Western euphemism for an illegitimate child, called an *old-field colt* and a *woods colt* in other regions. Originally the term meant a colt that wasn't the result of its owner intentionally breeding its parents.

cat-eyed An old, descriptive term for a paranoid gunfighter always aware of everything around him, his eyes constantly shifting around.

cat in the meal Something hidden or sinister; the expression comes from a story in the once-popular Webster's "blue-backed speller." "With all those politicians backing him, I'm sure there's a cat in the meal."

catlinite A Western clay-stone of pale grayish red to dark red color, *catlinite* honors American painter and writer George Catlin (1796–1872). Early used by American Indians for making pipes, it is commonly called pipe-rock. Catlin, a self-taught artist, is remembered for his primitive but authentic paintings of Indian life. An impresario, too, he displayed troupes of Indians in the East and Europe long before Buffalo Bill or Barnum.

cat's claw See ANGRY TREE.

cattle baron A synonym, first recorded in 1898, for a CATTLE KING; usually the word has a derogatory connotation.

Cattle Kate An old term for a woman cattle rustler; after "Cattle Kate Maxwell" (Ella Watson), who was hanged for rustling in 1889, though she may have been innocent. It is said that she traded sexual favors to rustlers for payment in cattle.

cattle king A rich cattle man with extensive holdings; the term is first recorded in 1874 and *not* named after the vast King ranch in Texas. See also REAL MCCOY; CATTLE QUEEN.

cattle moss Spanish moss.

cattle paper Notes and mortgages for which ranchers put up their herds as collateral.

cattle queen A rich cattle woman. On August 23, 1876, the *Bedrock*

Democrat of Baker, Oregon noted: "Mrs. Nash, of Corpus Christie . . . is fairly entitled to the name of 'the Cattle Queen of Texas.'" See also CATTLE KING.

cattle range A sparsely settled prairie region in the West where cattle graze.

cattle singer See quote. " . . . Shanghai Wiley, up from Texas, was the most famous cattle singer in the whole Southwest . . . Possessed of a remarkably high sweet tenor voice . . . he had been known to quiet a whole herd of restless cattle on the verge of a mad stampede. It was an art he had learned when a cowboy on the range. Many cowboys had it, but none possessed the magic soothing quality of Shanghai's voice. It was reputed to have in it the sorcery of the superhuman. It was told of him that in a milling herd, their nostrils distended, their flanks heaving, he had been seen to leap from the back of one maddened steer to another, traveling that moving mass that was like a shifting sea, singing to them in his magic tenor, stopping them just as they were about to plunge into the Rio Grande." [Edna Ferber, *Cimarron,* 1930]

cattle spinach A common name for the valuable browse plant saltbrush *(Atriplex polycarpa)* of the Southwest.

cattle thief A term first recorded in 1862, some 20 years before RUSTLER was given this meaning.

cattle town A Western town dependent on the cattle trade.

cattle war A war in cattle country usually caused by private individuals buying and fencing what had been free grazing ranges.

cattlo See quote. "'It's a word made up out of cattle and buffalo and that's what the critters are, they're bred up out of cattle and buffalo, bred years back to see if we couldn't fetch something the heat and ticks couldn't get to.'" [Edna Ferber, *Giant,* 1952] Also *catalo,* but the term *beefalo* is more common today.

cat wagon *Cat* was slang for a prostitute as far back as 1401, when a poem of the day warned men to "beware of cats' tails." Though this term associating the cat and commercial sex is less common, the connotation hangs on the word *cathouse,* a bordello. *Cat wagons* were cathouses on wheels, covered wagons pulled by horses that transported harlots while the West was being won.

cavy; caavy (1) A stray horse or steer. (2) A pony or saddle horse used on a roundup. (3) A bunch of horses; the borrowing of a Spanish word meaning the same.

cayuse An Indian pony; a poor stunted horse. Characters in Westerns sometimes use the word *cayuse* to describe a horse of little value, but *cayuse,* strictly, is a name for Indian ponies, a breed that Western pioneers knew as *kiyuse* and that was rarely properly trained by white men. The cayuse takes its name from the Cayuse Indians of Washington and Oregon, who bred the small horse. In 1847, blaming whites for a small-pox epidemic, the tribe attacked and killed 14 missionaries near the present city of Walla Walla, Washington. Subdued and put on a reservation in 1855, their ranks decimated by disease, they died as a people, with no full-blooded Cayuse Indian surviving today.

cayusein'; cayusin' A term used by Texans for the bucking of a horse. "That horse was really cayusein!"

celebrity wagon A sturdy wagon or coach once used on heavy roads and in rugged mountainous country.

Centennial State A nickname for Colorado because the state was admitted to the Union in 1876.

century plant This name for the agave (*Agave americana*) is a misnomer, referring to the legend that the plant blooms once every hundred years and dies shortly after it does. Actually, the plant rarely flowers in cultivation but in the wild flowers any time after 10 to 15 years, sometimes sooner, and doesn't die immediately afterward. The alcoholic drink pulque is made from the *Agave atrorrens* species, and tequilla and mescal are made from *Agave tequilla*.

chachalaca The popular name of a turkey-like bird common in Texas. *Ortalis vetula macalli* is called the *chachalaca* in imitation of the loud harsh cackling cry it makes and was first given the name by American Indians, the bird's name being *chachalacametl* in Nahuatl.

chain lightning Lightning bolts that appear to move very quickly in wavy and zigzag lines. The term is an Americanism coined about 1825 and is used in the Northeast as well as the West.

chalking the hat An interesting phrase used in the early West, especially on railroad trains, referring to the common practice of conductors making white chalk marks on the "stovepipes" or other hats of passengers who were traveling free of charge for one reason or another.

chalupa A Southwestern dish of Texas-Mexican ("Tex-Mex") cookery consisting of a fried tortilla spread with bean paste or ground cooked meat that is topped with shredded cheese, lettuce, chopped tomato and hot sauce. *Chalupa* means "small canoe" in Spanish but does not describe the shape of the dish, which is round and flat.

chamber lye A humorous term for wine, deriving from *chamber pot*.

chamise The evergreen bush *Adenostoma fasciculatum* common in California, where dense thickets of it are called *chamisal*. Its name is from the Spanish *chamiso* (burnt kindling wood) because the wood is used for kindling. The name is also used for the *wingscale bush,* the *buckbush,* the *squawbush* and the *toyon.*

chaparral Any dense growth of shrubs or small trees, a tangle, a thicket. The Spanish word is used mainly in the Southwest but has national use due to its use in Western stories and movies. ". . . the chaparral flats, a heaven for snakes and horned toads, roadrunners and stinging lizards . . ." [Larry McMurtry, *Lonesome Dove,* 1985]

chaparral bird; chaparral cock Another name for the ROADRUNNER in the Southwest.

chapote A wild fruit also known as the black persimmon *(Diospyros texana)* that grows on a small tree or shrub; the word derives ultimately from a Nahuatl Indian name for the fruit, which has been used as everything from a food to a hair dye.

chapping A game in which two cowboys slap one another with their leather chaps, each taking a turn, to see who gives up first. Also an old punishment of a cowboy imposed by a kangaroo court, the offender whipped with a pair of chaps.

chaps Joined leather leggings, often widely flared, worn by cowboys over pants as protection against chaparral or brush, burrs, rope burns and so forth while on horseback. The word ultimately derives from CHAPARRAL.

Charlie Dunns Custom-made cowboy boots worn by many celebrities, including Gene Autry, Slim Pickens, Arnold Palmer and Harry Belafonte, costing up to $3,000 and fashioned of leather and exotic skins like ostrich. The boots were made in Austin by Charlie Dunn, whose father, grandfather and great-grandfather before him were Texas bootmakers. Mr. Dunn, who died in 1993, age 95, is also remembered by the popular country Western song "Charlie Dunn," first recorded in the 1970s.

Charlie Taylor A butter substitute that cooks on the frontier in the old West made from sorghum and bacon grease; probably named after a chuckwagon cook of the day.

chase a cloud To be thrown high in the air by a bucking horse.

chaw Often used in place of *chew* as both a verb and noun, as in "He chawed on it" and "I gave him a chaw of tobacco."

chayote The edible green or white pear-shaped fruit of the chayote vine *(Sechium edule)* common in the Southwest; also called the *vegetable pear* and the *mirleton.* The word derives from the Nahuatl word for the fruit.

cheaters A humorous term for eyeglasses; used in other regions as well. Also a term for a horse's blinders.

check in To die. "Before I check in, I reckon a few of them will bite the dust."

cheechako A tenderfoot, the term mostly heard in the Pacific Northwest and deriving from a Chinook word meaning "just arrived."

cheerwater Liquor, dating back to the late 19th century and apparently modeled on *firewater*.

Cherokee outlet A 57-mile wide strip of land in what is now Oklahoma granted to the Cherokees by the United States in 1828 as a western outlet from their lands to the buffalo hunting grounds.

chesterfield Originally an English term for a large overstuffed kind of couch (named after an Earl of Chesterfield, who designed it), this word is now used (almost exclusively in northern California) as a generic term for any kind of couch.

chewing iron and spitting nails Very angry. "Angry? Judge, you was chewing iron and spitting nails!" [Lucia St. Clair Robson, *Ride the Wind*, 1982]

chew it fine To consider or explain something fully or thoroughly; derives from the expression *chew it over* (to think about it). "You've got to chew it finer than that before making a decision."

Cheyenne No one is certain about it, but the name of this North American Indian tribe of the Algonquian linguistic family, now found in Montana and Oklahoma, may derive from the French feminine for dog *(chienne)*. French traders in Minnesota may have named them so because the tribe, like many Indian tribes, ate dog meat. Another possibility is that *Cheyenne* comes from a Sioux Indian word meaning "people

of alien speech." For still another theory, however remote, see the following quote: "The plains warriors didn't torture. 'They takes scalps,' the old man had told him, 'and they cuts off a dead enemy's left arm, maybe only the left hand. Just that. Gets their name from that. Cheyenne means "Cut-Arm People" . . .' " [Theodore V. Olsen, *Arrow in the Sun*, 1969]

Cheyenne saddle A famous flat saddle, often highly ornamented, popular in the late 19th century and named after Cheyenne, Wyoming where it originated.

chia seed An oily seed from a species of salvia used in making a nourishing beverage; from a Nahuatl Indian word meaning the same.

Chicano An American of Mexican descent. One explanation claims this word is a contraction of the Spanish for "I am not a boy." Another suggests it comes from the ending of the word *Mexicano*, which the Aztecs pronounced "Meshicano," this eventually shortened to *shicano* and then *chicano*.

chicken feed Chickens were fed grain too poor for any other use by American pioneers, and these pieces of poor-quality grain had to be small so the chickens could swallow them. This grain obviously suggested the contemptuous term *chicken feed* for small change (pennies, nickels and dimes) to riverboat gamblers fleecing small-town suckers. The first mention of the expression is in *Colonel*

(Davy) Crockett's Exploits (1836): "I stood looking on, seeing him pick up chicken feed from the green horns." By extension, *chicken feed* has come to mean any small or insignificant amount of money, and even (rarely today) misleading information deliberately supplied or leaked by a government to spies employed by another government.

chicken-fried steak   A steak, often a cheap cut, breaded and fried; the dish is especially popular in the West and South.

chicken pulling   A game of Mexican origin played by Southwestern cowboys that consisted of burying a live chicken in soft ground up to its neck, the players riding by at a gallop and attempting to pick the chicken out of the ground, usually breaking its neck in the process. The game, also called *pulling the chicken*, fortunately isn't played much anymore, if it is at all.

chicken ranch   Unlike most sexual euphemisms, this synonym for a brothel takes its name from a real place. The original Chicken Ranch was a bordello in LaGrange, Texas, so named because poor farmer clients often paid for their visits with chickens. It is celebrated in the play *The Best Little Whorehouse in Texas.* The Chicken Ranch closed in 1974, inspiring, as Molly Ivins observed, a lot of bumper stickers that read: "BRING BACK THE CHICKEN RANCH—KEEP ON PLUCKING!"

chicken snake   Another name for the rat snake *(Callopeltis guttatus)* because it preys upon chickens and their eggs.

Chic Sales   Outhouses in the West and other areas of the country have been called *Chic Sales, Chic Sale* or *Chick Sales* since the 1920s after American vaudevillian Chick Sale, who had a comedy routine about building an outhouse and wrote a book about his "specialty."

Chihuahua   (1) A very small dog native to Mexico, especially the state of Chihuahua. (2) A slang term used on the frontier for a little town with a large number of saloons and dancehalls catering to soldiers. (3) A Mexican spur with large rowels often beautifully decorated in silver See also AY, CHIHUAHUA!

Chihuahua town   This derogatory term is used in the Southwest for the section of town where people of Mexican ancestry live.

chilacayote   A gourd used as a dessert fruit. Folklore has it that it is so named because it will bring on chills when eaten by a person who is overheated, but the name actually comes from a Nahuatl name for the gourd.

chilchote   A common designation in Texas for the green or sweet pepper; the word has its roots in the Nahuatl language.

child   Mountain men and others often called themselves "child" in the early West. "This child's getting old, and feels like wanting a woman's face about his lodge for the balance of his days . . ." [George Frederick Ruxton, *Life in the Far West,* 1848]

child of the earth A popular Southwestern name for the wind scorpion (*Eremobates* species).

chile (1) Any of various species of Capsicum, including the red or cayenne pepper; from a Nahuatl word meaning the same. Also spelled *chili.*

chili Short for *chili con carne,* a thick meat and bean stew spiced with chilies.

chili-belly A derogatory name for a Mexican. " 'There ain't many of them chili-bellies that will bother you once they're afoot.' " [Larry McMurtry, *Lonesome Dove,* 1985] Also *chili-eater* and *chili-chomper.*

Chinaman's chance The Chinese immigrants who built so many miles of American railroads often tried to make their fortune by working old claims and streams abandoned by white prospectors during the California gold rush of 1849. They had an extremely poor chance of finding any gold in such abandoned claims, and thus a *Chinaman's chance* came to mean "no chance at all." The poor lot of Chinese in a segregated society probably reinforced the phrase, for the Chinese had as poor a chance on the railroads and other places as they did in the gold fields.

China pheasant A name heard in the Northwest for a ring-necked pheasant. Also *Chinese pheasant.*

Chinese home run Because Chinese immigrants were forced to work for little pay in a segregated society, their name came to mean "cheap" in American slang and formed the basis of a number of expressions. *Chinese home run* is the only one of these that still has much currency. It describes a cheap home run, one that just makes it over the fence. No one is sure who coined the phrase. It either arose in some ball park on the West Coast at the turn of the century and was brought East by the cartoonist "Tad" Dorgan (who is also responsible for the words "yesman" and "hot dog"), or it originated in a baseball park with a fence a relatively short distance from home, possibly the old 239-foot right-field fence in Philadelphia's Shibe Park or the short right-field fence in New York's old Polo Grounds.

Chink A derogatory term for a Chinese person that possibly originated in the early West and probably derives from the Chinese exclamation *ching-ching! Chinee* was another such term.

chin-music Talk, especially elegant talk. See usage example at WALTZ THROUGH HANDSOME.

Chinook; Chinook wind Chinook, an important pidgin language, enabled 18th- and 19th-century American farmers and traders, French trappers and even visiting Russian seal hunters to converse with Indians in the Pacific Northwest. Chinook jargon was used for more than 100 years. Named for the Chinook Indians, who had large settlements along the Columbia River, this lingua franca combined various Chinook dialects, other Indian languages, English, French and probably Russian. *Chinook wind,* so called by early settlers because it blew from the direction of the Chinook Indian camps, designates a dry wind blowing from the west or north over the Rocky Mountains—warm in winter and cool in summer—while a *wet Chinook* is a warm, moist wind blowing from sea to land in Washington and Oregon.

Chinook salmon See KING SALMON.

chin-wag A person who talks too much, whose chin is always wagging.

chin whiskers Beard, a term that was apparently coined in California in gold-rush days.

chipper Prostitutes and loose women were called *chippers* in the early West; the expression survives today in the form of *chippie.*

Chiricahua An Apache Indian tribe originally residing in the mountains of Southwestern Arizona and often encountered today in fiction; named from an Apache word meaning "great mountain."

Chisholm Trail In the spring of 1866, Jesse Chisholm (c. 1806–68), a half-white, half-Cherokee Indian trader and government agent, drove his wagon loaded with buffalo hides through the Oklahoma Territory to Wichita, Kansas. The wheels cut deep into the prairie, providing rut marks for a route that was to become the most important and most famous of all Western cattle trails, extending from San Antonio, Texas to Abilene and other Kansas railheads. The trail was used for more than 20 years after the Civil War, 450,000 Texas longhorns having been driven up it in 1872 alone. Remnants of the trail, celebrated in folklore and cowboy ballads like "The Old Chisholm Trail," still remain along the Santa Fe railroad line.

cho cho A Basque word meaning a small child or a boy that is sometimes used by non-Basque speakers in parts of the West.

chock full of brag and fight An old expression for a wild, unruly person. "Chock full of brag and fight/ He wound up on the floor,/ A sorry sight."

choke 'em A colorful popular name in Texas for *dodder,* a sprawling, yellow thread-like plant of the genus *Cuscata,* because it literally chokes or smothers its host plants to death.

choke rag Cowboys invented this humorous disdainful word for a necktie.

cholo This Spanish word is used in the Southwest as a derogatory term for a Mexican of Spanish and American Indian heritage.

choosing match The selection of work horses by cowboys on a ranch, the choices made in order of seniority from the ranch stock.

chopping horse A horse used for separating cattle from the herd. Also called a *cutting horse* and a *carving horse.*

chop suey Though the words derive from the Chinese *tsa-sui,* meaning odds and ends, this dish isn't Chinese in origin; one source says it was invented by a dishwasher in a San Francisco Chinese restaurant at the turn of the century.

chousing Handling, taking care of. "I been chousing other people's cows, peeling other people's broncs, sweating my goddamned skin off for peanuts ever since I got big enough to hit out for myself." [Jack Schaefer, *Monte Walsh,* 1958]

chub A nickname applied to Texans a century ago, perhaps because Texans were noted for being big, fat or stocky men. In any case, the term is now used nationwide as a nickname for a chubby or stocky person.

chuck (1) Food or provisions in general; a meal. " 'Chuck, come and get it!' the cook cried." The term is an Americanism first used in about 1840 and probably derives from the cut of meat called *chuck.* (2) In the

Pacific Northwest and Canada, water or a body of water. This *chuck* probably derives from a Chinook word meaning "water" that sounds like *chuck* and is first recorded in about 1855.

chuck-a-luck An American dice game played with three dice. Players bet that a certain number will come up on one die, that the three dice will total a certain number or that the total will be an odd or even or high or low number. The game probably goes back to about 1840 in the West.

chuckaway A call to dinner. "The chuckwagon cook often cired: 'Chuckaway, John! If you don't come and git it, I'll throw it out!' "

chuck hole A hole in a field or a road, the term an Americanism first used in about 1830 when roads were far worse than they are now and probably deriving from *chuck* in the sense of "to toss up (a wagon or body) with a quick motion," plus *hole.* "The closest to excitement came that time I thought a road agent was stopping us and got ready for action to find out it was a cowboy whose horse had stepped into a chuck hole and broke its leg . . ." [Richard Matheson, *Journal of the Gun Years,* 1991]

chuck line rider An unemployed cowboy who rode from ranch to ranch, wherever he could get a free meal; cowboys who made this a profession were held in contempt by some but welcomed by many for the news they carried and the good stories they exchanged for a meal. Also called a *chuckliner*.

chuck wagon (1) The first chuck wagon was made from a surplus Civil War army wagon in 1867 by Charles Goodnight. By the 1880s the term was common for a wagon carrying provisions and equipment for cooking, the Studebaker Company manufacturing them by then for $75 to $100. (2) *Chuck wagon* is also recent Western slang, deriving from the chuck wagon of trail days and referring to the informal buffet-style meals served at some restaurants.

chuckwalla A lizard *(Sauromalus ater)* of the Southwest. The big lizard is not called the chuckwalla because the Indians use it for food (chuck), which they do, but after the Chuckwalla Mountains.

chuco A derogatory term for a Mexican. Short for *pachuco*.

chunk Any small stocky slow horse used for draft purposes. "You're not riding that chunk in the race, are you?"

chunked An old term used in the Southwest describing a very impudent person. "That boy's as chunked as you can get."

chunking distance Fairly close distance, as far from someone or something as one can chunk or throw a stone. ". . . he could not stand all night in chunking distance of Lorena

and not go see her." [Larry McMurtry, *Lonesome Dove,* 1985]

chunk of lead A bullet. " 'I'll pass a chunk of lead through him.' " [Max Brand, *Three on the Trail,* 1928]

Church of Jesus Christ of Latter-day-Saints See MORMON.

churn-dash calf A calf that hasn't received its full share of mother's milk and is fed from a pail or churn.

churn-twister A contemptuous cowboy term for a farmer, one of whose chores is churning butter.

Cíbola Coronado and other early Spanish explorers searched in vain for a fabled land of great wealth in the Southwest called Cíbola, or the Seven Cities of Cíbola, which later proved to be an area in western New Mexico inhabited by the Zuni Indians. The name, which derives from a native term for buffalo, was once suggested as a state name for the territory that became Colorado.

cimarron (1) The Latin *cyma*, the spring shoots of a plant, is the ultimate source for the Spanish word *cimarrón*, meaning wild, unruly, a solitary creature. The word is also used in these senses by some Western speakers. In American English, however, *cimarron* is mainly used for the big horn or mountain sheep *(Oris vanadensis)*. In this sense, it is first recorded in about 1840. (2) See quote. "He had dwelt . . . in that sinister strip, thirty-four miles wide and almost two hundred miles long, called No-Man's Land as early as 1854, and, later, known as Cimarron, a Spanish word meaning wild or unruly." [Edna Ferber, *Cimarron*, 1930]

cinch A strong belly band used on stock saddles with a ring on each end to which a strap running from the saddle is secured. *Cinch,* from the Spanish *cincha* (saddle girth) came to mean a firm hold or tight grip and then became an American term for something sure and easy, as in "It's a cinch."

City of Corruption An old name for San Francisco, California in the late 19th century, when vigilantes patrolled the streets.

City of Fair Colors A nickname for Short Creek, Arizona, famous at the turn of the century for a failed experiment in communal living.

City of the Angels A nickname for Los Angeles, California.

City of the Plains An old nickname for Denver, Colorado.

City of the Saints Salt Lake City, Utah, home of the Mormon church, or Church of Jesus Christ of Latter-day Saints.

City Where the West Begins A nickname for Fort Worth, Texas.

civit cat A synonym for the skunk in most parts of the West; also called the *civvy cat*. *Civit* here derives from an Arabic word.

civvy cat See CIVIT CAT.

clabber Curdled milk, milk that has soured and thickened. The word ultimately derives from the Irish *clabar* meaning the same. Also *clabber milk*.

claim A piece of land staked out by a miner or homesteader in the early West.

claim jumper One who illegally takes possession of another's land claim. "Occasionally, a claim jumper was hailed into court; but the practice of locating another man's ground became distinctly hazardous, it did not occur with the frequency that many writers of Western fiction would have us believe." [Philip Johnston, *Lost and Living Cities of the California Gold Rush*, 1948]

Clarkia Any of several western U.S. plants of the evening primrose family, the genus named after U. S. soldier and explorer William Clark of the Lewis and Clark expedition, 1804–06.

claw-hammer coat An old-fashioned coat with tails split in two like a claw-hammer. "Skinny old boy in a beaver high hat an' a claw-hammer coat, he was." [Frank Roderus, *Hell Creek Cabin*, 1979]

clean-up (1) A Western mining term meaning the removal of gold or any valuable mineral from gravel and rock. (2) A great financial success, this expression probably deriving from the mining term.

clear full Full to the top. " 'Jody, tonight see you fill the woodbox clear full. Last night you crossed the sticks and it wasn't only about half full.' " [John Steinbeck, "The Red Pony," 1938]

cliff dwellers Prehistoric people of the Southwest who were ancestors of the Pueblo Indians and were named *cliff dwellers* because they built their homes in caves or on the ledges of cliffs. The name is now humorously applied to residents of tall apartment houses in large cities.

clomb Climbed. "I clomb down and walked Blacky south across the meadow . . ." [Charles O. Locke, *The Hell Bent Kid,* 1957]

close herd See RIDE CLOSE HERD ON.

closet The seat in a privy or JAKES.

cloud mesa See quote. "One thing which struck him at once was that every mesa was duplicated by a cloud mesa, like a reflection, which lay motionless above it or moved slowly up from behind it. These cloud formations seemed to be always there, however hot and blue the sky. Sometimes they were flat terraces, ledges of vapour; sometimes they were dome-shaped, or fantastic, like the tops of silvery pagodas, rising one above another, as if an oriental city lay directly behind the rock. The great tables of granite set down in an empty plain were inconceivable without their attendant clouds, which were a part of them, as the smoke is part of the censer, or the foam of the wave." [Willa Cather, *Death Comes for the Archbishop,* 1929] See also MESA.

Coal Oil Johnny; Coal Oil Tommy A name for any character, especially a prospector, who was rich one day, broke the next day and rich again the third day.

coarse-gold A Western mining term for large grains or flakes of gold, including nuggets, as opposed to gold dust. During the gold rush of 1849, a California town was named Coarsegold because such gold was found there in abundance.

coarse-grained This logging term describes an irrascible person who is difficult to get along with.

coast (1) Used in northern California to mean a beach where one swims. "He went swimming at the coast." (2) When capitalized, short for the old Barbary Coast, the Pacific Coast and the West Coast.

coaster A nickname for the longhorned cattle of the coast country in Texas. Also called *Texas Coasters.* See SEA LION.

the coast of Nebraska The name early explorer John C. Frémont gave to the Platte River.

coast on the spurs A rodeo term meaning not to use spurs on a bronc or to use the spurs lightly.

coat-pocket whiskey A cheap pint of whiskey that fits in a coat pocket. "After too much heat and coat-pocket whiskey, Dirty Joe passed out on the worn grass of the carnival midway." [Sherman Alexie, "Amusements," 1993]

cock-a-doodle-doo An old term for the foreman of a ranch, who was considered the cock of the walk, at the top of the pecking order.

cock of the plains The sage grouse; the name has been used since the early 19th century.

cocktail An old cowboy term for the undesirable last watch of the night on the trail, the watch that ended at daylight; the expression derives from *cock's tail*, the last part of the bird.

code duello Dueling code. "He stepped out shooting. No gentleman editor's *code duello* now. No damned dime novel foolishness about who could make a fastest draw." [Jack Cummings, *The Surrogate Gun*, 1990]

Coeur d'Alene It is said that the Skitswish Indians of northern Idaho took the name Coeur d'Alene (French for "awl-heart") after some unknown chief of the tribe used the words to describe the size of a white trader's heart, which he compared to the small point of an awl.

coffin An old cowboy term for a large trunk.

coffin varnish A joking word for liquor of the poorest quality, rotgut.

cohab A derogatory expression dating back to the 19th century that was used mainly in Utah for a polygamous Mormon or anyone who lived in illegal cohabitation.

coil Old cowboy slang for a rope, ropes often being wound in coils.

cold as hell on the stoker's day off Quite cold. "His breath came as puffs of white frost . . . Cold as hell on the stoker's day off, Zeb Broadus thought." [R. C. House, *Warhawk*, 1993]

cold-blooded Said of an animal, especially a horse, that isn't a thoroughbred, that is the result of inferior breeding. Such a horse is called a *cold blood*, and a thoroughbred is called a *hot blood* or a *pure*.

cold brand A light brand in which only an animal's hair is marked, the process often done through a wet blanket.

cold deck A rigged deck of cards slipped into a poker game, the term first recorded in California in gold rush days.

cold-footed Cowardly; from *to get cold feet*. "Benton heard the words cold-footed again, obviously spoken, and something jerked in his stomach muscles." [Richard Matheson, *The Gun Fight*, 1993]

cold in the pants A colorful term Western mountain men used for gonorrhea. "But you ain't had two women this spree. A body'd think you was still feared of catchin' a cold in your pants." [A. B. Guthrie Jr., *The Big Sky*, 1947]

cold timberline The elevation in the mountains at which the growth of trees is prohibited or severely restricted by low temperatures. The *dry timberline* is some distance below this.

colear The act of throwing a bull or other animal by holding its tail and twisting it forcefully. Vaqueros brought this popular Mexican sport, *colea de toros,* to the Southwest.

color A term used by miners for gold, or a trace or flecks of gold, since the 1849 California gold rush. " 'Then I taken to huntin' for the Lost Adams gold. Found color here an' there, made a livin'.'" [Louis L'Amour, *The Haunted Mesa,* 1987]

Colorado The 38th state, admitted to the Union in 1876, takes its name from the Spanish *Colorado,* "red land" or "red earth." See also Cíbola.

Colorado Kool-Aid A joking name for Coor's beer, which is made in Colorado.

Colorado potato beetle A yellow, black-striped beetle (*Leptinotarsa decemlineata*) very harmful to potatoes that was originally confined to Colorado and vicinity before potatoes be-

gan to be extensively cultivated in the United States.

Colorado rook A euphemism for the crow, especially when it is featured on restaurant menus, as it has been in the past.

Colorado spruce The common blue spruce *(Pica pungens),* which is also called the *Colorado blue spruce* and, sometimes, the *Colorado blue.*

Colorado turkey A humorous name for both the great blue heron and the wood ibis.

colors Sometimes used as a synonym for small pieces of gold panned from a stream. " . . . he had come up with a show of color right off. The first pan netted him four or five colors and then the nugget." [Louis L'Amour, *Bendigo Shafter,* 1979]

Colt When Samuel Colt (1814–62) ran away to sea from his home in Hartford, Connecticut at 16, he spent his lonely nights on deck whittling a wooden model of the Colt revolver that was to make him famous. Young Colt had several metal models made of his gun upon arriving home and patented his invention. He built his armory into the largest in the world, his use of interchangeable parts and the production line making him one of the richest men in America. As for the *Colt,* the first pistol that could be effectively employed by a man on horseback, it played a more important part in the conquest of the West than any other weapon, the famed "six-shooter" becoming so popular that its name became a generic term for revolver. *Colt* for a young horse comes from the Old English *colt* meaning the same.

coma The bumelia, an evergreen tree common to Texas that grows up to 30 feet high and bears sweet black berries.

comadre A godmother, a close woman friend, the female counterpart of *compadre*.

Comanche moon The full moon of every month, perhaps because it was thought to aid the Comanches in their night raids. The Comanches, however, called the full moon the *Mexican moon*.

Comanche pill A humorous expression used in Texas for any laxative.

comanchero An old term for a man of Mexican-Indian origin; comancheros were often traders between the Indians and the Mexicans or whites.

Comanche yell A blood-curdling yell used by Comanche Indians in battle; said by some to be the basis for the *rebel yell*.

comb To rake a horse with one's spurs.

combings The last cattle driven in on the roundup, possibly because cowboys combed the brush for them.

come-along (1) A rope halter used by cowboys that tightens when a horse balks and loosens when he obeys a command. (2) A tool used to create tension to hold something in place and then tighten it (as a fence wire) or close it (as a railcar door).

come down in a pile To keel over, crumple down and die. "I'm getting old, won't be too long before I come down in a pile."

come over the trail with To know someone a long while. "I ain't callin' a man a liar, especially a man who come over the trail with me." [Louis L'Amour, *The Tall Stranger,* 1957]

come up at A term used in trading meaning to amount to or come to. "That comes up at two dollars each."

coming off Going to be. " 'Feels like it could be coming off hail,' Coy said." [Sam Brown, *The Crime of Coy Bell,* 1992]

commune A term for an outhouse used in Mexico and the Southwest.

compadre A Spanish term for a godfather or very close friend which has long been used in the West for one's partner or close friend and which has wide use throughout the country from its frequent use in cowboy novels and movies. *Comadre* is the female version.

compañero Spanish for a close companion or buddy. "I can't remember why I picked you for a compañero." [Larry McMurtry, *Buffalo Girls,* 1990]

compass cactus   Western settlers gave this name to the barrel cactus *(Echinocactus)* because it almost always leans southwest and they could tell directions by it.

compliment   An invitation, as in "I got a compliment to the dance."

compressed hay   A euphemism for dried cow dung. These cow chips were often used for fuel.

Comstock lode   A Nevada sheepherder and prospector named Henry Tompkins Paige Comstock first laid claim to the *Comstoke lode* that bears his name. In 1859, Old Pancake, as he was known, had taken possession of a cabin belonging to other prospectors who had discovered the lode but had died tragically before filing their claim. Comstock filed his claim, but he later sold all his rights for a pittance. The Virginia City mine became the world's richest known silver deposit, producing $20 million to $30 million annually at its peak and making great fortunes for many a "silver king." Virginia City mushroomed to 40,000 inhabitants, and anyone associated with the mines, hopeful prospector or millionaire, was called a *comstocker.*

Conestoga wagon; stogy   The heavy, covered, broad-wheeled style of wagon that carried numerous American pioneers westward. These wagons crossed many a waving "sea of grass" like "prairie schooners" and were named for the Conestoga Valley in Pennsylvania, where they were first made in about 1750. But as H. L. Mencken points out, *Conestoga Valley* derives in turn from the name of a long-extinct band of Iroquois Indians. The wagons, pulled by their six-horse teams, also supplied the West with manufactured goods and brought back raw materials, some carrying up to eight tons of freight. *Stogy,* a cheap cigar today, was coined by the Conestoga teamsters— either after the *Conestoga Valley tobacco* that they rolled into thin, unbound cigars for their long trips or after the wagons themselves.

con permiso   Spanish for "with your permission." "He stood at the end of the table and set his tray down. 'Con permiso,' he said." [Cormac McCarthy, *All the Pretty Horses,* 1992]

consarn   Damn, darn. "Consarn you, I'm not going!"

considerable   Considerably; a usage common in the West that actually dates back to the 14th century. "I could improve your education considerable, if you really liked to talk." [Larry McMurtry, *Buffalo Girls,* 1990]

conversation fluid   Used in the West and other regions for whiskey, especially potent moonshine that loosens the inhibitions and vocal cords.

cony   The little Rocky Mountain hare *Ochotana princeps.*

cookee   Western slang for a ranch or camp cook. Also *cookie.*

cool as a blue norther Cool and collected. "But it was Rusk, cool as a blue norther, who stopped him: 'Roy bub! you horse's ass, put up that gun.'" [James A. Michener, *Texas,* 1985]

coon Sometimes used as a term referring to oneself. "They hunted me, but believe me, nobody's goin' to trail this here coon across no desert. Nobody!" [Louis L'Amour, *The Haunted Mesa,* 1987]

cooncan A rummy-like card game played in the Southwest and South. It takes its name from a mispronunciation of the Mexican Spanish words *con quién* (with whom).

cooney See POSSUM BELLY.

Coors A beer made in Colorado and mainly popular throughout the West until relatively recent times. "He loved to guzzle yellow cans of Coors with his beautiful daughter and talk football, school work, America, money, romance, the revolving life of the Great American West." [Thomas McGuane, *Nothing but Blue Skies,* 1992]

coosie A ranch or trail cook, the word deriving from the Spanish *cocinero* (cook).

cooster A suitcase, an old cowboy term of unknown origin.

copper lily An orange- or copper-colored wildflower (*Atamasco texana*) common to Texas.

coral snake A common name for both the poisonous *Micruroides euryxanthus* and the king snake *(Lampropeltis pyromelana),* both found in the Southwest.

cordillera A mountain range; often used in the plural, *cordilleras:* "We passed through the cordilleras into the wilderness."

corked Tired; an expression used mainly in northern California. "I was really corked this morning."

corn dog A hot dog coated with cornmeal batter, deep fried and usually stuck lengthwise on a stick; very popular in the Southwest but now available in all regions.

corn freight When freight was shipped by mule in the old West, it was called *corn freight* because it had to be shipped with corn used to feed the mules; this method was more expensive than *bull-team freight* (ox-drawn freight), but mules were faster.

cornstalk shoot A traditional game once played by the Cherokees in Oklahoma in which bowmen shot arrows into bundles of cornstalks from a distance. The bowman whose arrow pierced the most stalks in a bundle won the contest.

corral *Corral* has for well over a century had many more meanings in the West than simply an enclosure for animals. In a letter to the *New York Tribune* in 1867, a rancher in the Montana Territory put it this way: "If a man is embarrassed in any way, he is 'corraled.' Indians 'corral' men on the plains; storms 'corral' tourists. The criminal is 'corraled' in prison, the gambler 'corrals' the dust of the miner."

cosh Kill; mutilate. " 'Bloody Bill Anderson once said that Flynn would cosh a Sister of Mercy for the gold in her molars.' " [Loren D. Estleman, *Sudden Country*, 1991]

Costa's hummingbird The Southwestern hummingbird species *Calypte costae* named after orthinologist Louis Marie Pantaléon Costa (1806–64).

cottonwood A Western poplar tree (*Populus Balsamifera*) with sweet-smelling buds that is also called the *Aspen poplar*, the *alamo* and the *cotton tree*, among other names.

cottonwood blossom In the old West, an outlaw hanged from the limb of any tree was called a *cottonwood blossom* after the cottonwood tree so common in the West and often used as a gallows tree. This use of the cottonwood led to the old saying *to have the cottonwood on one*, to have the advantage over someone.

cottonwood ice cream Among the most unusual American desserts of pioneer days was *cottonwood ice cream*, a sweet pulpy white mass scraped in the spring from the inner bark of the cottonwood tree.

cougar A Western name, from the French *couguar*, for the mountain lion (*Felix concolor*), which has also been known as the *California lion*, *puma*, *panther*, *painter* and even *red tiger*, among many names.

cougar juice; cougar milk Any strong cheap whiskey.

coulee A deep ravine or gulch with sloping sides, formed by running water, that is often dry in summer; can also be a small valley or a small stream. The word derives from the French *couler* (to flow). *Grand Coulee Dam* is at the end of the deep dry canyon called Grand Coulee that is cut by the Columbia River in the state of Washington. "Skimming over patches of cactus, soaring over a badger hole, plunging into the coulee and up the other side, he ran as if bears were after him." [Wallace Stegner, "Goin' To Town" in *The Collected Stories of Wallace Stegner*, 1990]

Coulter pine The big-coned southern California pine *Pinus coulteri* named after English physician Thomas Coulter, who discovered it in about 1830.

count coup A custom of the Apaches and other American Indians of touching a dead enemy with a COUP STICK. " 'Take the stick!' he commanded. 'Count coup!' Johnny hesitated. Hondo was suddenly glad that Angie was not present. 'Johnny,' he said distinctly, 'you must do as Vittoro says. Take the stick he offers you and tap the Indian with it.' " [Louis L'Amour, *Hondo*, 1953]

count over To count the number of cows in a herd when selling it to someone. "We counted over the herd to the new owner."

county attorney A humorous name, reflecting the cowboy's feelings about lawyers and law enforcement officials, for any dish containing cheap or unmentionable ingredients, including sweetbreads, guts and kidneys. Such dishes were also known as *district attorney* and *son-of-a-bitch stew*.

county hotel The county jail.

coup stick A decorated stick, usually made of willow, with which plains Indians sought to touch their enemies in battle as a sign of courage. (See also COUNT COUP.)

cover one's back with one's belly To sleep without blankets outside. "There I slept, covering my back with my belly, shivering all night."

cover one's dog A cowboy who gathered all the cattle in the region assigned to him was said to have *covered his dog.*

the cowards never started and the weak died on the way A popular saying about those who made their way West on the Oregon Trail beginning in 1843.

cow boss The owner or foreman of a ranch.

cowboy (1) A term first applied to members of Tory bands in New York

state who rustled cows, but by the mid-19th century, it came to mean a man who herds and tends cattle on a ranch in the West, most of his work done on horseback. Because of Hollywood Westerns, *cowboy* has also taken on the meaning of any reckless person, such as a speeding automobile driver. (2) See quote. "The word cowboy, once guarded with a vigilant jealousy, had come to apply as much to the handlers of sheep as to handlers of cattle. The average ranchhand was likely to be some of both. The hard knuckles of economics had driven most West Texas cowmen to discard their prejudice and turn to sheep. They found to their consternation that the two species mixed well, a proposition once considered akin to heresy. Now they raised cattle for respectability and sheep for a living." [Elmer Kelton, *The Time It Never Rained,* 1973]

cowboy A verb meaning to work as a cowboy. "What do you do for a living?" "I cowboy."

a cowboy all the way down to his liver A full-fledged 100% cowboy. "He was a cowboy all the way down to his liver. He broke and trained horses for anyone who would hire him . . . He rode West to punch cows and ride rough strings from Mexico to Canada . . ." [Max Evans, *Rounders Three,* 1990]

cowboy bible The books of paper cowboys carried for rolling their own cigarettes.

cowboy boots   Cowboys never called them this, at least not until the term was invented in the East in about 1912. Cowboys just called them *boots* or *cowhides* until then. In about 1860, however, cowboys did begin to wear boots with higher heels and pointed toes that better fit the stirrups. Edna Ferber describes a fancy pair in *Cimarron* (1930): "The gay tops were of shiny leather, and alternating around them was the figure of a dancing girl with flaring skirts, and a poker hand of cards which she learned was a royal flush, all handsomely embossed on the patent leather cuffs of the boots." See also JUSTINS.

cowboy cadillac   Any old truck.

cowboy change   Different-sized gun cartridges used by cowboys as small change in days past.

cowboy cocktail   Straight whiskey. "No need to mix a cowboy cocktail; you drink it right from the bottle."

cowboy coffee   Any very strong coffee.

cowboy hat   Cowboys simply called their hats *hats*, and there were many kinds of them, all of them with wide brims to keep the weather off their faces. *Cowboy hat* was coined in the East about 1900.

cowboy legs   Prominent bowlegs from a lifetime of riding a horse.

cowboy of the Pecos   A real cowboy from the hard country west of the Pecos River in Texas.

cowboy pen   The stalk of a plant, such as broomweed, used by cowboys to doodle in the soil.

Cowboy President   A nickname given to President Theodore Roosevelt, who was a North Dakota ranchman from 1884–86 and all of his life remained interested in cowboy life.

cowboy saddle   The original name of the common Western saddle, first recorded in the 1870s. Vaqueros developed this saddle with a high pommel and cantle from the war saddle of the Spanish conquistadores.

cowboys and Indians   No one knows exactly when children started playing cowboys and Indians in the 19th century (or possibly earlier), but the first recorded use of this name for the game has been traced to 1887.

cowboy shirt   Real cowboys didn't wear fancy bright-colored cowboy shirts until relatively recent times. The term isn't recorded until about 1930 when such shirts were popularized by cowboy movie star Tom Mix.

cow brute   A full-grown range cow or steer difficult to manage because it hasn't been handled since it was a calf; the word is used in other regions as a euphemism for a bull.

cow chips   Dried cow dung used as fuel by settlers in the early West; the term is first recorded in 1865.

cow country (1) Country where cattle roam freely in open territory, range country where cattle aren't fenced in. (2) A region of cattle ranches.

cowdog A dog specially trained to help handle cattle.

cowgirls When it was first recorded in 1884, *cowgirl* meant a female rancher or a rancher's daughter; it later came to mean a cowpuncher as well.

cowhand A synonym for *cowboy* first recorded in 1886.

cowhide Beat with a whip. " 'I'll horsewhip him, that's what I'll do! I'll cowhide him!' " [Benjamin Capps, *Tales of the Southwest,* 1990]

cowhides See COWBOY BOOTS.

cow horse See COW PONY.

cow hunt A roundup of cattle on the range.

cowlick (1) Places along branches or streams where drinking cattle eat or lick out great holes; the term is unrelated to the *cowlick* meaning an unruly tuft of hair. (2) A salt lick (block) purchased for cattle to lick.

cowman (1) A person who owns cattle, a rancher. (2) A cowboy.

cowpoke; cowpuncher *Cowpokes* and *cowpunchers* were originally cowboys who poked cattle onto railroad cars with long poles. The terms, first re- corded in 1880, were soon applied to all cowboys.

cow pony This cowboy horse used to work cattle weighs 700–900 pounds and is 12–14 hands high. The name is first recorded in 1874. Also called *cow horse.*

cow prod A cowboy. See also COW POKE.

cow rigging A cowboy's working clothes.

cow saddle The heavy saddle cow- boys use when at work roping cattle.

cow sense Both a cowboy and a good cutting horse can have cow sense, the practical knowledge of how to handle cattle; the term, like *horse sense,* has also come to mean common sense in general.

cow skinner A severe winter storm.

cow town A town that owes its exis- tence to the cattle industry, the term dating back to the mid-19th century. " 'Yes, that is how it is in cow towns.' " he observed. 'All this H—— raising is common because these towns are made so cowboys can blow off speed at the end of cattle drives.' " [Richard Matheson, *Journal of the Gun Years,* 1991]

coyote (1) Its name deriving from the Nahuatl *coyotl,* meaning the same, the *coyote (Canis latrans)* is a buffy-gray, wolflike canid distin- guished from the wolf by its smaller size, slender build, large ears and narrow muzzle. (2) A contemptible person, a liar or a cheat. (3) An Indian or one of some Indian ancestry. (4) A shallow mining tunnel, like a coyote hole. (5) In recent usage, a person who smuggles Mexicans across the border. Other names for the coyote include the *prairie wolf, medicine wolf* and *brush wolf.* In the West the word is usually pronounced *ki-yote.* "Hated and even feared, Old Man Ortiz was a power among his people though most privately condemned him as a coyote, a flesh-peddling profiteer . . ." [Elmer Kelton, *The Time It Never Rained,* 1973]

coyote around   To sneak around, move surreptitiously.

coyote days The early days in the unsettled West.

coyote dun See DUN.

coyote gold Gold dust found in coyote holes.

coyote house A small dugout with several boards placed over it for a roof; built and inhabited by settlers in the early days of the West.

coyotero An Indian of one of various Apache bands in Arizona.

Coyote State   A nickname for South Dakota.

coyotey Used to describe anything mangy, as in "He had two coyotey old horses."

coyoting Sneaking about. "Someone coyotin' around out there, for sure, he thought. Probably not so much waiting to give me an Indian haircut as to make free with my possibles [small personal property]." [R. C. House, *Warhawk,* 1993]

crawfish Crawl, apologize abjectly. " 'You're unreasonable . . . I can't crawfish for something I may have said unintentionally.' " [Zane Grey, *The Maverick Queen,* 1950]

crawl To stealthily advance on one's quarry, such as a herd of buffalo; a plains Indian technique that was imitated by white hunters.

crazy as a loon The common loon *(Gavia immer)* is noted for what one ornithologist calls its "mirthless laughter, a high, far-crying, liquid tremolo that sets your spine atingle." The loon has nothing to do with the word *loony* (crazy), which is a shortening of *lunatic,* but the bird does give us the expression *crazy as a loon,* which could have originated in the West and is first recorded there.

crazy as a peach-orchard boar Wild and crazy; a term used in the West and South.

crazy as a shithouse rat Very crazy. " 'These sumbucks are crazy as a shithouse rat,' he said." [Cormac McCarthy, *All the Pretty Horses,* 1992]

cream pea A small field pea that is cream-colored with a small, light-brown eye.

creasing (1) A method of capturing a wild horse by shooting it in the crest of the neck above the cervical vertebrae and stunning it. The practice is recorded in Texas as early as 1820. (2) Barely wounding someone. "He just creased him."

creosote bush A yellow-flowering shrub *(Larrea tridentata)* of the Southwest with resinous foliage thought by some to smell like creosote.

crevice To examine rock crevices hoping to find gold in them. "I've creviced and dug for gold and found none."

crib A cheap house of prostitution.

crick A pronunciation of *creek;* a running stream. "Let's go down to the crick."

critters Though Westerners have long favored this corruption of "creatures" to mean horses or cattle, *critters* has been used in this sense by Americans since at least 1782, when the term is first recorded. " 'I'll take your critters as far as Abilene, but I'll be damned if I'll take 'em to Colorado.' " [James Michener, *Centennial,* 1974]

crooked Cheated. " 'My men are well paid, my word is good, and no one can say that ever I crooked him.' " [A. B. Guthrie Jr., *Arfive,* 1970]

crossbred squatter An insulting term meaning a squatter with Indian blood. " 'Why, you crossbred squat-ter,' Wilson said, quick and sharp, 'are you telling me I'm wrong?' " [Jack Schaefer, *Shane,* 1949]

cross-buck saddle A pack saddle resembling a small sawbuck.

crow The name, bestowed by themselves, of a tribe of Siouan Indians; they were known to dance a crow dance wearing a crow-belt, which was a long bustle or tail made of crow feathers.

crowbait An old nag or other decrepit animal.

crowd To bother, pester, push or force into something. " 'Do I have to crowd you into slapping leather?' " [Jack Schaefer, *Shane,* 1949]

crucifixion thorn A thorny shrub (*Castela* genus) native to the Southwest whose spring branches are said to resemble Christ's crown of thorns.

crust Forwardness, nerve, impudence; the expression is used nationally now. "He's sure got a lot of crust."

culinary water A term heard mainly in Utah for treated water meant for direct human use as opposed to use for irrigation.

cultus A Chinook word meaning worthless. "He can't do nothing right, he's just cultus."

cuna A country dance, Spanish in origin, with a swaying motion similar to that of a cradle. Often called the *cradle dance,* the *cuna* takes its name from the Spanish word meaning cradle.

curl up To kill someone. "You'll never outdraw him. He'll curl you up."

Curly Bill spin See ROAD AGENT'S SPIN.

curly wolf An old cowboy term for a wild, tough guy, a badman or desperado, someone to beware of.

cuss Curse. " 'If you're planning to cuss, I'll ask you to do it outside,' the clerk said . . ." [Larry McMurtry, *Lonesome Dove,* 1985]

Custer Battle; Custer Tragedy Names for the battle of Little Big Horn in Montana on June 26, 1876, when a large force of Sioux wiped out U. S. forces serving under General George Armstrong Custer (1839–76).

cut (1) A group of cattle separated from the main herd for some purpose, such as branding or shipping. (2) As a verb, to separate animals from the herd. "Cutting was a ticklish and difficult job, the most exacting duty any horse could be called upon to perform. It demanded of the mount an apex of physical and mental control plus a calm dispatch that would not panic the animal being cut from the herd. A cutting horse had to spin and turn as quickly as the cow, always edging the reluctant animal away from the herd with-

out frightening it." [Richard Matheson, *The Gun Fight,* 1993]

cut a sign To come upon evidence of the presence of Indians or game. "Wherever he cut their sign, he steered us the other way."

cutback (1) Cowboy talk for cattle rejected for some reason. (2) An inferior worthless person.

cut finer than a frog hair Cut very fine. " 'She's cut finer than a frog hair,' Deakins said [of the coin]. 'Quarter of a silver dollar, exact.' " [A. B. Guthrie Jr., *The Big Sky,* 1947]

cut for sign To inspect ground for tracks and droppings (signs).

cut it wild aloose and see where it lights Free something from control and see what happens. "Me, I'd as soon cut the whole thing wild aloose and see where it lights. But they get the regulations and they'll bear down on you." [Elmer Kelton, *The Time It Never Rained,* 1973]

cut-nose woman An Indian woman of certain tribes whose nose was cut off because of her adultery. "He reckoned he . . . would . . . never have to cut Teal Eye's nose off . . . the way a Piegan did when he found his woman had lain in secret with another man. It was a sight, the squaws you saw with no end to their noses. Cut-nose women, they were called." [A. B. Guthrie Jr., *The Big Sky,* 1947]

cut out To separate a cow or horse from the rest of the herd; the term is first recorded in 1874 but was probably used earlier.

cut the alkali in the water A humorous expression for adding liquor to one's drinking water, which is often alkaline in the West.

cut the trail of To come upon, to meet up with. "We intended to cut their trail when they came out of the mountains."

cutting horses See quote. " 'They're what we call cutting horses. They're used to cut out certain animals from the herd . . . You don't have to touch the reins half the time. Just sway your body and your horse will turn your weight this way or that." [Edna Ferber, *Giant,* 1952]

D

dad drat it! An old-fashioned euphemism for *damn it!* that possibly derives from *God rot it!*

Dakota The largest tribe of Siouan Indians, their name deriving from an American Indian word meaning "allies."

dally man; dally roper A name for a cowboy who twists his rope a turn around his saddle horn on roping an animal; the expression derives from the Spanish *dale vuelta* (give a twist), which is also heard as *dally welta*.

dance hall hostess Western dance halls, like Dodge City's *Variety,* were often combined saloons, gambling houses, and brothels. By the 1870s, *dance hall hostess* became a euphemism for prostitutes like the Variety's Squirrel-Tooth Colie, Big Nose Kate, and Hambone Jane.

dancing devil A Southwestern expression for a funnel-shaped whirlwind of sand up to 50 feet high.

dangdest Darnedest. " 'Why, it never made no difference to *him*— he'd bet on *any* thing—the dangdest feller.' " [Mark Twain, "The Nortorious Jumping Frog of Calveras County," 1865]

danged Damned. " 'I've got to take that danged hog off the public streets.' " Benjamin Capps, *Tales of the Southwest,* 1990]

darning needle The dragonfly; used in the West as well as other regions.

datura See quote. " . . . a rank plant grew conspicuously out of the [desert] sand; a plant with big white blossoms like Easter lilies. By its dark blue-green leaves, large and coarse-toothed, Father Latour recognized a species of the noxious datura. The size and luxuriance of these nightshades astonished him. They looked like great artificial plants, made of shining silk." [Willa Cather, *Death Comes for the Archbishop,* 1927]

daunsy Moody, downcast in spirit. "He's mighty daunsy the last few days."

Davy Crockett David (Davy) Crockett, as the song goes, was "king of the wild frontier" from his earliest years. Born in 1786 in Limestone, Tennessee, Davy was hired out to a passing cattle driver by his Irish immigrant father when only 12; he wandered the frontier until he turned 15, finally returning home. He became a colonel in the Tennessee militia under Andrew Jackson during the Creek War and, after serving as a justice of the peace and state legislator, acted on a humorous suggestion that he run for Congress. He was noted in Washington for his backwoods dress and shrewd native humor, though many of the comments often attributed to him are largely apocryphal. His motto was "Be sure you are right, then go ahead." When defeated for reelection in 1835—mainly because he opposed Jacksonian banking and Indian policies—he moved to Texas, where he joined the Texas War for Independence from Mexico. On March 6, 1836, Colonel Crockett was killed with the defenders of the Alamo. The folk hero's famous autobiography, *A Narrative of the Life of David Crockett of the State of Tennessee* 1834), was probably dictated but is written in his robust style, complete with many examples of the tall tale.

a day late, a dollar short An old saying describing someone or something that just misses being successful.

day's busted The sun has risen. " 'Wake up, Wayne, old boy, day's busted . . .' " Zane Grey, *Western Union*, 1939]

deadfall A cheap saloon or crooked gambling house on the frontier.

dead forever Dead a long time. See usage example at DON'T KNOW SHIT FROM APPLEBUTTER.

dead Indian A synonym once used, often with humorous intent, for a good Indian. See also THE ONLY GOOD INDIAN IS A DEAD INDIAN.

deadman's hand James Butler "Wild Bill" Hickok, only 39, had come to Deadwood, Dakota Territory in 1876 to make a stake for the bride he had just taken, but lawless elements, fearing his appointment as town marshall, hired gunman Jack McCall to assassinate him, giving McCall $300 and all the cheap whiskey he needed for courage. Wild Bill was playing cards in the No. 10 saloon (his back to the open door for only the second time in his days of gunfighting) when McCall sneaked in and shot him in the back of the head, the bullet passing through his brain and striking the cardplayer across the table from him in the arm. Hickok's last hand, which he held tight in a death grip, was aces and eights, which has ever since been called the *deadman's hand*. McCall, freed by a packed miner's court, was later convicted by a federal court, his plea of "double jeopardy" disregarded on the ground that the miner's court had no jurisdiction. He was later hanged for his crime.

dead men don't talk A saying common in the Wild West, perhaps from the Spanish saying *los muertos no hablan* with the same meaning.

deadwood (1) To have the drop on someone in a gun fight; to have the advantage or upper hand over someone. The term was used long before the death of Wild Bill Hickock in Deadwood, South Dakota (see DEADMAN'S HAND). It may derive from the game of 10 pins in which a downed pin (deadwood) falls in front of the standing pins so that a ball bowled by the next bowler might strike it and knock all the other pins down with it. (2) See quote. "Wild Bill [Hickok] and Captain Massey are arguing mildly over the foreman's habit of sneaking looks at his opponent's [poker] discards, referred to as 'deadwoods'." [Loren D. Estleman, *Aces & Eights,* 1981]

Deadwood Dick *Deadwood Dick* became proverbial through many late 19th-century dime novels, especially those written by Edward L. Wheeler, and long stood for a fearless Indian scout and outlaw fighter. The prototype for Wheeler's westerns was Richard W. Clarke (1845–1930), who had been nicknamed *Deadwood Dick* long before his fictional exploits. Clarke, an Englishman attracted to the Black Hills by the gold diggings, won fame as both an Indian fighter and an express guard for gold shipped from the mines in and around Deadwood, South Dakota. Many of the *Deadwood Dick* myths have been debunked, but he was certainly a real character. Clarke was buried in a mountain grave near Deadwood.

deaf with hate See quote. "People who hear about this will not perhaps believe that I was deaf with hate. I have heard of this happening to people, that some senses can leave you. It shocked me for a little to realize that I had yelled and not heard the sound of my own voice." [Charles O. Locke, *The Hell Bent Kid,* 1957].

death camas The poisonous plant *Ziadenus venenosus,* whose root can be deadly; also called *crow poison, poison camas* and *white camas,* among other names.

death feast A feast held by various Western Indian tribes after the death of a great chief.

decoy brand A small brand hidden in an inconspicuous place on an animal's body in order to trick rustlers, in the hope that they would not find it and change it.

Denver mud The name for a patent medicine poultice used as a remedy for a cough or an infection. It is named for Denver, Colorado, but no one seems to know why; in fact, informants advise that the term isn't used much in Colorado.

Denver omelet An omelet made with chopped ham, onions and green pepper; in the East this is almost always called a *Western omelet.* It is said to have been invented on the trail to disguise the flavor of eggs going bad.

Denver sandwich Another name for the WESTERN SANDWICH.

dern Damn. " 'Dern, he's behaving like a deacon,' Soupy said." [Larry McMurtry, *Lonesome Dove,* 1985]

Derringer A short pistol often associated with gamblers in the West. Derringers are, of course, the small but deadly, large-bored guns so often concealed in the sleeves of gamblers and the bosoms of dance-hall girls in Westerns and that in real life have been the choice of a large variety of villains, including assassin John Wilkes Booth. The pistol, often carried in pairs, is named for Philadelphia gunsmith Henry Deringer, who invented it in 1835. Posterity cheated Deringer a bit, though, for the stubby gun came to be spelled with a double *r*. Deringer, who started his career selling squirrel rifles to Delaware river boatmen in exchange for lumber, had a prosperous business before his invention, but the little box-lock pistols made his one of America's largest armories. He alone is said to have fashioned 10,000 of them in his long lifetime—he lived to be 82; however, many imitations were made of his gun. One of these was a European make signed *Derringer,* the spelling that somehow became accepted. The original model has a 1½-inch barrel and .4 bore, but today any small pistol of a large caliber is called a *derringer.*

Deseret A place-name used in the Utah Territory by the Mormons in 1850. The word is a coined one from the *Book of Mormon* and means "honeybee," a symbol of hard work and cooperation. What is now Utah was called the State of Deseret, and Salt Lake City was called Deseret.

Deseret alphabet An alphabet of 41 characters invented for the Mormons by either Brigham Young or George D. Watt, an English convert to Mormonism, in 1857.

desert canary The humorous name for a burro or small donkey because of its loud unmusical bray.

desert candles The tall graceful *Yucca Whipplei* of the Southwestern deserts.

desert pavement An area of tightly packed stones that form a mosaic pavement on the Southwestern desert floor so firm that it leaves no footprints when walked or ridden upon.

desert rat (1) *Neotoma desertorum,* a rat found in desert areas in many Western states and often called the *desert brush rat.* It is one of many animals and plants named for the deserts where they are found, including the *desert ant, desert gray fox, desert oak* and *desert willow.* (2) A person, often a prospector, who has lived in the desert for many years.

desert varnish The polished surface of rocks caused by wind and water working on it for centuries; this surface, ranging in color from yellow to brown, is also called *desert gloss* and *desert glaze.*

desperado An outlaw, the borrowing of a Spanish word meaning the same.

Destroying Angel A historical term for a member of an alleged secret militant Mormon organization. Also called the *Destroying Band* and *Mormon Destroying Angels.* The group was said, in Mark Twain's words, "to conduct permanent disappearances of obnoxious citizens."

devil's bouquet A plant *(Nyctaginia capitata)* native to Texas, so named because of its musty, disagreeable odor. Also called *skunk flower.*

devil's darning needle See BRONCO GRASS.

devil's hat band An old name for barbed wire.

devil's head A common name for both the pincushion cactus *(Mammillaria wrighii)* and the barrel cactus *(Echinocactus texensis).*

devil's horse A name used in Texas for the praying mantis.

devil's tongue The Western prickly pear *(Opuntia humifusa),* which has many small bristles that are very painful when they penetrate the skin.

dewlap The skin hanging from the neck of a cow cut in various ways as an identifying mark. "They cut dewlaps in all of the cows."

dice-house A term used by many cowboys for the bunkhouse.

dicho A saying or proverb; borrowed from Spanish. " 'The lands of the sun expand the soul' is a dicho of our Latin neighbors."

dicker Deriving from *decem* (10), *decuria* was the Latin word for the bundle of 10 animal hides that Caesar's legions made a unit of trade in Britain and elsewhere, this word eventually corrupted to *dicker.* On the frontier in America, the haggling and petty bargaining over *dickers* of pelts became the meaning of the word itself.

die game Die bravely. ". . . all executed men who do not 'die game' are promptly called cowards by unreflecting people . . ." [Mark Twain, *Roughing It,* 1872]

die-out See DIE-UP.

die-up The death of great numbers of cattle due to a drought or a blizzard. "We lost thousands in the die-up of 1872–73." Also called a *die-out.*

die with throat trouble To be hanged. "Someone bad as that's gonna die of throat trouble."

differential grasshopper; differential locust *Melanoplus differentialis,* a large destructive grasshopper of the Western states.

Digger Indian A small Paiute tribe near St. George, Utah was first called the Diggers because they practiced agriculture instead of hunting for food; the name was said to be an English translation of their Indian name. Later, *Diggers* was applied to all agricultural tribes and eventually the name became a derogatory one for an Indian.

dimes An old term for money. "He's got the dimes; he's a real wealthy man."

Dine See NAVAJO.

dinero Spanish for money. " 'I could send for a friend of mine who has a map and get plenty of dinero.' " [J. Frank Dobie, *Coronado's Children*, 1930]

dink A term for an animal or person found wanting, from a small or deformed calf to a horse that doesn't perform well to a person who leaves much to be desired. "I'm sorry I voted for that dink."

dipping A term in the West and the South for using snuff by putting it into the mouth.

dirt grubber A farmer. "A bunch of dirt grubbers hired him an' brung him down from Oregon or some such place." [Frank Roderus, *Hell Creek Cabin*, 1979]

Dirty Thirties The 1930s, when terrible dust storms afflicted the Western plains.

discovery dance A Plains Indians dance celebrating the discovery of game or an enemy tribe.

disremember Forget. " 'Rickety can be rode, they say . . . but I disremember anybody that's done it . . .' " [Max Brand, *Alcatraz*, 1923]

district attorney Any dish contained cheap or unmentionable ingredients, such as sweetbreads, guts and kidneys, and named because of the cowboy's feelings about legal authorities.

Also called *county attorney* and *son-of-a-bitch stew*.

ditch riders Someone employed to check and maintain an irrigation system, cleaning the waters of debris and allotting the water.

dive Another term for the bunkhouse used by cowboys.

divide (1) A mountain range or ride. (2) A section of high ground separating two watersheds.

divinity A soft white candy made with egg whites and usually containing nuts, so named because its taste is "heavenly" to many.

Dixie A name given by Mormon settlers to the southern part of Utah, so named after the U.S. South or Dixie.

Dixie wine Wine made by Mormon settlers in southern Utah; also called *Dixie punch*.

dobe (1) A mud brick used in making ADOBES. (2) A Mexican silver dollar.

dobe wall To execute someone by firing squad, as was done in Mexico against adobe walls. "They dobe walled him as soon as they caught him."

does a bear shit in the woods? Absolutely, certainly. " 'Can you ride or not?' said Rawlins. 'Does a bear shit in the woods? Hell yes I can ride

. . .' " [Cormac McCarthy, *All the Pretty Horses*, 1992]

doesn't know A from bullfrog Has knowledge of very few things, is ignorant. "He doesn't know A from bullfrog about horses."

doesn't know beeswax from bullfoot Is ignorant or stupid.

dofunnies An old term for a cowboy's knives, trinkets and so forth.

dogbit Bit by a dog. ". . . I got dogbit by a bulldog took a chunk out of my leg the size of a Sunday roast . . ." [Cormac McCarthy, *All the Pretty Horses* (1992).

dog dance A historical term for a wild Sioux dance in which the heart and liver were cut from a dog and eaten raw by warriors.

dogfight A term used by cowboys for a fistfight; many cowboys, preferring to fight with weapons, thought dogfights were beneath them, reasoning that if they were intended to fight like dogs they would have been born with longer teeth and claws.

dogging Short for BULLDOGGING "When I started dogging I was looking for a passion . . . rapidly became a crackerjack bulldogger . . . and soon fixed upon four seconds as a pure limit, a goal to aim for. To chase and throw a steer within four seconds would equal perfection . . ." [Larry McMurty, *Cadillac Jack*, 1982]

doghouse Another cowboy term for the bunkhouse.

doghouse stirrups Wooden stirrups used in the early days of the West; they were said facetiously to have enough wood in them to build a doghouse with.

dogie The American cowboy has been shouting "git along, little dogie" for more than a century, but etymologists differ about the origin of the word *dogie* for a motherless calf. Some think it derives from "dough-guts," referring to the bloated bellies of such calves; others think that *dogie* is a clipped form of the Spanish *adobe* (mud); possibly it referred to cows so small that they were playfully called "doggies," and the pronunciation changed. Since some American cowboys were black, there is also the possibility that the Bambara *dogo* (small, short) is the source, or the Afro-Creole *dogi*, meaning the same. A dogie can be a calf, a yearling, a motherless calf, a poor worthless calf, a steer, or even a lamb or horse. See also DOUGH GUT.

dog my cats! A common euphemistic exclamation for *damn it!*

dog my skin! An old exclamation. "Dog my skin, ef thar was one in eight." [Bret Harte, "Spelling Bee," 1889]

dog soldiers (1) Members of a Cheyenne warrior society, the word often applied loosely to any Cheyenne or Indian warrior. The origin of the name is unknown. (2) Outlawed members of certain Western Indian tribes who banded together.

dollop glass A whiskey shot glass. "Ladino bent over a small wet spot on the carpeting and retrieved the dollop glass, but shook his head as Specs reached for the bottle again." [William Hopson, *The Last Shoot-Out,* 1958]

domino An old euphemism for "to give birth." "She's fixin' to domino in about three months." The reference here is to the end of a long game of dominoes.

Donation Land Act A congressional act of 1850 giving a married couple 640 acres of homestead land if they met certain conditions; it was the first such act of its kind and is said to have inspired many marriages.

done went Went. "He done went there."

Donner Pass; Donner Lake The scene of one of the most gruesome tragedies in Western history is named for the two Donner families who were part of a California-bound wagon train of emigrants that set out across the plains from Illinois in 1846. The Donner party, beset by great hardships, paused to recoup their strength at what is now *Donner Lake* in eastern California's Sierra Nevada mountains, only to be trapped by early snows that October. All passes were blocked deep with snow, and every attempt to get out failed. Forty of the 87 members of the party, which included 39 children, starved to death during the winter, and the survivors, driven mad by hunger, resorted to cannibalism before expeditions from the Sacramento Valley rescued them in April. The Donner party's gruesome yet heroic adventures have figured in much native literature. California's Donner State Historic Monument commemorates the event; the *Donner Pass* is traversed by U.S. Highway 40 today.

don't chew on something that's eatin' you Don't dwell on problems. "My daddy used to tell me not to chew on somethin' that was eatin' you." [Cormac McCarthy, *All the Pretty Horses,* 1992]

don't count on a rain 'til it's floatin' chip up around your belly button A West Texas saying, *chips* here being cow chips from the pasture.

don't fence me in Give me freedom, elbow room, a song and expression often associated with the West. Originally it was a line of a poem written by Bob Fletcher, a Westerner. Cole Porter bought the rights to the poem, revised the lyrics and wrote the music for the song, which wasn't used until a decade later, in the film *Hollywood Canteen* (1944). The next year it was featured in the Roy Rogers' movie *Don't Fence Me In.* "Meanwhile, in a sad irony," Frank Richard Prassel notes in *The Great American Outlaw* (1993), "Porter had been left crippled by a riding accident."

don't give a hoot and a holler Don't care at all. " 'Thing is, I didn't give a hoot and a holler what happened after I kicked off.' " [Richard S. Wheeler, *Stop*, 1989]

don't give a hoot in hell Don't care at all. "I don't give a hoot in hell how you put it down. That's your problem." [Jack Schaefer, *Monte Walsh*, 1958]

don't go a cent on An old term used when one declines an offer. "I don't go a cent on that."

don't know shit from applebutter To know nothing, be stupid or ignorant. " 'You don't know shit from apple butter,' said Rawlins. 'Booger kid's been dead forever.' " [Cormac McCarthy, *All the Pretty Horses*, 1992]

don't signify Doesn't make sense, seems unlikely, is unimportant. " '[The river] is dry now. Like powder.' He shrugged. 'Don't signify.' " [Jeanne Williams, *Home Mountain*, 1990]

don't you worry around Don't worry. " 'I'm all right,' Mrs. Thompson said. 'Now don't you worry around.' " [Katherine Anne Porter, *Noon Wine*, 1937]

doodads Trinkets, gadgets, devices, jewelry, etc. " 'Texas girls are mighty dressy. Wait till you see them, they go to Chicago and New York for their doodads.' " [Edna Ferber, *Giant*, 1952]

dope (1) A preparation of pitch that was applied to skis much like wax is today to make them slide faster. (2) To apply a substance to something with the intention of improving or fixing it. "Let me dope that sore on your leg."

dot and carry one A Western method of travel in which a rider would ride a distance, tie up his horse to rest and proceed on foot. Then his companion would reach the rested horse on foot and ride him past the walker, tie the horse up again and walk. When the first rider reached the tied rested horse, he would then ride it past the second rider and tie it up . . . and so on until they reached their destination.

double-damned lie A total lie. " 'That's a double-damned lie. I never wrote her a scratch.' " [Mari Sandoz, *Son of the Gamblin' Man*, 1960]

double-distilled liar An emphatic term for a pure, unadulterated liar. " 'Why you double-distilled liar,' said Monte Walsh." [Jack Schaefer, *Monte Walsh*, 1958]

double jack A long-handled heavy sledgehammer that is swung with both hands.

doughboy This word for a U.S. Army infantryman may have originated in the West from the term *adobe*, which Spaniards in the Southwest called military personnel, though this is only one of several possible explanations for the term.

Dougherty wagon An ambulance or passenger wagon used in the Southwest in the early days of migration;

named for its inventor, his first name unknown.

dough god A type of bread cooked over an open fire. "Mrs. Nelberger came to the door with a pan in her hand and asked, quite humbly, if she could put this here dough god to bake on top of our stove . . . so [she] put her dough god in the oven, since mother was not baking." [David Lamson, "Haywire," 1943] Also called a *dough gob* and a *dough goddy*.

dough gut An old cowboy term for a calf that has lost its mother and is fed with the cattle, the sudden change in diet causing its stomach to swell; one story has it that the term DOGIE for a calf derives from *dough gut*.

douse Put out, extinguish. "Douse that cigarette."

downer (1) An animal, such as a cow, that is off its feet, especially in a loaded cattle car. (2) A sick or injured animal that can't stand after a long drought or a hard winter.

down one's Sunday throat Logger's talk for swallowing something the wrong way. "It went down his Sunday throat, and he near choked to death."

down the river Another name for the poker game of seven-card stud.

down to a gnat's eyebrow Something very small, fine or insignificant; descriptive of something done very precisely. "He dropped that tree right where he wanted it, down to a gnat's eyebrow."

downwinder A term applied to people in the Southwest "who claim they were harmed by wind-carried radioactive fallout resulting from open-air testing of atomic bombs in the 1950s and early 1960s," according to a *New York Times* article of 12/29/93.

drag The tail end of a herd of cattle; the cowboy in charge of these cows is called the *drag-driver*, having the worst place to ride because of the dust kicked up by the cattle.

drag it See LIGHT A RAG.

drank Drink. "I went outside with a couple o' fellers to take a drank." [James Still, "Lost Brother," 1937] Heard in Texas but used more in the South than the West.

drat A euphemism for *damn*. "Drat him!" [Clarence B. Kelland, *Valley of the Sun*, 1940]

draw (1) To draw a pistol from a holster on one's belt, an expression that originated in the West in the mid-19th century. (2) A dry streambed or gully.

draw one's steel Draw a gun. " 'Sit quiet,' said the dealer, scornfully to the man near me. 'Can't you see he don't want to push trouble?' He had handed Trampas the choice to back down or draw his steel." [Owen Whister, *The Virginian*, 1902]

dressed up like a sore thumb Dressed very gaudily, overdressed for a place or occasion, out of place. "She came into the bar dressed up like a sore thumb."

drift (1) A herd that strays from its range. (2) Cattle that persistently move slowly in response to a storm. (3) To drive cattle slowly.

drifter Originally a cowboy riding or drifting through the West looking for work.

drinking hole Any bar. "Describing the place as a lounge sure was euphemistic . . . The place was a bonafide honky-tonk. It didn't possess a single feature that would elevate it to any higher caliber of drinking hole than that." [Sandra Brown, *Texas Lucky!*, 1990]

driver A cowboy who moves cattle that are on foot from one place to another.

drizzles Involuntary urination, wetting of the pants. " 'You boys will get the drizzles if you don't relax,' he said." [Larry McMurtry, *Lonesome Dove*, 1985]

drop band A flock of pregnant ewes that are going to drop, that is, give birth to lambs, in a short time.

drop of a hat No one has offered a convincing explanation for this very common American expression, and both *Webster's* and the *Oxford English Dictionary* ignore it entirely. It has been suggested that it is Irish in ori-

gin and that since the words are most often heard in the form of "he's ready to fight at the drop of a hat" the phrase parallels challenges like "roll up your sleeves," "take off your coat" and other expressions used at the start of a fistfight. Another possible explanation lies in the duels with guns, knives, whips or fists so common in the 19th century. The referee who judged these duels usually dropped a handkerchief or hat as a signal for the fight to begin. The expression appears to have been used in the United States first in the West and was first recorded in 1887.

drouth Drought. ". . . the once powerful frame of a man in whom some inward drouth had dried up the last few water holes of life and power." [Conrad Richter, *The Sea of Grass*, 1937]

drouthed out Ruined by drought. "All the drouthed-out land in West Texas ain't worth one tear in that girl's eye." [Elmer Kelton, *The Time It Never Rained*, 1973]

drug Dragged. "They drug him out."

drunk as a biled (boiled) owl ". . . the Comanches . . . all got drunk as a covey of biled owls." [J. Frank Dobie, *Coronado's Children*, 1930]

dry camp A place for camping where there is no water available.

dry-gulch To ambush someone, killing or harming him. "They dry-gulched Bill Morrow just outside of town."

drygulch whiskey A cheap, potent, locally brewed whiskey. "He mouthed the words to the tune of 'Joe Bower's,' a song much heard among the Texas drovers . . . but the quality of his singing was not as good, because his voice was not oiled with drygulch whiskey as the Texans' always were . . ." [Douglas C. Jones, *Roman,* 1986]

drylander An old term for a farmer who farms without irrigation because of a poor supply of water.

ducking A hard cotton fabric used to make clothing, sacks, etc.; also called *duck.*

dude An often contemptuous term for an Easterner or city slicker, especially one who vacations on what is called a *dude ranch;* the term dates back to the late 19th century.

dude ranch At first a term for tourist ranches in the West but now used to describe such places everywhere, from the Catskills to the Texas Panhandle.

dugout A pioneer dwelling built into the ground. "Their dug-out was a wretched place to live in . . . A hole is dug in the side of a hill, a few forked posts are put in the corners, poles are laid in the forks, brush and straw as thick as will keep out rain, and with a door in front and a chimney cut in the bank, the house is ready for occupation." [Percy G. Ebbutt, *Emigrant Life in Kansas,* 1886]

dulce A Southwestern term for a sweet or candy, a borrowing of the Spanish word meaning the same.

dump Another term used by cowboys for the bunkhouse.

dumpling mover A term used in Texas for a very heavy but brief ran.

dun A dun-colored horse, usually a dull grayish brown with a black tail. "He pointed at this big dun horse . . . I say dun; in the north they generally call them *buckskin,* but on the ranges in the Southwest they call them *dun,* or *coyote dun.*" [Benjamin Capps, *Tales of the Southwest,* 1990]

dust Short for *gold dust.* "We panned out some dust from the old mine."

dust along; dust out To depart quickly. "He dusted out of there quicker than a wink."

dust bowl Severe dust storms beginning in 1934 destroyed crops and dried the soil in the southern High Plains of the United States, largely because this land in Kansas, Colorado, Oklahoma, New Mexico and Texas had been poorly farmed for years. The Great Depression, drought, and the dust forced large numbers of people to migrate from the area, which was first called the *dust bowl* in a story written by Associated Press reporter Robert Geiger in April 1935. The dust storms lasted almost a decade, and dust from them blew as far as 300 miles out into the Atlantic, where it coated ships.

dust devil See quote. "The strong wind blew out of the northwest, sweeping the hotter air of the desert toward the mountain. Heated unevenly by the baking sunlight on the white earth of the bottom of the long-gone lake, the wind in places lost its smooth southeast flow and began to eddy and swirl. The swirls grew and pirouetted like invisible dancers and then, as their strength grew, birthed giant dust devils that dizzily spun white dust around and upward in vortices of counter clockwise-whirling turbulent pools of air four to five hundred feet deep. The ghostly columns, like giant dancing worms, wiggled and zig-zagged along to the southwest with the wind." [F. M. Parker, *Skinner*, 1981]

duster (1) A dust storm. (2) A dry hole, that is, an oil well that comes up dry, yielding no oil.

dust pneumonia A pneumonia caused by breathing dust-laden air; it took a heavy toll of human life and livestock in eastern Colorado and western Kansas in the 1930s. See also DUST BOWL.

E

ear down To hold a horse still by biting its ear. "I yelled at Wrangler [his partner], 'Ear him down; the son of a bitch is settin' my ears afire!' Wrangler came sailing in looking like a bowlegged hog crossed with a short-shanked bear. He finally got the [horse's] ear in his mouth and held on till I got a hackamore on the bay's head." [Max Evans, *The Rounders*, 1960]

ear-notched Tame, domesticated, broken, part of the herd. 'Sleeper was 'ear-notched, but mostly maverick,' men said of him." [Max Brand, *One Man Posse*, 1934]

ear sewer A colorful term heard in northern California for the dragon-fly; also called the *snake doctor*.

ears like a fox A keen sense of hearing. " 'Ah, lad,' he said. 'Hush now. The man will hear ye. He's ears like a fox.' " [Cormac McCarthy, *Blood Meridian, or, The Evening Redness in the West*, 1985]

earthquake weather A term used in California for the hot, humid weather without wind long believed to precede an earthquake.

ear to the ground Ramon Adams wrote in *Western Words* (1944 edition) that old plainsmen often placed a silk neckerchief on the ground, put an ear to it and thus could hear the sounds of men and horses miles away. Even if plainsmen and American Indians didn't hear distant footfalls by putting their ears to the ground, so many writers of Westerns have attributed this skill to them that the practice has become well known. The phrase is first recorded in 1900 in the *Congressional Record*, meaning "to use caution, to go slowly and listen frequently." Since then someone with *an ear to the ground* has become someone trying to determine signs of the future, trying to find out what's coming.

eat dog for another Various American Indian tribes ate dog meat and at least one was called *the Dogeaters* by their enemies. When white men sat at Indian councils where dog meat was served, those who didn't relish the dish could, without offending their host, put a silver dollar on the dish and pass it along, the next man taking the dollar and eating the dog. From this practice arose the American political expression *to eat dog for another*.

eat grass See EAT GRAVEL.

eat gravel To be thrown by a bucking horse or a steer; also *eat grass*.

eat lead Get shot. "The wrangler drew his six-shooter and pointed it at the barkeep's face. 'This is all I need to get a drink around here,' he said. 'Now pour or eat lead.'" [Larry D. Names, *Boomtown*, 1981]

E Clampus Vitus A humorous fraternity formed during California gold rush days mainly for the purpose of drinking; the name was probably formed on the analogy of *E Pluribus Unum* combined with the suggested convulsions of St. Vitus's dance.

educated in his books Had school or book learning. "[He's] tall, strong and better educated in his books than me." [Louis L'Amour, *The Lonesome Gods*, 1983]

eeef A pronunciation of *if*. See usage example at KEEL.

Egypt of the West The interior area of the United States between the Alleghenies and the Rocky Mountains; the term was coined by President Lincoln in an 1862 message to Congress.

eight square rifle A rifle with an octogonal barrel, used in the West toward the turn of the century; often called for short an *eight square*.

eitherhanded as a spider Ambidexterous. "He had the pistols stuck in his belt at the back and he drew them one in each hand and he is eitherhanded as a spider, he can write with both hands at a time . . ." [Cormac McCarthy, *Blood Me-*

ridian, or The Evening Redness in the West, 1985]

elbow room Plenty of room to move about in the open country, something a cowboy required miles of.

El Dorado The legendary treasure city of South America, whose name was applied by prospectors to the American West in the 19th century.

elephant tree A small Southwestern tree *(Bursera microphylla)* with gray bark and a stout tapering trunk that looks like an elephant's trunk.

embarcadero A port or landing place, especially one serving an inland Western city, a borrowing of the Spanish word meaning the same.

emigrant In the U.S., *emigrant* has meant at various times: (1) Someone moving farther West from the more settled East. (2) An American settler in Texas. (3) One who settles in Oregon. (4) A Mormon settler in the West. (5) A settler in California. (6) A settler in Kansas before the Civil War.

Emigration Road A nickname for the Oregon Trail, which brought so many settlers West and was called by a traveler in 1862 "the best and longest natural highway in the world."

emmer See EMORY.

emory (1) The Emory oak of the Southwest, named after American engineer W. H. Emory (d. 1889). (2) A pronunciation of the wheat called *emmer (Triticum turgidum dicoccon)* grown as a forage crop in the West.

enchilada A Spanish word first used in the Southwest and now widely known throughout the United States for a tortilla rolled and stuffed with meat or cheese and served with a chili-spiced sauce.

encina The Spanish word for the coast live oak *(Quercus agrefola)* of California. An *encinal* is a grove of such oaks.

endowment The course of instruction about Mormon rules and dispensations given to people wanting to join the church.

equalizer A pistol, possibly from the common Western saying that a "Colt makes all men equal." Yet another story traces the derivation to the Smith & Wesson pistol. Inventors Daniel B. Wesson and Horace Smith founded the Smith & Wesson Arms Company at Springfield, Massachusetts, in 1854. Their Smith & Wesson pistols replaced the Colt to a large extent and have been famous ever since. The term *equalizer* for a gun may come indirectly from their names. It is said that the term derives from a remark made by Chicago gangster Tim Smith, who died in a gangland killing on June 26, 1928. "Smith and Wesson made all men

equal," this nonrelated Smith is supposed to have said.

estancia A Spanish word used in the Southwest for a large cattle ranch.

estufa An underground meeting room in Pueblo Indian villages in which a sacred fire always burns.

et Ate. " 'I have et okra,' Jasper replied, 'but I have never yet et no gourd.' " [Larry McMurtry, *Lonesome Dove,* 1985]

ethyl A Western term for premium grade gasoline *(high test* in the East), even though ethyl is no longer used as a gas additive; from *tetraethyl lead.*

euchre To cheat, deceive; from the name of the card game *euchre* once much in vogue in the West.

Eureka State A nickname for California alluding to the motto "Eureka" on the state shield.

Evergreen State A nickname for the state of Washington from its abundance of evergreen trees.

ever whichway; every whichway In all directions. "He turned ever whichway."

everywheres Everywhere. Mark Twain used the pronunciation in his famous story "The Celebrated Jumping Frog of Calaveras County" (1865).

exalted A humorous term for hanged.

extry A pronunciation of *extra*.

eyeballer Someone who is very nosy, who meddles in other's affairs.

eyeballing Cutting off the upper eyelids of cattle to prevent them from escaping into the brush, which would cut their unprotected eyes.

F

fadedy Heard in East Texas for *faded*. "He had on those fadedy jeans."

fag along To move fast, depart quickly. "There he went fagging along."

fairground To rope and tie a steer; probably from the rodeo competitions held at fairgrounds. "I fairgrounded that cow before you could wink."

fairy primrose The small, sweet-scented yellow and magenta flower *Primula angustifolia* common in high Colorado country.

fallen hide A term used for the hide of a dead cow. Wrote Frank Dobie in *A Vaquero of the Brush Country* (1929): ". . . the custom of the country was that any man could take a 'fallen hide' . . . when he found it, no matter what brand the animal wore."

fallen timber Places where large numbers of trees have fallen in high winds or hurricanes, making passage difficult on foot or horse.

Fall Indians A group of Indians formerly living in Oregon, also called the *Gros Ventres of the Prairie,* who, according to one writer, "were the most relentlessly hostile tribe ever encountered by the whites in any part of the West, if not in any part of America. The trapper always understood that to meet with one of these Indians meant an instant and deadly fight."

false pond A Western term for a mirage.

fan (1) J. Frank Dobie explained the Western gunfighter's term *to fan* in *A Vaquero of the Brush Country* (1929): "To 'fan' a gun the person gripped it in his left hand and with rapid passes of his right hand knocked back and released the hammer. The gun used in 'fanning' had, of course, no trigger. A man might 'fan' for pastime, but seldom for his life." (2) To flourish a knife. (3) To move out smartly. (4) To whip, spank, punish. "Those little fellows needed fanning."

fandango (1) A Spanish-American dance in triple time; the music for such a dance. (2) A ball or dance popular in the Southwest.

Fanny Heath raspberry Raspberries have not been cultivated for nearly as long as apples, peaches and pears. Called a brambleberry and considered a nuisance in England, it was not until about 1830 that the delicate, delicious fruit began to be developed in America. The *Fanny Heath* variety is a tribute to a determined pioneer woman who emigrated to North Dakota in 1881. This young bride had been told that she could never grow anything on the barren alkaline soil surrounding her house, but 40 years later her homestead was an Eden of flowers, fruits and vegetables. After her death in 1931, the black raspberry she developed was named in her honor.

fantods A state of nervous irritability; nervous movements. "When I walked I got the fantods and saw Julia, my baby sister, the day she was arrow-shot. She was very clear to me and stayed a long time." [Charles O. Locke, *The Hell-Bent Kid,*1957]

far A pronunciation of *fair*. "[He's] a far-minded man." [Bret Harte, "Tennessee's Partner," 1870]

farewell-to-spring A showy flower *(Clarkia amoeua)* of the evening primrose family native to the West.

farm to the walls of the barn Plant a crop extensively, using all available land. "I burned the feed bunks and farmed right up to the walls of the barn." [Thomas McGuane, *Nothing but Blue Skies,* 1992]

a far piece A long distance. " 'It is a far piece, ma'am,' Bick agreed . . . 'But when you get there you never want to live anywhere else.' " [Edna Ferber, *Giant,* 1952]

farting against the wind Undertaking an exercise in futility. "Powder Pike laid a rough hand on Flagg's shoulder. 'You're fartin' against the wind, Charlie. We've got used to government money like a kid gets used to candy.' " [Elmer Kelton, *The Time It Never Rained,* 1973]

fart-knocker A cowboy term for a hard fall from a horse.

Far West The area of the Western United States west of the Great Plains—the Rocky Mountain and Pacific states region.

faunch Rant and rave. " 'I guess you know that damn teacher of yours hung a haymaker on Kraker . . . What maybe you don't know is that Kraker's faunchin' to swear to a charge.' 'Why not let him faunch?' " [A. B. Guthrie Jr., *Arfive,* 1970]

feather duster An old Western term for an Indian, after the feathers many Indians wore in ceremonial dress.

feathers in his britches Said of someone restless. " 'You sure got feathers in your britches these days, Robert Henry,' his grandfather told him . . ." [Mari Sandoz, *Son of the Gamblin' Man,* 1960]

feller A common pronunciation of *fellow*.

fence lifter Any heavy rain that washes away soil.

fence rider A cowboy who rides along fences making repairs where needed.

fence war A feud among cattlemen over the fencing in of what had been open cattle ranges by some ranch owners; also called *fence cutting war.*

fetched out Popped out, appeared. ". . . I'd no thought of drawing that gun. It just fetched out when the need came." [Louis L'Amour, *Bendigo Shafter,* 1979]

fever tick The cattle tick *(Margarapus annulatus)* that causes Texas cattle fever.

fiddlefooted Descriptive of a wanderer or rolling stone or of a skittish horse. " 'But he's fiddle-footed. Remember. He said so himself. He'll be moving on one of these days and you'll be all upset if you get to liking him too much.' " [Jack Schaefer, *Shane,* 1949]

field Indian An old term used in California for Indian agricultural laborers.

fiesta A Spanish word meaning a festivity or celebration, now widely known throughout the United States but first used in the Southwest.

fiesta flower A deep purple or violet Southwestern flower *(Pholistoma auritum)* said to be worn by señoritas on their dresses at fiestas in early times.

50-50 A term used in California for a "creamsickle" made of half frozen, flavored water and half ice cream.

54-40 or fight James Polk won election to the American presidency in 1844 with this slogan, which referred to the ousting of the British from the whole of the Columbia River country up to latitude 54° 40' north. After his election Polk discarded the slogan and settled the Oregon question without going to war. The sarcastic Whig slogan "Who is James K. Polk?" inspired the myth that Polk was a political nonentity and weak president. In truth, he was one of the hardest-working of all presidents, attained almost all his stated aims and added more territory to the United States than any president except Jefferson.

57 varieties of a fool A complete fool; probably from the popular Heinz 57 varieties of canned food. ". . . and he would concede that she was not a particularly pretty girl according to the standards people seemed to go by any more. But he figured any man who judged a woman by a tape measure was fifty-seven varieties of a fool." [Elmer Kelton, *The Time It Never Rained,* 1973]

fight fire with fire An Americanism, possibly deriving from the use of backfires to help extinguish great prairie and forest fires in the early West. Settlers would set fire to a circle or strip of land in the path of a blaze but at a good distance from it, then extinguish it and leave a barren patch so that the advancing fire would have nothing to feed on and so would burn itself out. Fighting fire with fire could be a dangerous practice for the backfire might get out of control itself, so the expression came to mean any desperate measure involving great risk.

fightin'est See usage example at RUNNIN'EST

fight shy of Avoid. "That's the place to fight shy of. You're gettin' into cliff-dweller country . . ." [Louis L'Amour, *The Haunted Mesa*, 1987]

file one's teeth for (someone) To prepare or plan revenge on someone. "He knows you did it, and he's filing his teeth for you."

fill a blanket To roll a cigarette, an old expression.

fine-haired sons of bitches A derogatory term for gentlemanly, "civilized" types in the early West. " 'I despise all you fine-haired sons of bitches,' Blue Duck said." [Larry McMurtry, *Lonesome Dove*, 1985]

finish one's circle To die. "He finished his circle after 90 full years."

fire dance A Plains Indian dance employing a bundle of flaming reeds that varied from tribe to tribe. One observer of the dance wrote: "Each man started slapping the man ahead of him with the burning torches and the man would pretend to writhe in discomfort and leap high."

firehole A term used for the holes in the ground that contain hot water in Yellowstone National Park.

fire one's shuck To criticize one sharply, to light into a person. "He's sure gonna fire your shuck."

firewater Though much used in the West, this expression didn't originate there. A traveler in North America in 1817 reported that "[the Indian chiefs] called the whiskey fire water." An accurate description of whiskey's taste going down, especially the whiskey Indians were traded, *firewater* is probably a translation of the Algonquin Indian *scoutiouabou* meaning the same.

fish A yellow oilskin rain slicker that cowboys carried rolled and tied on their saddles. It was named for the picture of its trademark, a fish.

fishing falls A name used especially for falls of the Snake River in Idaho, after the great quantities of salmon taken there.

fist and skull An early Western expression referring to a fight in which no weapons are used, a fair fight. "He told us about a fist and skull fight that he won."

fits like a hog in a saddle An old simile meaning something that doesn't fit at all.

Five Civilized Tribes A collective name given to the Cherokee, Creek, Choctaw, Chickasaw and Seminole Indian tribes because of their adoption of European culture; in spite of this, they were deported to the Indian Territory from 1830 to 1850. Also called *Five Civilized Nations.*

five-shooter   Far less famous than the legendary *six-shooter,* the *five-shooter* was a revolver that fired five times before it had to be reloaded. The name is first recorded in 1848.

fixtures   An old term for clothing. In *Tall Tales of the Southwest* (1930), edited by Franklin Meine, a narrator says, "The idea of pulling off my boots before the girl was death. And as to doffing my other fixtures, I would sooner have my leg taken off."

flasharity   Fancy riding clothes, a dude outfit.

flat   An early Western expression meaning to reject a suitor or lover. "She flatted him."

flathead   A name for members of a tribe of Salishan Indians of Montana and members of the Chinook Indian tribe; the name derives from their supposed practice of flattening their children's heads at birth. The word was extended to mean a simpleton or a fool among Western settlers.

fleece   (1) An early term for the pure fat obtained from a bear. (2) Fatty buffalo meat.

flickertail   A ground squirrel *(Citellus richardsoni)* of the Western prairie; so named because they disappear into their holes with a final flick of the tail.

Flickertail State   An old nickname for North Dakota, because of its many *flickertail squirrels.*

floating town   A wild temporary town built along the advancing railroad in Colorado and other states.

flock   A lot, a great deal. " 'He's gone and had a flock of bad luck.' " [Max Brand, *Speedy,* 1931]

flour gold   Gold powder, fine particles of gold.

flying   In referring to cattle brands, *flying* means a letter is wavy or flowing in appearance, as in the *Flying H* brand.

flying light   An expression used of the pony express in the early West. "Both horse and rider went 'flying light' . . . fer even the postage on his literary freight was worth *five dollars a letter.*" [Mark Twain, *Roughing It,* 1872]

fofarraw   (1) Tawdry baubles and trinkets; gaudy dress. "He traded his furs for all that fofarraw." (2) An uproar of fuss. "The new law set off a fofarraw of protest." (3) An old perhaps obsolete term for vain, conceited. "She was too fofarraw for me." The word probably derives from the Spanish *fanfarrón* (braggart). It is also spelled *foofarar.*

fofarraw house   A brothel. "A purty little whore at St. Louis, at a fofarraw house called a place of entertainment, she give it to me, a regular case." [A. B. Guthrie, *The Big Sky*, 1947]

fog (1) To hurry, go quickly, rush. "He come fogging into town last night. (2) To repeatedly fire a gun. "The deputies had them trapped and kept fogging them for nearly an hour."

fogging Obscuring or hiding something. " 'Quit foggin, Doc,' came a voice from the crowd. 'Show us what you got behind that curtain.' " [Jack Schaefer, *Monte Walsh*, 1958]

folden pants A baby's diapers.

fold up To buck. "The horse folded up and threw him."

fool hay A name used for various weedy grasses (such as witch grass) in the Far West because they deceive farmers into thinking they will make good hay when they do not.

fool hen Certain quail and grouse that are easy to kill because of their lethargy or tameness.

fool hoeman An old contemptuous term for a farmer.

fool's gold A term coined in the West around 1875 for iron or copper pyrites, which are sometimes mistaken for gold; used figuratively to mean anything that deceives a person. " 'That's fool's gold. See how green those flakes look in the light? Real gold don't do that.' " [Anke Kristke, "Dust" in *Women of the West*, 1990]

fool's water Another colorful term for strong hard liquor, this one contributed to the language by the Crow Indians and, according to one early writer, "a term at once attesting to their nice moral discernment and good sense."

footburner An old humorous term for a plow that a farmer walked behind.

footermans A cowboy term descriptive of how one travels when traveling on foot. "No real cowboy wants to go footermans anywhere."

Foot Indians A name formerly given to Indians who inhabited the plains and did not use horses.

footrags Socks. "He hadn't changed his footrags for a month."

footslaves Indians, usually captured from another tribe, who followed the warriors on horseback, carrying their possessions. "When the wind was in the north you could hear them, the horses and the breath of the horses and the horses' hooves that were shod in rawhide and the rattle of lances and the constant drag of the travois poles in the sand like the passing of some enormous serpent and the young boys naked on wild horses as jaunty as circus riders and hazing wild horses before them and the dogs trotting with their tongues aloll and footslaves following half naked and sorely burdened and above all the low chant of their traveling song which the riders sang as they rode, nation and ghost of a nation passing in a soft chorale across the mineral waste to darkness bearing lost to all history and all remembrance like a grail the sum of their secular and transitory and violent lives." [Cormac McCarthy, *All the Pretty Horses*, 1992]

foot trail A trail made and used by persons on foot rather than by animals or wagons.

fore-and-after; fore and aft schooner Other names for the big Army wagons called prairie schooners, "because the two ends of the wagon inclined upward, like the bow and stern" of a schooner sailing ship.

fore pay Payment in advance. *Bartlett* (1850) notes, " 'There are two bad paymasters, no pay and fore pay.' This proverbial expression is frequently heard in the West."

foretop The driver's seat of a stage or other vehicle pulled by horses. "It was worth a lifetime of city toiling and moiling, to perch in the foretop with the driver and see the six mustangs scamper." [Mark Twain, *Innocents Abroad*, 1869]

fork Cowboy talk meaning to mount and ride one's horse. Andy Adams writes in *The Log of a Cowboy* (1903): "So fork that swimming horse of yours and wet your big toe in the North Platte."

fort (1) In the early West, every military post in Indian country was called a *fort,* even if there were no fortifications and it only consisted of

a few wooden buildings and a parade grounds. (2) To secure oneself. " 'He forted up behind his horse,' Dog Face said." [Larry McMurtry, *Lonesome Dove*, 1985]

for Texas! A popular cry of Texas Rangers in battle. "As they ran they screamed whatever occurred to them. 'For Texas' was the most popular. Followed by 'Remember the Alamo,' which had become an all-purpose phrase." [Lucia St. Clair Robson, *Ride the Wind*, 1982]

for to To, the "for" being redundant. "I'd like for to see you."

Fort Whoop-Up A humorous name for a dive selling rotgut whiskey to Indians.

40 miles of bad road A very ugly or unattractive person or place. "She looked like 40 miles of bad road, and he looked like he went on 10 miles longer."

49er (1) A person who went to California in 1849 during the gold rush. (2) Someone in favor of the use of the 49th parallel of latitude as a compromise boundary line in the Oregon boundary dispute with Great Britain.

40 rod lightning Whiskey in the early West could literally kill a man and was thus given colorful names, none more vivid than *40 rod lightning*—which likened it to a rifle or shot that could kill a man at 40 yards.

42 A game of dominoes that is popular in Texas and probably originated there; named for the total sum of the "counters" in the game.

Fort Yuma See quote. "Fort Yuma [in Southwest Arizona] is probably the hottest place on earth . . . There is a tradition . . . that a very, very wicked soldier died there, once, and of course, went straight to the hottest corner of perdition,—and the next day he *telegraphed back for his blankets*." [Mark Twain, *Roughing It*, 1872]

four cows and calves In the anonymous *Brusky Joe's Reminiscences* (c. 1870) the author notes that he "used to hear the early settlers tell how a cow and calf was legal tender for ten dollars. Even if a man paid in gold— say forty dollars for a horse—he might say he gave 'four cows and calves' for it. So the banks were logically just cowpens."

four-five-six A game played with three dice similar to the card game "21."

fourflusher A *flush* in poker is five cards all of the same suit, the hand taking its name either from a flush, or flight of birds, or more likely, from the Latin *flux* (a copious flow). A four-card *flush* is worthless, but in open-handed poker, if four cards of the same suit are face up on the table a player is in an excellent position to bluff, nobody knowing whether he has a fifth card of the same suit as his concealed "hole" card. Gamblers in the American West at the turn of the century bluffed so often with such *fourcard* or *bobtail flushes* that the term *fourflusher* spread from the gambling tables into politer society, where it came to signify anyone who bluffs or pretends, especially someone who pretends to be more than he is while living on money borrowed from others.

four-legged word Any long, polysyllabic word, often scholarly, frequently pretentious.

the fourth Thursday A euphemism for menstruation heard in Texas.

fractured like a watermelon in a cowlot Broken to almost unrecognizable pieces. "It didn't matter that his own Spanish . . . was fractured like a watermelon in a cowlot." [Elmer Kelton, *The Time It Never Rained*, 1973]

Fredonia In 1827 a group of adventurers tried to set up a Texan republic called Fredonia; the name Fredonia had been invented in about 1800 by Dr. Samuel Latham Mitchell as a term for the United States, "a land where things are freely done," and borrowed by the unsuccessful adventurers.

free-for-all In the West a *free-for-all* means a free fight, not a horse race in which all comers may compete. As Stewart White put it in *The Blazed Trail* (1902), "In a free-for-all knock-down and drag-out, kicking, gouging, and biting are all legitimate."

free grass Free pasture rights on public land.

free range Open public range, free for grazing, that belongs to the government; also called *free grass*.

freeze An old term meaning to long for or ardently desire. "I freeze to go back home, I'm half froze for buffalo meat and mountain doings."

freezeout A poker game requiring each player to drop out when he loses a predetermined amount of money, until one player is left with all the winnings. The game appears to have first been played in the West, in about 1855.

Fremontia The black greasewood of the desert, named after explorer John C. Frémont (1813–90).

fresh Said of a cow that has had a calf. " 'She's fresh enough.' 'Do you mean she's new?' 'No. No . . . Fresh means she's had a baby.' " [A. B. Guthrie Jr., *Arfive*, 1970]

fretting Worrying. " 'Sure, Cal, sure,' said Hat. 'Quit fretting yourself.' " [Jack Schaefer, *Monte Walsh*, 1958]

frijoles A Spanish word for beans of the *Phaseolus* genus, especially kidney beans, used in the Southwest and sometimes pronounced "freehollies."

frijoles refritos Refried beans, that is beans cooked and mashed and then fried, often with onions and other seasonings; a borrowing of the Mexican-Spanish meaning the same.

Frisco A nickname for San Francisco dating back to the 1850s.

from Fort Kearney, west, he was feared a great, great deal more than the Almighty A Western saying about the notorious desperado "Captain" J. A. Slade. Wrote Mark Twain of these words in *Roughing It* (1872): "For compactness, simplicity and vigor of expression, I will back that sentence against anything in literature."

frontage road A road running parallel to a highway that gives access to businesses.

frontier Although the word in the sense of "a new or sparsely settled region" is usually associated with the American West, *frontier* is first recorded in the East, in 1671.

Frontier Day A celebration initiated in Cheyenne, Wyoming in 1897 to keep alive the customs of the early West.

front porch A humorous term for a large belly, a potbelly.

frozen words An old story from the Texas Panhandle tells of a winter so cold that spoken words froze in the air, fell entangled on the ground and had to be fried up in a skillet before the letters would reform and any sense could be made of them. The idea is an ancient one, used by Rabelais and familiar to the Greek dramatist Antiphanes, who is said to have used it in praising the work of Plato: "As the cold of certain cities is so intense that it freezes the very words we utter, which remain congealed till the heat of summer thaws them, so the mind of youth is so thoughtless that the wisdom of Plato lies there frozen, as it were, till it is thawed by the refined judgment of mature age."

fruit tramp   A migrant fruit picker.

frying pan   The term usually used for a skillet in Texas and other Western states.

fryin' size   Said of a young person or a runt. "He's just about fryin' size, and he's struttin' around givin' orders."

fry thin   Punish severely. " 'Darn his fat soul! I'll fry him thin for this!' cried the iron hand of justice." [Max Brand, *The Trail to San Triste,* 1924]

fucking the dog   Loafing, shirking work on the job, malingering; heard in Texas, other Western states and other regions as well.

full as a tick   Stuffed with food. " 'You all want more of this?' said John Grady. 'I'm full as a tick.' " [Cormac McCarthy, *All the Pretty Horses,* 1992]

full blood   A term for a person of pure Indian descent.

full ear   A calf that hasn't been branded or earmarked.

full of bounce   Energetic, resilient. "And me edging past twenty and full of bounce and knowing I was good." [Jack Schaefer, *First Blood,* 1952]

funning   Kidding. "You all are just funnin'. I knowed you was all along." [Cormac McCarthy, *All the Pretty Horses,* 1992]

fur   A common pronunciation of *far.* "It's a fur piece down the road."

fuss   A fight. "Better get yourself well . . . We'll need all hands for this fuss." [Louis L'Amour, *The Tall Stranger,* 1957]

fussbudget   A finicky person.

G

gachupin A Mexican-Spanish word for a Spaniard, used in the Southwest; it is said to derive originally from a Nahuatl word meaning approximately "a man wearing spurs," as the first Spanish horsemen did.

Gadsden Purchase The purchase in 1853 from Mexico of land now part of New Mexico and Arizona; named after negotiator James Gadsden, then U.S. minister to Mexico.

gal Affectionate nickname for a cow. "That old gal is ready to give birth right soon."

galleta Grasses of the genus *Hilaria* used for hay in the Southwest, a borrowing of the Spanish word for the same.

galliwampus A mythical monster of Texas, once described by O. Henry as "a mammal with fins on its back and eighteen toes on its feet."

galon See quote. " 'The Mexicans call a big horse [used for hauling] a galon . . . The [American] teamsters would yell to their big horses, 'G'long! G'long!' Get along, get along, see? So the Mexicans thought a heavy horse was a galon.' " [Edna Ferber, *Giant*, 1952]

galoot A big, stupid man.

> "Hare-lipped Sal, she was a beaut,
> She wore a number nine.
> She kicked the hat off a Texas galoot
> To the tune of Auld Lang Syne."
> [Old Western song, quoted in Jack Schaefer's *Monte Walsh*, 1958]

Gambel oak A small white oak (*Quercus gambelli*) with colorful autumn leaves found at high elevations from Montana to northern Mexico; named for naturalist William Gambel (1821–49).

game of the arrow American artist George Catling recorded this favorite (though little known) amusement of the Plains Indians: "The young men . . . assemble on the prairie (and) . . . step forward in turn, shooting their arrows into the air, endeavoring to see who can get the greatest number flying in the air at one time, thrown from the same bow."

ganted Thin, gaunt, drawn. " 'You look real ganted I was saying to Bick.' " [Edna Ferber, *Giant*, 1952]

garbanzo A Spanish word for the chick-pea used in the Southwest.

Garden of the Gods An area near Colorado Springs, Colorado noted

101

for over a century for its great natural beauty.

gaschupin An upper-class person of Spanish descent.

gasser Used in Texas and Oklahoma for an oil well that yields gas as well as oil.

gat More commonly associated with gangsters, *gat* was a term used by gunfighters in the West; it is apparently a humorous exaggeration of the Gatling gun of the Civil War. "But the minute he saw me lower my gat, he raised his and started pumping lead at me . . ." [Max Brand, *The Black Signal,* 1925]

Gateway to the West An old nickname for Pittsburgh, Pa.; also called *Gate City of the West.*

gaum A mess, a sticky mess. "You're making a gaum out of that candy."

gazook A gawky, strange or stupid person. "That old gazook is always bothering us."

geed up Lame or out of commission; possibly from the horse command *gee* (stop).

Gem State; Gem of the Mountains Nicknames for Idaho.

Gene Autry Popular Western singer and film star of the 1940s and 1950s after whom Gene Autry, Oklahoma is named, perhaps the only Western

city named after a movie star, unless one counts Tarzan, Texas.

General Grant Tree One of the largest redwoods in California, named after American general and president Ulysses S. Grant; the General Grant National Park was created around it, this later becoming the Kings Canyon National Park.

Genius of the Divide See quote. "For the first time, perhaps, since the land emerged from the waters of geologic ages, a human face was set toward it with love and yearning . . . Then the Genius of the Divide, the great, free spirit which breathes across it, must have bent lower than it ever bent to a human will before. The history of every country begins in the heart of a man or a woman." [Willa Cather, *O Pioneers!,* 1913]

gentile As used by the Mormons, *gentile* means anyone who is not a Mormon.

gentle as a milkpen calf Very gentle, harmless. "Hell, that old pony just stopped and stood there. 'See there, boys,' Jim Ed yelled. 'Just like I said—gentle as a milkpen calf.' " [Max Evans, *The Rounders,* 1960]

gentling Taming an unbroken horse.

Geronimo! Chiricahua Apache leader Geronimo is said to have made a daring leap on horseback to escape U.S. cavalry pursuers at Medicine Bluffs, Oklahoma. As he leaped to freedom down a steep cliff into a river below, he supposedly cried out his name in defiance of the troopers. There is no mention of this incident in the great warrior and prophet's autobiography, which he dictated to a white writer before his death while under military confinement at Fort Sill, Oklahoma in 1909. But by that time, Geronimo was an old man, well over 70, and had converted to the Dutch Reformed Church; little remained of the brave leader who in protecting his people's land against white settlers had terrorized the American Southwest and northern Mexico with cunning, brutal raids and whose actions became Western legend. The cry *Geronimo!* is part of that legend and was adopted as the battle cry of American paratroopers leaping from their planes in World War II. The 82d Airborne at Fort Bragg, North Carolina first used it, taking it either from the oral legend about Geronimo or from the popular movie featuring the Indian warrior that was being shown near the paratrooper training center at the time.

get Originally Western slang meaning to kill or to hunt down and kill a person. Philip Paxton in *A Stray Yankee in Texas* (1853) wrote: "A Texan does not kill his game, he *saves* or *gets it*, or *makes it come*." The term is now widely used to mean to kill a person.

get a halo gratis A cowboy expression meaning to be killed.

get a hunch, bet a bunch A saying said to derive from the game of faro. "A daring player or a confident high roller would bet both win and lose at the same turn. The practice gave rise to the saying 'get a hunch, bet a bunch.'" [Matt Braun, *The Brannocks,* 1986]

get off the dime Get busy, get going, hurry up. This California phrase, first recorded in the 1920s, is also heard as *get off the nickel*. "Quit your loafing, men, get off the dime."

get oneself harnessed To get hitched, get married. "He got himself harnessed last year."

get one's spurs tangled To be confused, disoriented. "He took so many blows in the head he got his spurs tangled."

get shut of Get out of, finished with. "Well, he plans to go quick as he can get shut of school." [Thomas McGuane, *Keep The Change,* 1989]

get someone cold To have a clear advantage over someone. "Put up your hands. I got you cold."

get the deadwood on To get the advantage of. "He got the deadwood on him in that deal."

get there with both feet To carry out something successfully; the old expression is first recorded in 1887.

get up and dust To move out or move about quickly, an expression dating back to the 1880s. "Get up and dust, we got a lot of work to do."

get yourself on a hair trigger Be ready to act instantly. "Get yourself on a hair trigger—and heaven help you!" [Max Brand, *Mountain Guns,* 1930]

ghost dance An Indian ceremonial religious dance. "The Ghost dance was a ceremonial religious dance connected with the Messiah doctrine which originated among the Paviotso in Nevada in 1888 and spread rapidly among other tribes until it numbered among its adherents nearly all the Indians of the interior basin from the Missouri River to beyond the Rockies." [Grant Foreman, *The Last Trek of the Indians,* 1946]

ghost town A term first applied to, and still usually associated with, a Western town abandoned by its inhabitants, usually because a mine nearby has petered out or the railroad passed it by; the term appears to have been first recorded in about 1870–75.

giant bird's nest Another name for the pinedrops tree (*Pteropora andromeda*) because of its mass of matted fibrous roots.

giant cactus Another name for the SAGUARO.

Gila A name, from the Gila River in Arizona, attached to a number of animals, including the Gila bat, Gila chipmunk, Gila monster, Gila trout and Gila woodpecker.

Gila monster The bright-colored Southwestern desert lizard *Helod-erma suspectum,* which is venomous and changes color to conform to its environment.

gimlet To ride a horse heavily and make its back sore; also called *to beefsteak.*

girling An old-fashioned term for courting or chasing women. "They spent their time drinking, gambling, fighting and girling."

git along, little dogie See DOGIE.

git-up end A horse's rear end.

give Jesse To scold or physically beat someone. "He gave him Jesse."

give the gate To divorce; divorced. "She gave him the gate."

give tongue To speak. "The big man was saying, 'How about it there, you that hasn't give tongue . . .'" [A. B. Guthrie Jr., *Arfive,* 1970]

gizzard Guts, spirit, courage. "He had no gizzard, no sand in his craw."

glory hole A large, open surface mining pit; so named either because of a previous nautical usage or because such a hole, usually funnel-shaped, resembles in shape a morning glory flower.

goat A folk name for the pronghorn (*Antilocapra americana*), an antelope ruminant of the plains that is an endangered species in some areas.

go-back A historical term dictionaries often fail to note for someone who returned East after failing to make a go of it in the West. See also GO WEST YOUNG MAN.

go back on one's hash (1) To criticize the food one is served. (2) To weaken in the face of hardships.

the gobble See quote. "[Yancey] opened his mouth, and there issued from it a sound so dreadful, so unearthly as to freeze the blood . . . It was a sound between the gobble of an angry turkey cock and the howl of a coyote. Throughout the Southwest it was known that this terrible sound, famed as the gobble, was Cherokee in origin and a death cry among the Territory Indians. It was known, too, that when an Indian gobbled it meant sudden destruction to any or all in his path." [Edna Ferber, *Cimarron*, 1930]

goddam An Indian expression for a white man, because the white explorers and settlers used "God-damn" so frequently in their speech. A few centuries before, the French called the English the same for the same reason. So it goes.

go-devil An old term for a railroad handcar used at great speeds on steep grades in northern Idaho.

go-easter Eastern-style bags or baggage cowboys often bought in days past when they traveled to the East.

gofer matches Paper or book matches; because they are unreliable, you strike one and "gofer" another.

going West A historical term meaning the action of going West to make one's fortune. See also GO WEST, YOUNG MAN.

gold belt A kind of money belt used by Western miners to carry gold dust and nuggets. "His gold belt lies fat and long upon the bar. He is setting them up in honor of the goddess of fortune." [Max Brand, *The Making of a Gunman*, 1929]

goldbrick Con men working Western mining properties toward the end of the 19th century sometimes sold gullible investors lead or iron bricks coated with gold paint, representing them as the real thing. One Patrick Burke of St. Louis is recorded as having paid $3,700 for such a "gold" brick in 1887. This all-too-common confidence scheme gave the name *goldbrick* to any swindle or fakery. Later, soldiers picked up the expression and used the phrase *to goldbrick* in its present meaning of avoiding work or shirking duty. The phrase is first recorded in 1914 in this sense, applied to army lieutenants appointed from civilian life.

gold digger Long before *gold digger* meant a mercenary woman, a use first recorded in 1915, it signified a miner in California gold fields such as Jackass Gulf, Puke Ravine, Greenhorn Canyon and Rattlesnake Bar. In fact, the term *gold digger,* for a miner, is recorded in 1830 during America's first gold rush, which took place in northern Georgia.

golden banner A common Western flower *(Thermopsis devaricapa)* with bright yellow bloom.

Golden Bible The Book of Mormon, which is said to have been translated by Joseph Smith from an original that was engraved on golden plates; the term is first recorded in 1830, before the Mormons came to Utah and built the temple there.

Golden Gate The strait at the entrance to San Francisco Bay from the Pacific Ocean; also a name for the Golden Gate Bridge spanning the strait.

Golden Gate Bridge A 4,200-foot bridge that connects northern California with the San Francisco peninsula. The bridge is not golden but named after the Golden Gate Strait connecting the Pacific Ocean and San Francisco Bay. The Golden Gate Strait, discovered by Sir Francis Drake in 1579, was so called long before it gained new popularity during the 1849 gold rush.

golden hills See BRITTLEBUSH.

Golden Land See GOLD FEVER.

gold fever A term, first recorded in 1847, for the excitement produced by the gold rush to the *Golden Land* (California) when gold was discovered there. Also called the *gold mania*. The lust for gold was of course

one of the main reasons for the exploration of the New World, long before the California gold rush. This is reflected in what may be the first American proverb—"gamble the sun before sunrise"—though it isn't recorded in *Bartlett's* or any other book of quotations. The expression surely is old enough, dating back to 1533, when Pizarro conquered Cuzco, the capital of the Inca empire, and stripped the Peruvian metropolis of gold and silver. One cavalryman got as his share of the booty a splendid golden image of the sun "on a plate of burnished gold spread over the walls in a recess of the great temple" and which was so beautifully crafted that he did not have it melted down into coins, as was the usual practice. But the horseman came to symbolize the vice of gambling. That same night, before the sun had set on another day, he lost the fabulous golden image of the sun at cards or dice, and his comrades coined the saying *"Juega el Sol antes que amanezca"* (He gambles (or plays) away the sun before sunrise), which crossed the ocean from America on Pizarro's gold-laden galleons and became proverbial in Spain.

gold fields Yellow-flowered California plants of the *Baeria* genus that bloom so profusely that they make vast fields of gold; more prosaically called *scrambled eggs*.

gold mania See GOLD FEVER.

gold rush The rush of migrants to California in the late 1840s when gold was discovered there. See GOLD FEVER.

gold story A tall tale or fish story, because of the exaggerated stories of huge gold nuggets and the like found in the California gold fields.

gondola A long wagon, deep in the middle, used for hauling in the early West.

gone beaver Someone hopelessly lost, finished, done for, a term commonly used by trappers in the Far West. "Well now, I figured I was gone beaver, knowin' no better." [A. B. Guthrie Jr., *The Big Sky*, 1947]

gone coon An old expression indicating someone lost, ruined or distressed. "I'm a gone coon if he finds me."

gone to Texas Hiding out from the law. See also G.T.T.

gone up the flume Died. " 'You see, one of the boys has gone up the flume.' " [Mark Twain, "Buck Fanshaw's Funeral," 1872]

good and far A long distance away. "You'd claim Indians object to killing a white man when they run into him good and far from human help?" [Owen Wister, "A Western Tale," in *Harper's Magazine*, January 1894]

goodbyes Droppings, excrement. "Grub came first, meat and potatoes and gravy and bread pudding with raisins in it like goodbyes from rabbits." [A. B. Guthrie Jr., *Arfive*, 1970]

good Indian A term once commonly used in the West for a friendly Indian; variation included an *honest Indian* and a *dead Indian*. See also the ONLY GOOD INDIAN IS A DEAD INDIAN.

good leather Good qualities, character. "As they pressed down the earth over his grave, and threw the last sprig of green down upon it, one of the pall-bearers remarked: 'There was good leather in that man.' " [Sam Davis, "Mark Haverly," 1886]

good man An old Southwestern term for an arbitrator in a dispute; a translation of the Spanish *hombre bueno* meaning the same.

good medicine See MEDICINE.

goodnighting Students of the old West may be aware that bulls on long cattle drives often suffered from chaffing of the testicles, which frequently swelled so large that the animal sickened and died. The remedy was to cut off the testicle bag, push the testicles up into the body and sew the cut—a process that enabled the bulls to travel well and did not impair their breeding. This remedy was called *goodnighting*, after cattleman Charles Goodnight, who invented it, and is surely among the most unusual of words named after people.

goods trader A term for a trader among Indians in the early West.

go on a high lonesome To go on a drunken spree.

go on the fight To become belligerent, feisty; often said of animals. "She might go on the fight if you bother her now."

goose drowner A very heavy rain.

goose hair bed A mattress or pillow filled with goose down or goose feathers.

the goose hangs high Said when everything is going very well for someone. See usage example at HAVE GOT THE WORLD BY THE TAIL OF A DOWNHILL PULL.

go over the grade To turn over, capsize. "The stage went over the grade, but nobody was seriously hurt."

gopher (1) The paririe dog (*Cynonys ludovivianus*). (2) Ground squirrels and burrowing rodents of the *Citellus*, *Geomys* and *Thomonys* genera. (3) A small-scale miner in California working small mines called *gopher holes*.

go quick plant An old folk name for rhubarb, probably because of its laxative effect.

gores See quote. "Well I know, and you know, that all along a line that's being surveyed, there's little dabs of land that they call 'gores,' that fall to the surveyor free gratis for nothing. All you've got to do is to survey in such a way that the 'gores' will fall on good fat land, then you turn 'em over to me . . ." [Mark Twain, "The Professor's Yarn," 1883]

gore the other man's ox An old proverb meaning make the other man pay, work, and so forth, but don't make me accountable for anything.

goshed A euphemism for "damned." " 'I'll be goshed,' he thought, 'if I caught on to half that when I was streakin' around in short pants.' " [Owen Wister, *Lin McLean*, 1898]

go south (1) To lose or be defeated. "We're winning five to nothing, we've got them going south." (2) To disappear; from the notion of outlaws escaping lawmen by disappearing south into Mexico. See GO WEST.

gospel sharp A sleazy sanctimonious preacher, perhaps modeled on *card sharp*. Also *gospel shooter*.

gospel shooter See GOSPEL SHARP.

got aged out Grown too old to work in a hard job. "He wasn't a young man anymore, he had got aged out at breaking horses."

got behind Was out-maneuvered. "Well, old Idaho Joe got behind, as the saying goes. He got to riding over here when Cimarron was already over yonder. He hit the ground rolling and scrambled for the fence." [Benjamin Capps, *Tales of the Southwest*, 1990]

gotch-earred An animal such as a horse or donkey with clipped, drooping ears; from the Spanish *gacho* (turned downward).

gotch-eyed Descriptive of a person with eyes looking in different directions.

got his kettle on Angry, boiling over, planning retribution. " 'Say, I know Bick's got his kettle on for me, I ain't aiming to meet up with him—yet.' " [Edna Ferber, *Giant,* 1952]

go to hell across lots To go straight to hell or the devil. "Isaac in his sermons grew solemner, and swears in his mind that the Gentiles [non-Mormons] were going to hell across lots." [Wallace Stegner, *Mormon Country,* 1942]

go under To die. "Old Gabby had gone under that winter."

go up the flue To die, the spirit departing like smoke going up a chimney flue.

go up the flume An old expression meaning to fail, to come to grief.

governor A historical term for an Indian chief heading a tribe or pueblo.

go west To die. An unknown poet may have coined the phrase *to go west,* "to die," in the trenches of World War I. The expression was common then, possibly suggested by the setting of the sun in the west. But the phrase is much older. In the United States, Indian legend had it that a dying man had gone to meet the setting sun, and later, when explorers and prospectors didn't return from dangerous country west of the Mississippi, they were said to have *gone west.* In 16th century England, the phrase was used of criminals going to be hung at Tyburn, which is west of London, and an early 14th-century English poem with the refrain "his world is but a vanity" had the lines: "Women and many a willful man,/ As wind and water are gone west." The idea behind the expression is even older. The Egyptians spoke of the west as the home of departed spirits, and among the Greeks the association of death with the west was proverbial, as in *Ulysses:*

> My purpose holds
> To sail beyond the sunset, and the paths
> Of all the western stars, until I die.

Even our word *Occident,* for "the west," is associated with death. It comes from the Latin *occidens,* "the place where the sun died at the end of each day," which is from the verb *occidere,* "to die." See GO SOUTH.

go west, young man In America, *go west* came to stand for new life and hope instead of death with the expansion of the frontier. There is some controversy about who said *go west, young man* first, however. Horace Greeley used the expression in an 1855 editorial in his *New York Tribune:* "Go west, young man, and grow with the country." Later, as the phrase grew in popularity, Greeley said that his inspiration was John Babsone Lane Soule, who wrote "Go West, young man" in an 1851 article in the *Terre Haute Express.* Greeley even reprinted Soule's article from the Indiana newspaper to give credit where it was due, but several writers insisted that Greeley had given them identical advice before Soule had written the piece. Journalist William S. Verity said that the great editor had coined the expression a full year before Soule.

grab-it-and-growl A humorous term for a diner or any small greasy spoon with poor, indigestible food.

gracias Spanish for "thank you," frequently used in the Southwest.

grade up with To be equal to. "When a man married a queen he ought to grade up with her." [O. Henry, *Heart of the West,* 1904]

grama grass Any low grass of the genus *Bouteloua* growing on the Western plains.

Grand Canyon State A nickname for Arizona.

Granddaddy The nickname of the oldest and biggest saguaro cactus in the United States, located in the desert of the Saguaro National Monument East in Arizona. About 300 years old and 40 feet high, with 52 arms, the cactus was said to be dying of bacterial necrosis in December 1992 with only a few months at most to live.

Grande Short for the Rio Grande. "Hope keeps the illegals coming across the Grande every night."

grandmother story An Indian expression, see quote. "The absentee Shawnee cherished a prophetic tradition generally known as the 'grandmother story' as told by a Shawnee woman, having reference to certain present and eternal judgments that would be visited upon the unfortunate head of any Indian who laid aside the blanket to adopt the white man's dress." [Grant Foreman, *The Last Trek of the Indians,* 1946]

Grand Tetons French voyageurs early named these mountains in northwestern Wyoming the *Grand Tetons,* the "big breasts," because of their resemblance to a woman's breasts. For the same reason, the rounded hillocks or mounds west of the Mississippi River are called *mamelle,* from the French, *mamelle* (woman's breast). "In Jackson Hole [Wyoming] there is a Catholic church named Our Lady of the Grand Tetons by somebody who didn't know what tetons are." [Wallace Stegner, [*All the Little Live Things,* 1967]

grant ring A term once used in the West for groups that secured large land grants through fraud.

grapevine Some 15 years after Samuel Morse transmitted his famous "what hath God wrought" message, a long telegraph line was strung from Virginia City to Placerville, California, so crudely strung, it's said, that people jokingly compared the line with a sagging grapevine. I can find no record of this, but in any case, grapevines were associated with telegraph lines somewhere along the line, for by the time of the Civil War a report *by grapevine telegraph* was common slang for a rumor. The idea behind the expression is probably not rumors sent over real telegraph lines but the telegraphic speed with which rumormongers can transmit canards with their own rude mouth-to-mouth telegraph system.

grass-bellied   Full, like a cow that has grazed a long time. " 'I'm grass-bellied with spot cash,' [Lin said]." [Owen Wister, "A Journey in Search of Christmas," 1897]

grass bloom   The shiny coat an animal gets because it has fed well on grass for a period of time.

grass dance   A Sioux Indian dance by warriors featuring tufts of grass symbolic of scalps.

grassers   Cattle that have been fed on grass rather than feed.

Grasshopper Battle   A historical term for a battle fought in 1873 between the Shawnee and Delaware Indians, supposedly started by an argument among children over the ownership of a pet grasshopper.

grasshopper fruitcake   A humorous name Western settlers gave to an Indian cake made from berries and crushed grasshoppers; also called *grasshopper pie*.

grasshopper Indians   A name for the Ute Indians, because they used grasshoppers for food.

grasshopper mouse   A Western name for a mouse *(Onychomys leucogaster)* that feeds on grasshoppers.

Grasshoppers' Library   See quote. "Who presides over the genial branches of the Grasshoppers' Library in the sunshine of the Pecos, beside the elms and oaks on Waller Creek, down the mesquite flats of the Nueces River, up the canyons of the Rio Grande, under the blue haze of the Guadalupes, deep in the soft Wichitas, over the hills of the San Saba, and in many another happily remembered place where I pursued 'scholarly enquiries', I cannot name. I wish I could, for in the wide-spreading Grasshoppers' Library I have learned the most valuable things I know." [Frank Dobie, *Coronado's Children*, 1930]

Grasshopper Year   See quote. "They had come in droves that August of 1874 (which would, as a result, be referred to ever after as the 'Grasshopper Year'), like nothing she had ever before seen . . . millions upon millions of the hideous, chirring insects [across the Kansas prairie] . . ." [Rebecca Brandewyne, *Heartland*, 1990]

grass sack   A term used in central Texas and elsewhere for a burlap sack.

graveyard dead   Dead without a doubt. " 'You aim to shoot me,' said the black. 'You don't get your black ass away from this fire I'll kill you graveyard dead.' " [Cormac McCarthy, *Blood Meridian, or, The Evening Redness in the West*, 1985]

gravy-licker   Someone who takes something for nothing, especially a government dole, instead of working for it; like a cat that hangs around the kitchen licking up gravy instead of hunting for food. "His dark eyes smoldered . . . 'I didn't think you'd ever class me as a gravy-licker.' " [Elmer Kelton, *The Time It Never Rained*, 1973]

graze   Grazing land. " 'I'm giving you two days to get them (sheep) off of my graze.' " [Jack Cummings, *The Rough Rider*, 1988]

grazing fee   A fee paid for the right to graze cattle on another's land, especially on Indian lands.

greaser   A derogatory offensive name for Mexicans and Mexican-Americans first recorded in 1836 in what is now Texas. *Greaserdom* is a derogatory historical name for New Mexico. An unlikely explanation says that *greaser* derives from men hired by Mexican freighters to run alongside their wagons and grease the wooden axles. " 'Say, greaser,' said the boy [aiming his gun], 'you got a tassel on the side of your hat that you don't need. So I'm gunna take it off for you.' " [Max Brand, *The Black Signal*, 1925]

greaserdom   See GREASER.

greasewood   The spiny resinous Western shrub *Sarcobatus vermiculatus*, often used for firewood in the Southwest. "At noon he alighted and collected enough greasewood to boil the Bishop's coffee." [Willa Cather, *Death Comes for the Archbishop*, 1927]

greasy The pronunciation of *greasy* as *greazy*, with a *z* instead of an *s* sound for the next to last letter, is a characteristic of Southern speech but is also occasionally heard in Texas and the Midwest. The usual pronunciation in the West, however, is with the *s* sound.

greasy-sack outfit A small, second-rate ranch outfit; so named because such outfits had no chuck wagons and carried their food on the trail in cotton bags called greasy-sacks. "Reckon how she'll take to a greasy-sack outfit like this." [Elmer Kelton, *The Time It Never Rained*, 1973]

Great American Desert The idea of a Great American Desert in the West discouraged many people from settling in the region, which they thought was uninhabitable. The term *Great American Desert* was used in newspapers and geographies as early as 1834. Before this, the area, which is actually part of the fertile Great Plains, was called the Great Desert, this term recorded 50 years earlier. ". . . the tales had been rampant about the *Great American Desert* and the hardships encountered by parties of gold-seekers racing to the California fields." [Frank Roderus, *J. A. Whitford & the Great California Gold Hunt*, 1990]

Great Basin A 12,275-square-mile region in the West including most of Nevada and parts of Utah, California, Oregon and Idaho; so called because it has no drainage to the ocean.

Great Divide A name for the continental divide of North America; the Rocky Mountains.

Great Father An Indian name for the president of the United States. "This war . . . was brought upon us by the children of the Great Father . . ." [Spotted Tail of the Brule Sioux, quoted in Dee Brown, *Bury My Heart at Wounded Knee,* 1970]

great hand for Like, favor. " 'I'm a great hand for goatskins,' he said. 'They make good settin' and they make good pallets.' " [J. Frank Dobie, *Coronado's Children,* 1930]

Great Knives A name various American Indians gave U.S. soldiers, in reference to their bayonettes.

great medicine An American Indian term for anything especially effective. The explorers Lewis and Clark noted that "whatever is mysterious or unintelligible (to the Indians) is called great medicine." See also MEDICINE.

Great Medicine Trail A name Indians gave to the Oregon Trail.

Great Plains The semiarid region east of the Rocky Mountains in the United States and Canada.

Great Register of the Desert See INDEPENDENCE ROCK.

Great Roundup Death; also *the Last Roundup* and *ride the long trail.* "When Blue gets drunk he becomes sentimental about all his friends who have been called to the Great Roundup or who rode the long trail . . ." [Larry McMurtry, *Buffalo Girls,* 1990]

Great Salt Lake A large, shallow, salty lake in northwest Utah, west of which is the Great Salt Lake Desert.

great sand and sagebrush! An old exclamation. " 'Gr-eat sand and sagebrush! do you mean it?' " [Mark Twain, "A Horse's Tale," 1906]

great seizer A colorful old term meaning the sheriff; perhaps a play on *Great Caesar.*

great smoke See quote. "He's the main trump, the big card, the great smoke in their whole nation." [Max Brand, *Mountain Guns,* 1930]

Great Spirit The chief deity in the religion of many North American Indian tribes. "Standing Bull . . . held up the pipe to the Great Spirit and chanted a sacred song . . ." [Max Brand, *Fugitive's Fire,* 1928]

Great White Father Now a humorous term for the U.S. president; said to have been used seriously for the same by American Indians in the 19th century.

greenbroke Said of a horse recently and barely broken. "Just halfway decent greenbroke horses." [Cormac McCarthy, *All the Pretty Horses,* 1992]

greener A greenhorn, tenderfoot, someone new to the West. See usage example at PULLING THE BADGER.

Greenhorn Canyon A California gold field.

green river (1) A famous hunting knife first made at Green River, Wyoming. (2) To kill someone by knifing him.

gringa The feminine of GRINGO. " 'Now I work as a dancehall girl. You see how much better it is that you are a gringa?' " [Jack Cummings, *The Rough Rider,* 1988]

gringo Many scholars trace this disparaging term for an American to the Spanish *gringo* (gibberish), which is a corruption of the Spanish word *Griego* (a Greek). *Gringo,* by this theory, would be related to the old saying "It's all Greek to me," indicating that the Yankees were strange and unfamiliar in their ways to the Mexicans who so named them. But another etymologist boldly claims "green coat" as the base for *gringo,* and yet another theory says that the first two words of the Robert Burns lyric "Green grow the rashes O," a song sung by American soldiers in the Mexican War, is the origin of the contemptuous word—somehow one can't imagine battle-hardened veterans riding along singing: "Green grow the rashes O / The happiest hours that ere I spent / Were spent among the lasses O!" If the "gibberish" theory is to be challenged, the most likely contender is Major Samuel Ringgold, a brilliant strategist dreaded by the Mexicans during the Mexican War until he was killed at the Battle of Palo Alto in 1846. Ringgold's name, pronounced with a trilled *r* and without the last two letters, as it normally would be by a Mexican, might yet prove the correct source for the word. " 'We have trouble with gringo names, just like gringo faces, they all look alike; their language sounds like Chinese.' " [Carlos Fuentes, *The Old Gringo,* 1985]

grit Courage, bravery, sand. " 'They say he has grit.' said I. 'I wanted a man with grit.' " [Charles Portis, *True Grit,* 1968]

grizzly bear *Ursus horriblis,* a large ferocious bear found in the Rocky Mountain area.

grizzly lager A humorous name for any potent homebrewed beer.

grocery sack A brown paper grocery bag. "Scraping wellcleaned ribs into a big brown grocery sack, Charlie saw Tom peer intently out the window." [Elmer Kelton, *The Time It Never Rained,* 1973]

ground cuckoo See ROADRUNNER.

grub-line rider An unemployed cowboy who looks for free meals on the grub line from ranch to ranch.

grubstake Supplies given to a prospector by a backer in return for a share in any gold or silver he might find. "Grubstake me, and I'll make you a rich man."

grulla mare A dark-colored horse. "Into this bright scene came old man Overstreet on a bony little grulla mare . . ." [Thomas McGuane, *Keep the Change*, 1989]

G.T.T. (1) A historical term common in the 19th century standing for "Gone to Texas," apparently derived from *G.T.T.* signs that emigrants hung on the doors of their homes and businesses when they went West. (2) Initials entered by lawmen in their record books when a wanted man couldn't be located. (3) A designation for any disreputable man. "Now finally the settlers over there began to organize for mutual protection . . . against the more overbearing ranch hands who were often Texas badmen, mostly GTT's meaning 'Gone to Texas,' men who had fled there from the law or other vengeance." [Mari Sandoz, *Son of the Gambling Man*, 1960]

guayave A bread made by Pueblo Indians from a species of agave; its shape gave rise to the word being used by Southwest settlers for a roll of money.

guess off To estimate the weight of a herd of cattle.

the guide See quote. " 'The evening star,' he said in English, slowly and somewhat sententiously, then relapsed into Spanish. 'You see the little star beside Padre? Indians call him the guide.' " [Willa Cather, *Death Comes for the Archbishop*, 1927]

gulch A ravine, canyon or gully where gold is mined or prospected.

gumbo Sticky heavy soil. "The car shot into a morass of prairie gumbo—which is mud mixed with tar, fly-paper, fish glue, and well-chewed chocolate covered caramels. When cattle get into gumbo, the farmers send for the stump dynamite and try blasting." [Sinclair Lewis, *Free Air*, 1919]

gunbroke Said of a horse that isn't disturbed when a gun is fired.

gun fanner This term for a Western gunfighter is first recorded in 1903 and refers to the way gunfighters fired their weapons by removing or tying back the trigger of their revolvers and thumbing or fanning the hammer.

gun fight; gun battle Expressions originally used in the West for a fight with guns, the participants called *gun fighters, gun fanners* and, infrequently, *gun handlers*.

gunnysack The usual word in the West for what is called a *burlap bag* in the North and a *crocus sack* in the South—a large sack made from loosely woven coarse material such as burlap. *Gunny* here ultimately derives from the Sanskrit word *goni* (jute or hemp fiber). "In my hometown of Missoula, Montana, older brothers all over town trained their younger brothers to jump from garage roofs using gunnysacks for parachutes." [Norman Maclean, *Young Men and Fire*, 1992]

gunsel A cowboy word for a braggart.

gun-toter This isn't a truly Western term for a gunfighter, having been first recorded in a Western movie in 1925.

gusher A profusely flowing oil well, a very successful profitable one, the term apparently first used in the West.

gussied up All dressed up.

gut hook Spurs; also called *gut lancers* and *gut wrenchers*.

gut-shrunk Very hungry. "I was gut-shrunk and couldn't wait to get to the chuck wagon."

gut twister A wild bucking horse, usually in a rodeo, that twists up a rider's guts. "But you couldn't keep up with that horse; he was a gut twister . . ." [Benjamin Capps, *Tales of the Southwest*, 1990]

guying Ridiculing, making fun of; originally a British expression referring to effigies of Guy Fawkes hung and burned on Guy Fawkes Day. "[She'd] talked her damnedest to keep Charlie from eating . . . She never stopped guying him about his weight." [Elmer Kelton, *The Time It Never Rained*, 1973]

gwinter An imaginary animal, employed to trick a tenderfoot. "They kidded the greenhorn about a vicious gwinter that had a short leg in front and one behind, so it could better circle a mountain, catch a man and tear him to bits."

gyp See GYPWATER.

gypped Made ill by drinking large quantities of water containing gypsum or other alkaline salts.

gypwater Water highly saturated with gypsum and other alkaline salts, which causes a severe upset stomach when drunk in large quantities; also called *gypsum water* and *gyp*. "Rawlins leaned from the saddle and wet his hand in the river and tasted it. 'It's gypwater,' he said." [Cormac McCarthy, *All the Pretty Horses*, 1992]

H

habañero pepper The hottest of hot peppers by scientific measurement. They originated in Mexico and are now widely grown in the Southwest, especially in New Mexico, the largest chili-growing state in the United States.

hacienda A Spanish word for a ranch or the principal residence on a ranch.

hackamore Any of several halters used for breaking horses, from the Spanish *jáquima* (headstall).

hair brand A temporary brand on cattle, where the hair not the hide is burned.

hair in the butter An expression used in Texas to describe a very delicate or sensitive situation. The words refer to the difficulty of removing a single hair from a piece of butter. "The Great Iranian Arms Caper is not only hair in the butter, I'd say someone's thrown a skunk in the churchhouse as well." [Molly Ivins, *Molly Ivins Can't Say That, Can She?*, 1991]

hair lifter A humorous term for an Indian who scalped his enemies but also applied to whites who "lifted" scalps as well.

hair raiser Same as *hair lifter* above. "I've raised the hair of more than one Apache." [George Ruxton, *Life in the Far West,* 1848]

hair-raising This Americanism probably came into the language too late, about 1910, for it to be associated with Indians or Indian hunters taking scalps. There is no evidence that horrible accounts of Indians or whites "lifting or raising hair" inspired the synonym for "frightening." Most likely the term is a streamlining of the old expression *to make one's hair stand on end*.

hairy money Hairy money—money with hair on it? Yes. Hairy money was a term for beaver pelts in the American fur trade out West. The skins were worth a lot of money and even used as a medium of exchange.

half a bubble off; half a bubble off plumb Someone who is mildly eccentric, in reference to the bubble in a carpenter's level. Also *a bubble off plumb*.

half-breed An offensive term for the offspring of an American Indian and a white person; first recorded in 1760, though later much used in the West, and now used as offensive slang for the offspring of parents of different racial origin. See also HALF-STRIPE.

half-stripe A derogatory term for a person of mixed American Indian and white ancestry. See also HALF-BREED.

half woman and half rainwater An old saying descriptive of someone, usually a man, who is soft, effete, unlike the macho men of the West; rainwater is a soft, not a hard, water. " 'You're a tough one, Hogan, a real tough one,' my father said. 'Half woman and half rainwater. Tell them you lied and you can walk away from here.' " [Wayne D. Overholser, *Cast a Long Shadow*, 1956]

halo Chinook jargon meaning no, none, not any.

handcarter Settlers, especially Mormons, who were too poor to buy horses, mules or oxen and therefore pushed or pulled their families and material possessions in handcarts when emigrating to the Far West in the mid-19th century.

hand-fighting Fighting without weapons. " 'Why I reckon we're both gun-handy . . . I'd have preferred hand-fightin' you, but that would scarcely give you an even break.' " [Louis L'Amour, *The Tall Stranger*, 1957]

hand out Apparently this expression meaning a free meal or anything free, given charitably, originated in the West, at least the first quotations attesting it are recorded there.

handsome Nice, good. " 'That's handsome of you,' Burch said." [Luke Short, *Ramrod*, 1971]

hang and rattle To ride an unbroken horse. "But I damn sure seen him hang and rattle a time or two." [Cormac McCarthy, *All the Pretty Horses*, 1992]

Hangtown fry A famous omelet made of eggs, fried oysters, bacon and onions that was invented during the gold rush in Placerville, California, which was nicknamed Hangtown because a good number of men were hanged there—or so the story goes.

ha'nts Haunts, ghosts. " 'I found some [gold] all right an' there's aplenty where it came from if'n you aren't skeered of ha'nts and the like.' " [Louis L'Amour, *The Haunted Mesa*, 1987]

happy as a frog Very happy and content. " 'Shoot, my baby sister's happy as a frog,' Josie said." [Larry McMurtry, *Cadillac Jack*, 1982]

happy as a jackass eatin' sawbriars Very happy, content.

happy hunting ground Indian heaven, according to writers of Westerns anyway, though the term was first recorded in a Washington Irving story (1837). "Yet even so I gave seven of the Red Skins one way tickets to their Happy Hunting Ground." [Richard Matheson, *Journal of the Gun Years*, 1991]

happy trails This farewell has been popular for many years, thanks in part to the song "Happy Trails" sung by many Western country singers, including Roy Rogers. "Happy trails, Hans," the hero (Bruce Willis) says to the villain in the movie *Diehard 2* (1991) as he dispatches him.

hard-boiled A *boiled* or *boiled shirt* was, on the American frontier, a shirt boiled in water, in contrast to one newly washed in cold water. Later the term came to mean a stiff or hard-starched white shirt. By 1886 we find Mark Twain using the term *hard boiled,* probably suggested by a hard-boiled shirt, for "a rigid narrow person," and by 1898 *hard-boiled* was being used to mean hard-headed and heartless.

hard-boiled hat A stiff derby hat. "That fellow in front of the drug store over there with the hard-boiled hat on." [Andy Adams, The *Log of a Cowboy,* 1903]

harder'n climb'n a peeled saplin' heels upward An old expression from frontier days describing something very difficult.

hard money An old term meaning metal coins, not currency.

hard-proved hand A cowboy proven under the most difficult circumstances. "Do you think [he'd] . . . have anything but an all-around hard-proved hand up here . . ?" [Jack Schaefer, "Stubby Pringle's Christmas," 1990]

hard rocker A historical term for a miner who worked hard rock formations underground.

harness bull An old term for a policeman or sheriff. "The harness bull collared him and threw him in the hoosegow."

Harry of the West A nickname of American statesman and politician Henry Clay (1777–1852); also *Gallant Harry of the West.*

Harvey A famous chain of Western restaurants originated by Fred Harvey (b. 1835) in the 1870s.

has more wrinkles on his horns Said of someone who has become older and wiser with experience, like wild cattle whose horns wrinkle with age. "He's smarter now, has more wrinkles on his horns."

have a bear by the tail This is another of those colorful expressions that arose in America during the first half of the 19th century. *To have a bear by the tail* is to be in a bad situation—you're in trouble whether you hold on or let go!

have a burr under one's saddle Said of someone in a bad mood.

have the bulge on To have the advantage especially because one is packing a gun. " 'Well, you've ruther got the bulge on me.' " [Mark Twain, "Buck Fanshaw's Funeral," 1872]

have the colly wobbles To be blue or depressed. "She's got the colly wobbles since he rode away."

have the cottonwood on one See COTTONWOOD BLOSSOM.

have the world by the tail on a downhill pull To have everything going exceedingly well for you. "In Texas, nothing gave a man status like the ownership of cattle. Now there was status enough for everybody. The goose was hanging high, and they had the world by the tail on a downhill pull." [Elmer Kelton, *The Time It Never Rained*, 1973]

hawse A common pronunciation of *horse*. "Put that hawse in the stable."

hazer A ranch hand who drives in or *hazes* horses that are to be broken, keeping them away from fences and other obstacles. "Rope them together [boys] and haze them out of here." [William Faulkner, *The Unvanquished*, 1938]

headache! A warning to "watch it!" used by loggers, oil men and others in the West because a heavy object is overhead or coming down: Be careful or you'll get a headache, get hit in the head by it. Similar to "heads up!"

headright A right given by a government to a piece of public land; so called because the right was granted to the head of the family settling upon the land. "Under former laws of Texas, a headright was the inheritable right given to immigrating heads of families to grants of free land." [Burton Roscoe, *Belle Starr*, 1941]

heap Very, a lot; said to be a feature of Indian speech in early times. "An Indian is always a 'heap' hungry or thirsty—loves a 'heap'—is a 'heap' brave—in fact, 'heap' is tantamount to very much." [Blackwood's Magazine, LXIII, 1848]

heap hogs Hogs on a garbage heap. " 'White men are mostly wasters, as well as bein' greedy . . . I know an old Indian onct who said white men were heap hogs.' " [Zane Grey, *Western Union*, 1939]

heap-walk-man A colorful Indian term describing a U.S. infantryman.

heathen Chinee An old derogatory term for a Chinese person, especially one considered devious; the term apparently derives from the Bret Harte poem "Plain Language from Truthful Jones" (1870): "For ways that are dark / And tricks that are vain / The heathen Chinee is peculiar."

he couldn't say "hell" with his hands tied Said of a person who can't talk without excessive hand gestures.

he'd fight till hell freezes over and then skate with y' on the ice A very pugnacious, tenacious person.

hedgehog cactus Any of some 200 cactus species of the genus *Echinocactus* native to the Southwest but most often the Southwestern barrel cactus *(Echinocactus Texensis)*

he'd steal the butter off a blind man's bread, and put him on the wrong road home Said of a no-good person, someone with no scruples at all; quoted in Frank O'Rourke's *Last Ride* (1958).

heel (1) To arm oneself. "He was well heeled, wearing two pistols." (2) To rope an animal by the hind feet. (3) To be provided with money. "With all those expenses, I'm not so well-heeled now."

heeler In the early days of Texas, dogs were trained to catch and herd cattle. Often of the bulldog breed, they were called *heelers* because they typically caught the heel of the cow in their jaws.

heel fly Several warble fly species that lay their eggs on the heels and legs of cattle, troubling them and making them hard to manage.

heem A pronunciation of *him*. See usage example at KEEL.

heidi Howdy, a pronunciation often heard in Texas.

heifer In addition to its common meaning, *heifer* once meant a young female buffalo in the West.

hellacious Severe, dreadful, terrible. "He gave him a hellacious beating."

to hell and gone All over the place, everywhere. " 'And one of the best advertisements I can have is for good rodeo hands like you to be seen pulling my trailers to hell and gone.' "

[Elmer Kelton, *The Time It Never Rained,* 1973]

Hell and Texas Civil War General Phil Sheridan said that if he owned Hell and Texas, he'd "rent out Texas and live in Hell."

hell-bent Determined in a reckless driven way. "He was hell-bent for war with Mexico."

hell-bent for breakfast Very fast. "I was going lickety-split, hell-bent for breakfast, trying to head off a gotch-earred brown stallion and his bunch . . ." [J. Frank Dobie, *Coronado's Children,* 1931]

hell-bent for leather With great speed, especially on a horse, the term suggested by hard use of a leather whip while riding a horse.

hell fire and damnation! A common expletive.

hell-for-leather To travel, especially to ride, at a very fast pace. " 'I saw that kid Greene . . . come by here hell-for-leather half an hour ago,' Mapes said." [Walter Van Tilburg Clark, *The Ox-Bow Incident,* 1940]

hell for stout Rugged, reliable. ". . . Tom's old trailer . . . might not look like much, but it was hell for stout." [Elmer Kelton, *The Time It Never Rained,* 1973]

hell heard him holler He screamed extremely loud. " 'Show me someone as can stand up to a pitchfork,' Pike said . . . 'They tell me hell heard him holler.' " [A. B. Guthrie Jr., *Arfive*, 1970]

helling around Living a reckless, often violent, dissipated life. "A man was liable to go sporting and helling around till he waked up." [Owen Wister, *Lin McLean*, 1898]

hell-on-wheels (1) Union Pacific Railroad construction gangs in the 1860s lived in boxcars that were pulled along as the line progressed. Traveling and living with these hard-drinking, often violent men were gamblers, prostitutes and other unsavory characters. The wild congregation assembled in the boxcars suggested the population of hell to settlers, and the transient town was called *hell-on-wheels,* a colorful term soon applied to any violent, vicious person or lawless place. (2) A name given to a vicious, difficult horse. "I called him Hell-on-Wheels."

hello the house A common greeting upon approaching a house in the early West. " 'Hello the house,' Hartzell called. He listened and watched for some sign of another human being." [F. M. Parker, *The Predators,* 1990] Also *hello in the house.*

hell-raisingest Most unruly, troublesome. "He's the hell-raisingest man I know."

hells' half acre (1) A 19th-century term for a low saloon, a dive. (2) A small or distant place. "He lived way out there in hell's half acre." (3) Any disreputable or crime-ridden place.

hell-to-split Very fast. "He cut hell-to-split across the pass."

hell with the fires out A colorful expression for the Southwestern desert. "That's desert! . . . It's been called 'hell with the fires out' . . . but you can live with the desert if you learn it." [Louis L'Amour, *The Lonesome Gods,* 1983]

help To serve or put food on a plate. "Shall I help your plate?"

hell wind A tornado.

hen skin A comforter stuffed with chicken feathers. "All there was was a thin hen skin on the bed."

hen wrangler A person who does menial chores on a ranch.

hep A common pronunciation of *help*. "Kin ah hep you?"

hereford A breed of cattle and a word with its own distinctive pronunciation, in Texas, where it is heard as *Hearford* and *Herford*. See also Introduction.

he wears a two-inch belt and Big Jim suspenders Said in Texas of someone who is very cautious.

hiaqua Shell money used by North Pacific Coast Indians; the term derives from a Chinook word.

hidalgo A Spanish word for a Spanish nobleman or big landowner in the West.

hide and tallow factory   A place where cattle were slaughtered for hides and tallow during hard times in Texas.

hide-hunters   Rustlers who killed steers for their hides or skins. ". . . Anthem rode out of a thick of scrub oak and mesquite and down into a washed out arroyo where two raggedly dressed hide-hunters were busily skinning a fresh-killed steer whose hide wore the Slash A brand . . ." [James Reno, *Texas Born*, 1986] Also a professional hunter, like Buffalo Bill Cody, who hunted animals for their hides.

highbinder   (1) A mean, vicious horse. (2) A mean person, usually a man.

high grade   A thief who steals ore from gold mines; so named because such thieves only stole high grade ore.

high-headed   Excessively proud. " 'Yes, you're too damn proud . . . It's the number of gents that have broke their hearts for you . . . Is that what made you so damn high-headed?' " [Max Brand, *Trouble Trail*, 1926]

high land   Land, especially farmland, in the hills. " 'Most of the land is rough and hilly . . . Down there they have a little certainty, but up with us there is a big chance. We must have faith in the high land, Emil.' " [Willa Cather, *O Pioneers!*, 1913]

high-line rider   A desperado who always rode in high country to keep an eye out for lawmen who might be after him. See also HIGH PLAINS DRIFTER.

high lonesome   An all-out drunken spree. "Old Dad and Jim Day got on a high lonesome and started to paint the town red." [J. M. Franks, *Seventy Years in Texas*, 1924]

high-muck-a-muck   *Hiu muck amuck* meant "plenty to eat" in the language of the Chinook tribes in the far West north of the Columbia River. Fur traders there probably began to use it without regard to its original meaning but in the sense of "a big man, a chief," pronouncing the *hui* in the phrase as "high." Perhaps the reasoning was that an important person was thought to have plenty to eat or the best things to eat.

high noon   Many people associate this term for a high point, a peak or pinnacle or a crisis or confrontation, with the classic Western movie *High Noon*, though it is in fact first recorded in 14th-century England.

high-nosed   Conceited, stuck up. "He's gotten high-nosed since they found oil on his ranch."

high plains drifter   A person, often an outlaw, who rode the high plains from place to place in the early West in order to be aware of possible enemies around him. See also HIGH-LINE RIDER.

high road to hell A hard or dangerous road, such as one across a desert. " 'This looks like the high road to hell to me,' said a man from the ranks." [Cormac McCarthy, *Blood Meridian, or, The Evening Redness in the West*, 1985]

High Sierra The main range of California's Sierra Nevada mountains.

hightail it Mustangs, rabbits and other animals raise their tails high and flee quickly when they sense danger. Trappers in the American West noticed this, over a century ago, probably while hunting wild horses, and invented the expression *to hightail it*, to leave in a hurry, to make a fast getaway. Another theory is that the expression was suggested by cattle bothered by heel flies. " 'He's had such a tight rein, I expect she's hightailed it.' " [Bill Crider, *A Time for Hanging*, 1989] See also HEEL FLY.

hit out Start out, commence. "They hit out for Omaha."

hit the grit Hit the trail, left. ". . . they packed up their stuff and hit the grit after the stallion . . . a big, long-legged, red son of a wide-stepping chunk of a hurricane." [Max Brand, *Rogue Mustang*, 1932]

hit the leather Jump in the saddle and ride, fast. "Mount up! Hit the leather! We're goin' on!" [Louis L'Amour, *Kilkenny*, 1954]

hit the trail To set out, depart. "He hit the trail for Mexico."

hoary marmot A large marmot (*Marmota caligata*) of the Northwest with grayish (hoary) hair on its chest and shoulders and noted for the sudden shrill whistling sound it makes.

hogan A Navajo dwelling, usually earth-covered and built with the entrance facing east. "The Navajo hogans, among the sand and willows. None of the pueblos would at that time admit glass windows into their dwellings. The reflection of the sun on the glazing was to them ugly and unnatural—even dangerous." [Willa Cather, *Death Comes for the Archbishop*, 1927]

hogleg A large, long handgun or six-shooter; originally the famous Colt Single-Action Army pistol, also called the "Peacemaker."

hog-nosed skunk A Southwestern skunk (*Conepatus mesoleucus*) with a long snout with which it roots like a hog.

hog plum A name given to the wild plum tree and its fruit.

hog ranch (1) An old Western term for a brothel; also called a *chicken ranch*. (2) A rude structure on the edge of an army base that also sold whiskey.

hog wallow Besides its usual meaning, a *hog wallow* in the West means a depression with poor drainage in a plain or prairie; the name stems from the popular belief that razorback hogs caused the depressions many years ago. Thus there are terms like *hog wallow prairie, hog wallow mesquite* and so forth.

hold on till the last whistle Stick with something until the end; probably derives from the final whistle blown in rodeo competitions indicating that the cowboy has lasted the alloted time.

hold up (1) To rob at the point of a gun; it possibly originated in the West with the robberies of trains and stages. (2) To take advantage of someone in any way.

hole Often used in Western place names, such as Jackson Hole, Wyoming, usually in the meaning of a deep valley, a place surrounded by mountains.

hole up A hiding place; to hide. "It seemed sense that the Lohman boy would go north for a hole-up." [Charles O. Locke, *The Hell Bent Kid,* 1957]

holler To give up, to cry "I quit" in a fight. "I once heard a Western man say he had 'hollered on drinking', meaning that he had quit the practice." [John Bartlett, *Dictionary of Americanisms,* 1858] Also *holler calf rope.*

hollow horn A hollowness of the horns in cattle, said to cause their general poor health.

holy doggie! An old exclamation. "'Lookit—Holy Doggie, look at him!'" [Edna Ferber, *Cimarron,* 1930]

hombre A man, the word a borrowing of the Spanish word meaning the same.

home range (1) The area where one lives. (2) A place where cattle are usually kept.

home state One's native state. "I come from your home state of Idaho."

Homestead State An old nickname for Oklahoma because so much of the state was settled by homesteaders under the Homestead Act.

honda An eye (a metal ring or a slip knot) at one end of a lariat through which the other end is passed to form a lasso; probably from the Spanish word *hondón* (an eyelet, the eye of a needle).

honest Indian See GOOD INDIAN.

honky-tonk A name for a cheap, noisy dance hall, burlesque house or nightclub; the expression is first recorded in the West and may be a rhyming compound based on *honk,* though its origin is uncertain. See also DRINKING HOLE.

hoodlum wagon An extra wagon used on roundups to carry bedding and other supplies.

hoodoo A pillar of rock of fantastic shape caused by erosion; many can be seen in the Yellowstone Park region where there are sites called *Hoodoo Mountain, Hoodoo Basin* and *Hoodoo Rocks.*

Hoodoo Bar An 1850 mining site on the Yuba River in California; the name *hoodoo* here is said to be an Indian pronunciation of *How do you do?*, but it could derive from the *hoodoo stick* divining rods miners used in trying to find gold.

hoofed locusts A colorful expression for sheep. "The sheep—'hoofed locusts'—actually were a menace to the raising of other livestock. Nibbling the bush grass to its roots and, with their sharp hoofs, chopping these roots into sterility, they converted into a semi-desert any locality they frequented." [Philip Rollins, *Gone Haywire*, 1939]

hoopy An old, beat-up or broken-down car or truck; the term is heard mostly today in Texas. "I got in my old hoopy and headed out for the lake."

hoosegow *Hoosegow* is a Western word of the 1860s that derives from Spanish *juzgado* (a court or tribunal), which to Mexicans means "a jail" and was borrowed in this sense by American cowboys. Our slang word *jug* for a jail probably also comes from *juzgado* and was recorded a half century or so earlier. " 'You can make nice or not,' he said in a jolly way . . . 'but it's down to the hoosegow we go.' " [Thomas McGuane, *Nothing but Blue Skies*, 1992]

hoot-owl trail The night trail, the trail of crime and wrongdoing. "They had ridden the 'hoot-owl trail' and tasted the fruits of evil and now justice had caught up with them and

demanded payment." [Charles Portis, *True Grit*, 1968]

Hopi A member of a Pueblo Indian people of northern Arizona; from a native word meaning "the powerful ones."

hoppergrass Grasshopper; a word sometimes used in the West and South and formed by metathesis, the transposition of letters in this case.

hoppers Grasshoppers. "I hear that up on the Niobrara River the hoppers are so thick they're damming the whole 300-foot-deep canyon, dropping pebbles in, to flood the county and grow their own green stuff." [Mari Sandoz, *Son of the Gamblin' Man*, 1960]

horned toad See HORNY TOAD.

horn, hide and hair Everything. " 'There's nothing I don't know about a ranch—horn, hide and hair.' " [Edna Ferber, *Giant*, 1952]

horn off Drive away, ward off, as buffalo bulls might do to other bulls in a herd.

hornswoggle An old-fashioned word meaning to cheat or swindle but also used in expletives, like "Well, I'll be hornswoggled!"

horny toad The horned toad, a lizard of the genus *Phrynosoma* with hornlike projections on its head. "He could not imagine this country [the Southwest] without . . . the roadrunner . . . the prickly pear and the live oaks, the jackrabbit and the horned toad. They were all an integral part of it, biding their time to take it back if man ever relaxed his hold." [Elmer Kelton, *The Day It Never Rained,* 1973] Also *horned lizard.*

horse apple Another name for the Osage orange. See also BODARK.

horse heaven A place in Washington state once noted for the droves of CAYUSE ponies roaming there.

Horse Indian A name given to Plains Indians, who expertly rode and used horses.

horse opera Any cheap Western movie, dating back to the first motion pictures featuring a lot of horses and gunplay. See also SPAGHETTI WESTERN.

horse pistol A large pistol. "If I had a big horse pistol like yours I would not be scared of any booger-man." [Charles Portis, *True Grit,* 1968]

horse pucky Horseshit, manure. "Don't give me any of that horse pucky."

horse restaurant A colorful term recorded in 1856 California for a livery stable.

horse sense *Horse sense* for good plain common sense comes from the American West, about 1850, inspired by the cowboys' trusty intelligent little cow ponies, trained even to do a good deal of cattle-herding

work without directions from their riders (as noted in *The Nation,* as far back as August 18, 1870).

horse wrangler A cowboy; also *wrangler;* from the Spanish *caballerango,* a hired hand who looked after horses.

hoss (1) A common pronunciation of *horse.* (2) An affectionate nickname for a friend. "Git ready, old hoss, but hold fire till I give the sign." [A. B. Guthrie Jr., *The Big Sky,* 1947]

hoss op'ry See HORSE OPERA.

hosteen A term of respect for an old man, used in the Southwest; from the Navaho *hastqui'n* meaning the same.

hostile Indians Though much used in the West for Indians unfriendly to settlers, this term is first recorded in the East as far back as 1796.

hostiles Applied by whites to unfriendly, warring Indians. "This killer also knew that the desert and surrounding mountains were swarming with hostiles. They didn't like the reservation at San Carlos . . ." [Lewis B. Patten, *Ride a Tall Horse,* 1980]

hot as billy hell Hot as hell, very hot. "It was hot as billy hell out there, but we had work to do."

hot blood A thoroughbred horse. See also COLD-BLOODED.

a hot of a day A very hot day. " 'My! It's a hot of a day!' " [Edna Ferber, *Giant*, 1952]

hot of summer The heat of summer. " 'It all but stops except for a few weeks maybe in the hot of summer . . .' " [Edna Ferber, *Giant*, 1952]

hotroll A cowboy's bedding and belongings.

houlihan Rope used by cowboy. "Smithwick made a loop and pitched his houlihan. The rope seemed to drop out of the sky over the head of Plumb Rude." [Thomas McGuane, *Keep the Change*, 1989]

hour by sun An hour before sunset or after sunrise. "It's two hours by sun, and we got to be done by noon."

houstonize On April 13, 1832, Sam Houston, the soldier and political leader who became president of the Republic of Texas, fought and gave a beating to Congressman William Stanberry. As a result, *houstonize* became a synonym, now only an historical curiosity, for "to beat someone up, especially a Congressman." Sam Houston's name is better honored, of course, by the city of Houston, Texas.

how This ejaculation, which is now used chiefly as a facetious greeting in imitation of American Indians' speech, was first used by Western Indians and had a number of meanings. Some etymologists believe it is an Indian corruption of "how do you do"; others say the Indians took it from the old Army expression "how," a toast meaning "here's to your health"; and still others say it is simply the Sioux *hao* or the Omaha *hau*. It is first recorded in 1817 as meaning "come on" or "let us begin."

howdy Generally regarded as an expression born in the American West, *howdy*, a contraction of "how do you do?," began life as a Southern or Eastern expression and was taken West by Civil War veterans. It is first recorded in 1840.

howdy do Hello. " 'Howdy do, sir. I'm Miz Thompson . . .' " [Katherine Anne Porter, *Noon Wine*, 1937]

the how-so of it How it works. " '[The river's] in flood? How so?' 'Snow in the mountains . . . Snow melt and rain. That's the how-so of it.' " [A. B. Guthrie Jr., *Arfive*, 1970]

hoya A Spanish word used in the Southwest for a mountain valley or park.

huero A person with fair complexion and light or red hair; from the Spanish *quero* meaning the same.

hull Saddle. "He swung the saddle down . . . The first vehicle along was a Model A Ford truck . . . and the driver leaned across and rolled down the window part way and boomed at him in a whiskey voice: 'Throw that hull up in the bed, cowboy, and get in here.' " [Cormac McCarthy, *All the Pretty Horses*, 1992]

hum Heck, hell, as in "What the hum do you mean?"

humpt it! Move fast, run fast. " 'Go on!' shouted Summers. 'Humpt it, you goddam fools . . . Goddam it, run . . .' " [A. B. Guthrie Jr., *The Big Sky,* 1947]

hungrier than a woodpecker with a headache Very hungry indeed.

hunkers The knees, haunches or calves. "Get down on your hunkers [kneel down]."

hunt the top rail An old term for to flee quickly, as if jumping over the top rail of a fence on a horse. "The three of them went for their guns, and it was time to hunt the top rail."

hurdy-gurdy houses According to Mark Twain in *Roughing It* (1872), these were disreputable Western dance halls with bars, dancing and prostitutes.

hurricane deck A humorous term for a horse's saddle.

hyas kloosh A Chinook term used in the old Northwest meaning very good, fine.

hydrophobia skunk A Southwestern name for the spotted skunk *(Spilogale putorius)* because of the belief that its bite causes hydrophobia in humans.

hymns The songs cowboys sing to calm cattle; these songs were often bawdy lyrics set to religious tunes.

I

ice cream social A social gathering with ice cream as the principal refreshment, usually but not always held to raise money for a local church or school; the term is used in the North and North Midland as well.

Idaho *Idaho* may be the only state name that is a complete fraud—at any rate, its name may mean nothing at all. Many sources derive the word *Idaho* from a Shoshonean Indian word meaning "gem of the mountain," but the Idaho State Historical Society claims that there never was any such Indian word and that *Idaho* and its translation was the phony creation of a mining lobbyist who suggested it to Congress as the name for the territory we now know as Colorado. Congress rejected the name, but it caught on among gold prospectors along the Columbia River, and when it was proposed in 1863 as the name for what we know today as Idaho, Congress approved it and the *Idaho Territory* was born. The origin of the word may actually be Shoshonean, however, though it does not mean "gem of the mountain" or "Behold! The sun is coming down the mountain," as another writer suggested. Idaho residents, in fact, ought to forget about the real Shoshone word that *Idaho* may have derived from, for that word would be *Idahi,* a Kiowa curse for the Co-manches that translates roughly as "eaters of feces," "performers of unnatural acts" or "sources of foul odors."

Idaho brainstorm A tornado, a whirling sandstorm, a dust twister; also called a *dancing devil.*

if his IQ slips any lower, we'll have to water him twice a day Said of someone exceedingly stupid. Columnist and Texan Molly Ivins says it in her *Molly Ivins Can't Say That, Can She?* (1992) and either invented it or is passing it along. She was referring, of course, to a politician.

if ignorance ever goes to $40 a barrel, I want the drillin' rights on that man's head Used in Texas to describe someone extremely ignorant; attributed to former Texas agriculture commissioner Jim Hightower.

if I had my druthers An old Western expression, also heard in the South, meaning "if I had my choice;" the "druthers" in the phrase is a corruption of "rathers."

if you ain't the lead horse, the scenery never changes See quote. "My old man used to say, 'If you ain't the lead horse, the scenery never changes.' Now it looks like I might lose the place. I need to get out front

with that lead horse. I feel like I've been living in a graveyard."
[Thomas McGuane, *Keep the Change,* 1989]

if you don't like the weather wait five minutes A saying heard in Montana and North Dakota.

I god Apparently a euphemistic pronunciation of "By God." " 'I god, Woodrow,' Augustus said. 'As long as you've worked around horses it looks like you'd better know them to turn your back on a Kiowa mare.' "
[Larry McMurtry, *Lonesome Dove,* 1985]

ill Cross, vicious, ill-tempered. "That dog of his is ill—it's bit two people."

I'll be there with bells on Early 18th-century Conestoga wagons usually arrived at their Western destinations with bronze bells ringing, giving rise to this Americanism. These same Conestogas are responsible for traffic moving on the right side of the road in the United States rather than on the left as in Britain. According to one authority, the Conestogas were "best guided from the left and so afforded a clear view ahead only when driven from the right side of the road. Drivers of other vehicles found it not only wise not to argue but convenient to follow in the ruts made by the heavy wagons and habit soon became law."

I'll shoot through the barrel and drown you! A common gunfighter's threat in the early West to adversaries who ducked behind water barrels that had

been placed along the streets for use in case of fire.

Ima Hogg Perhaps this is the best known of humorous American names, for *Ima Hogg's* father was the governor of Texas and she was a prominent socialite. It is not necessarily the *best* humorous real American name, for we have hundreds of gems like the following to choose from: Lance Amorous, Fannie Bottom and Dill L. Pickle (who was a pickle salesman). There was even someone named La Void.

I may not be a cowboy, but I can take one's place till he gets here See quote. "When I was a young man the word 'cowboy' was only used as a great point of honor. One of the favorite sayings from top hands was, 'I may not be a cowboy, but I can take one's place till he gets here.' "
[Max Evans, in the "Author's Notes" to *Rounders Three,* 1990]

I'm here to tell you I assure you, I can testify. "My, oh my, folks, but that boy c'n bite, I'm here to tell you." [Frank Roderus, *Hell Creek Cabin,* 1979]

I'm shootin' you straight I'm telling you the truth.

I might would I may. "I might would come to the party."

immigrant A term used in the 19th century to mean one who has migrated from the East to the West.

immigrant cattle Cattle brought to a range or ranch from a great distance away.

impsonite A black variety of the mineral asphalite named after the Impson Valley in Oklahoma where it is found.

in This sound is frequently used instead of *en,* especially by Texans, as in the words innernational, (international), innerjy (energy), interprise (enterprise), intry (entry), tin (ten), twinny (twenty), cint (cent), wint (went), tinnis (tennis), timperature (temperature), Winsdy (Wednesday), innertainment (entertainment) and ind (end).

in a hole In debt or some other kind of trouble. The expression can be traced to Western gambling houses of the mid-19th century where the proprietors took a certain percentage of each hand for the house. This money, according to a gambling book of the time, was put in the "hole," which was "a slot cut in the middle of the poker table, leading to a locked drawer underneath, and all checks deposited therein are the property of the keeper of the place." When one had put more money into the poker table hole than was in his pocket, he was *in a hole.*

in a tight In a difficult position. "That old badger's in a tight."

in cahoots with In partnership, often shady partnership, with, from the French *cahorte* (gang).

incense cedar An important white cedar *(Libocedrus decurrens)* of the Pacific coast, growing on mountains from Oregon south; also called the *post cedar,* because it is used for fence posts.

Independence Rock A natural granite landmark rising 128 feet high near the Sweetwater River in Wyoming. Over 100,000 pioneers chiseled their names on this "Great Register of the Desert" while making their way west along the Oregon Trail beginning in 1843.

Indian At least one writer has speculated that *Indian* may have been suggested to Columbus as a name for the Taino people he encountered because they were so friendly, peaceful and gentle, *una gente in Dios* (a people of God). But there is no proof of this, most etymologists believing these people were mistakenly named by Columbus because he thought he had reached the Indies of Asia, the first but not the worst mistake immigrants made regarding the native Americans. See also NATIVE AMERICAN.

Indian agent A U.S. official who represents the government in dealing with an Indian tribe or tribes.

Indian bread Pioneers called the strip of fatty meat extending from the shoulder along the backbone of the buffalo *Indian bread* because the Indians favored it. As one writer put it: "When scalded in hot grease to seal it, then smoked, it became a 'titbit' the buffalo hunter used as bread.

When eaten with lean or dried meat it made an excellent sandwich." "This heah's the depouille . . . or Injun bread . . . Mighty good." [Frank Yerby, *Western,* 1982]

Indian breadroot A plant *(Psoralea esculenta)* also called *breadroot* that was a staple in the diet of Indians of the West.

Indian-broke Descriptive of a horse broken by Indians, trained to be mounted from the right side, where Indians usually mounted from (whites customarily mounting their horses from the left side).

Indian country A term used by Western pioneers to describe any place where hostile Indians were likely to be encountered.

Indian fungus A common fungus *(Echinodontium tinctorium)* found on Western conifers and thought to have been used as a dye by Pacific Northwest Indians.

Indian giver Tradition holds that American Indians took back their gifts when they didn't get equally valuable ones in return. Some Indians were no doubt *Indian givers;* others, however, got insulted if they received *more* than they gave. Instances of Indians *Indian-giving* are hard to come by, and even the *Handbook of American Indians* (1901) published by the Smithsonian Institution, defines the practice as an "alleged custom." Perhaps the expression is explained by the fact that *Indian* was once widely used as a synonym for bogus or false. Many of the nearly 500 terms prefixed with *Indian* unfairly impugn the Indian's honesty or intelligence—even *honest Injun* was originally meant sarcastically, and *Indian summer* means a false summer. The term may also have first applied to white men who revoked treaties with Indians. See also NATIVE AMERICAN.

Indian paintbrush *Castilleja linariaefolia,* a plant of the figwort family that is the state flower of Wyoming; also a name given to other plants of the genus.

Indian post office Indians in the American West often piled sticks and stones in a mound to indicate that they had been at a certain point and would return there in a certain number of days, depending on the number of rocks and sticks piled there. Cowboys called such a mound an *Indian post office* because messages could be left there.

Indian saddle A rudimentary type of saddle used by Plains Indians.

Indians don't count An offensive boast of gunmen in the early Southwest, who supposedly kept a count of all but Indians and Mexicans that they killed. Also *Mexicans don't count.*

Indian territory A former U.S. territory of about 31,000 square miles now in eastern Oklahoma.

Indian-up To sneak or creep up on someone as quietly as an Indian. "He

Indian-upped on them, and they didn't have a chance."

Indian warrior A western U.S. plant *(Pedicularis densiflora)* of the lousewort family with densely clustered brilliant red flowers that suggested "redskins" to some.

Indian whiskey Cheap rotgut often sold to Indians by cynical traders as good liquor. E. C. Abbott and Helene Huntington Smith in *We Pointed Them North* (1939) tell a story about early Western traders making it from the following recipe: "Take one barrel of Missouri River water, and two gallons of alcohol. Then you add two gallons of strychnine to make them crazy—because strychnine is the greatest stimulant in the world—three bars of tobacco to make them sick—because an Indian wouldn't figure it was whiskey unless it made him sick—five bars of soap to give it a bead, and half-pound of red pepper, and then you put in some sage brush and boil it until it's brown. Strain this into a barrel and you've got your Indian whiskey." Also called *Indian liquor.*

I never shot a man who didn't need it A saying repeated in a number of Westerns but actually said first by outlaw Clay Allison, who is also remembered for pulling a dentist's tooth at gunpoint after the dentist pulled the wrong tooth in his mouth.

Injun A common early Western pronunciation of *Indian.*

inkslinger A writer or editor. " 'You scared him off with that editorial . . . He may be gone fer the moment, inkslinger, but he'll be back.' " [Larry D. Names, *Boomtown*, 1981]

innernational A common pronunciation of *international.*

in Texas the cattle come first, then the men, then the horses and last the women An old Texas saying quoted by Edna Ferber in *Giant* (1952).

in the boot The growing stage when wheat is developing inflorescence. "A bad frost fell when the northern Texas wheat was in the boot."

irrigation An old Western expression meaning the refreshment of a dry body or mouth with liquor. "I was in great need of irrigation and stepped up to the bar."

iron in your barrel Sexual energy; an erection.

is all Often used at the end of a sentence as a short form of "that's all." "I came here for some sugar, is all."

istle; ixtle A fiber from plants of the Agave or Yucca genus used in making carpets and other items. The word derives from the Nahuatl *ichtli* meaning the same.

I-talian A pronunciation of *Italian.* " 'Since when did you become an I-talian?' Bobby Lee asked . . ." [Larry McMurtry, *Texasville*, 1987]

It's gettin' a bit Western The wind is blowing up to near blizzard conditions.

it sounds to me! An expression of disbelief. " 'I know,' replied Bud, using the cowpuncher's expressive phrase of skepticism, 'but it sounds to me!' " [O. Henry, "The Passing of Black Eagle" in *The Best Short Stories of O. Henry,* 1945]

it's such a fur piece you've got to ride a pregnant mare to get back A very long distance to travel.

I've seen cows get well that was hurt worse than that An old cowboy retort when one is served a rare steak.

J

jacal See quote. ". . . beneath it stood a *jacal* such as the Mexicans erect—a one-room house of upright poles daubed with clay and roofed with grass or tule reeds." [O. Henry, "The Passing of Black Eagle" in *The Best Short Stories of O. Henry,* 1945]

jackalope A mythic creature that is half jackrabbit and half antelope. Pictures on postcards show a jackrabbit with antlers. "He was gone before daybreak, following a Haliburton drilling equipment truck with a sign on its rear that said it braked for jackalope." [Thomas McGuane, *Keep The Change,* 1989]

jackaroo A cowboy or BUCKAROO.

Jackass Gulf A California gold field.

jackass mail A stagecoach pulled by mules over rough terrain; also *jackass express.*

jackass rabbit See quote. ". . . we saw the first specimen of an animal known familiarly over two thousand miles of mountain and desert . . . as the jackass rabbit. He is well named. He is just like any other rabbit, except that he is from one third to twice as large, has longer legs in proportion to his size, and has the most perposterous ears that were ever mounted on any creature *but* a

jackass." [Mark Twain, *Roughing It,* 1872] Also called *jackrabbit.*

jacket To cover an orphan lamb with the skin of a dead lamb so that the dead one's mother will nurse the orphan.

Jack Mormons Mormons who are not active church members. "Jack Mormons, the Mulders did not tithe or go to meeting . . ." [Wallace Stegner, *Recapitulation,* 1979]

jackrabbit An abbreviation of *jackass rabbit,* the large hare of North America so named because of its long jackass-like ears and legs. *Jackass-rabbit* is first recorded in 1847 by a traveler in the West: "[We] started a number of hares (called Jackass rabbits) and had no little amusement in witnessing some animated runs." Within 15 years the same hares were being called *jackrabbits.* They were also called *mule rabbits.*

Jackson Hole, Wyoming See HOLE.

jag A partial load; a small amount. "He had a jag of hay to take in."

jakes An outdoor privy, an outhouse; the word of British origin. "He went down the walkboard toward the jakes . . . Then he opened the rough board door of the jakes and stepped in. The judge was seated upon the closet . . ." [Cormac McCarthy, *Blood Meridian, or, The Evening Redness in the West*, 1985]

jalapeño A hot green or orange-red pepper *(Capsicum annuum)* used in Mexican cooking and well-known in the Southwest.

jamoka Coffee; a combination of *java* and *mocha*.

janders A pronunciation of *jaundice* heard in northern California.

jaw Talk, often excessively. " 'Go ahead and jaw.' " Barton cut in savagely . . . 'Don't mind me atall.' " [William Hopson, *The Last Shoot-out*, 1958]

jaw cracker A humorous old name for itinerant dentists.

jawing Talking. " 'What're you boys jawin' about?' Fyle asked merrily." [Frank Roderus, *Hell Creek Cabin*, 1979]

jay A common expression in the early West for a man, a person. "What men say about my nature is not merely an outside thing. For the fact that I let 'em keep on sayin' it is a proof I don't value my nature enough to shield it from their slander and give them their punishment. And that's a poor sort of a jay." [Owen Wister, *The Virginian*, 1902]

Jayhawker State A nickname for Kansas, after the antislavery guerrillas called *Jayhawkers* in the state before and during the Civil War.

Jefferson (1) A proposed name for the territory that became Colorado, which was part of what was sometimes called the Jefferson Territory before the Civil War in honor of Thomas Jefferson. (2) A name proposed for the territory that became Montana, which was also part of what was called the Jefferson Territory before the Civil War.

Jeffrey pine A conifer growing in the high mountains of the West with long needles and large cones. *Pinus jeffrey* is named for Scottish botanist John Jeffrey, who collected plants in the Pacific Northwest in the mid-19th century.

jerk one baldheaded To treat someone roughly. "If I get my hands on him, I'll jerk him baldheaded." Also *snatch one baldheaded*.

jerkwater town Steam engines often made stops in small Western stations for no other reason but to obtain water, the fireman jerking a cord attached to a long spigot extending from the water tower to fill the engine's water tender. Similar practices, universal in the early days of railroading, gave rise to the Americanism *jerkwater town*, first recorded in 1896, for any small, out-of-the-way place where no train stopped except to "jerk water."

jerky (1) Dried and smoked strips of dried beef, first recorded in 1850. Much used by travelers in the West, *jerky* is simply the Anglicization of the Mexican-Spanish *charqui* (dried meat), which was often used instead of *jerky. Charqui,* in turn, comes from the Incan *echarqui* for dried meat. Today jerky is sold commercially throughout the United States. "Fumbling with my pack I got out another piece of the precious jerky . . ." [Louis L'Amour, *Jubal Sackett,* 1985] (2) An old term for a wagon without springs.

jessamine A name in the Southwest for a shrub of the family *Apocynaceae* with fragrant white flowers.

a Jesse James A robber or bank robber, after Jesse Woodson James, who became a kind of American Robin Hood in his own brief lifetime. A member of the Confederate Quantrill gang in his youth, he and his brother Frank later led the most notorious band of robbers in the country's history. The gang's daring bank and train robberies caused many deaths, but James was regarded as a hero by a public that hated foreclosing banks and greedy railroads. In 1882, changing his name to Thomas Howard, Jesse went into hiding at St. Joseph, Missouri. There, six months later, Robert Ford, "the dirty little coward that shot Mr. Howard," killed him for a reward. Jesse James was only 35 when he died. He is still a folk hero, commemorated in a popular ballad, folktales, movies, novels and at least one play. Besides being slang for a robber, a *Jesse James* is a truckman's name for a police magistrate and has been applied by baseball players to umpires.

jicama The large, turnip-shaped root of the tropical American legume *Pachyrhizus erosus* eaten as a side dish and in salads. The plant ultimately takes its name from the Nahuatl *Xicamatl.*

Jicarilla An Apache tribe with members now mostly in New Mexico; the tribe possibly takes its name from the Spanish *jicara* (chocolate cup) after the shape of a hill where they once lived in present-day southeast Colorado or northern New Mexico. Or it may have been named from the Spanish *jicarillos* (little baskets) because of the basket-weaving skills of tribe members.

jigger A contemptuous term for a person, guy. " 'That towheaded jigger with the fancy drinking ideas don't have to ride very far to get trouble if that's what he's looking for.' " [Wayne D. Overholser, *Buckaroo's Code,* 1947]

Jim Hill mustard A popular name in the Northwest for wild mustard; named after railroad builder Jim Hill.

jimpsecute A colorful old term meaning to call courting on one's true love; the courted one often called her courter a *juicy-spicy.*

jingle bob (1) An ear mark made on cattle by cutting the ear on the upper side so as to break the back of the ear and make it hang down. (2) Spurs that jingle as a cowboy walks.

jingler A wrangler, a herder, a cowboy.

jingle your spurs! Hurry up, get a move on it.

jittery as a bird in a butter churn Very nervous. " 'You always look so calm, Noah, I'm jittery as a bird in a butter churn.' " [Lucia St. Clair Robson, *Ride the Wind*, 1982]

john Slang for a Chinese male during the California gold rush.

John B. A cowboy hat or STETSON, named after its first manufacturer, John B. Stetson.

John Henry One's signature: often called a *John Hancock* in other sections of the country.

John Law A name used for any law officer.

Johnny Navajo This collective name for the Navajo Indians was used by white settlers in the 19th century.

a John Wesley Hardin A fabled gunfighter. After John Wesley Hardin (1853–95), killer of some 40 men, the first when he was only 12. Hardin, famous for his *quick cross draw* (crossing his arms to opposite sides and pulling his guns from his vest pockets) died when he was shot in the back of the head while playing cards. See also WILD BILL HICKOK.

jojoba A Southwestern shrub *(Simmondsia chinensis)* with edible seeds containing a valuable oil; from a Spanish word for the shrub.

jornada Southwesterners used this Spanish word, meaning literally "a day's journey," to mean a day's travel across a desert without stopping for water.

Joshua tree *Yucca brevifolia,* a desert, treelike plant that grows only in the Mojave Desert and is named after the biblical Joshua's spear pointed at the city of Ai. ". . . these were plants of a strange kind, two or even three times the height of a man, yet with strange limbs, twisted oddly. They were like no trees I had seen before, having instead of leaves, sharply pointed blades. 'They are called Joshua trees,' my father explained." [Louis L'Amour, *The Lonesome Gods*, 1983] Also called *tree yucca*.

Judas eye See quote. " 'What is a Judas eye?' 'Glass, boy. With a wicked shine in it as like as if he could still see with it.' " [Loren D. Estleman, *Sudden Country*, 1991]

Judas steer A steer that leads others into the slaughterhouse.

judge A title that was often bestowed gratuitously on any lawyer in the early West.

Judge Colt The Colt revolver as a symbol of law enforcement. "Judge Colt was the law, and the Winchester rifle was order."

judge of the plains The title of 19th-century California officials who settled cattle disputes.

jughead A stupid horse; a stupid person. " 'We have no broncs here. I buy my horses already broken.' 'What about that horse that threw you?' 'He is not a bronc. He is just a jughead.' " [Elmer Kelton, *The Time It Never Rained*, 1973]

juice To milk. "Mr. Ross blew out a thoughtful plume of smoke, then asked, 'You savvy how to juice a cow? . . . Pail one, I mean?' " [A. B. Guthrie Jr., *Arfive*, 1970]

the juice ain't worth the squeeze Said of something that requires too much effort to be worth it; heard mainly in the South and West.

juicy-spicy See JIMPSECUTE.

jumping bean The seed of certain Mexican plants of the genus *Sapium* and *Sebastiana* that jump or move about because of the movements of a moth lava inside the seed. Also *Mexican jumping bean*.

jumping cactus The cholla cactus of the Southwest, so named because when the loose stems on the ground are touched the entire stem may move.

jump up dust Leave quickly. "They saw the posse coming and jumped up dust into the hills."

Juneteenth June 19, in honor of the emancipation date of blacks in Texas, where it is celebrated annually by many African-Americans.

Justins Cowboys began to wear fancy boots by the end of the 19th century, some handtooled leather ones costing them two months pay, about $50. The most famous of these were made by Fort Worth boot-maker Joseph Justin and called *Justins* in his honor. The term is still in use today.

juzgado See HOOSEGOW

K

kachina doll A Hopi Indian doll. Carved from cottonwood root in the shape of a *kachina*, an ancestral spirit, it is used as a household decoration or given as a gift to a child.

kangaroo court Although this expression may have originated in Australia, it was first recorded in the United States during the California gold rush. Perhaps Australian 49ers did bring it with them to the gold fields. According to this story, the source for the term are kangaroos in Australia's back country, who when out of spear range sat staring dumbly at men for long periods of time before leaping off for the horizon; their staring was thought to be similar to the dumb stares of jurors sitting on a mock jury, and their leaping away suggested the quick decisions of such an extralegal court. But there are no quotations supporting the use of *kangaroo court* in Australia at any time. The expression could have been coined in America, in fact, based on the several uses of the word *kangaroo* in England for anything unusual or eccentric. Another guess is that Americans familiar with the kangaroo's jumping habits, or Australians here with gold fever, invented *kangaroo court* as a humorous term for courts that tried "claim-jumpers," miners who seized the mining claims of others. *Mustang court* means the same.

kangaroo rat A long-tailed rodent (genus *Dipodomys*) of the Western desert with long hind legs adapted for jumping.

the Katy The Missouri, Kansas & Texas Railroad line. "[It had] just arrived via the Missouri, Kansas & Texas Railroad, familiarly known throughout the [Oklahoma] territory, by a natural process of elision, as the Katy." [Edna Ferber, *Cimarron*, 1930]

Katy-bar-the-door Watch out, take precautions, big trouble is coming. "When these clouds hit that front, it's liable to be Katy-bar-the-door." [Elmer Kelton, *The Time It Never Rained*, 1973]

keel The way Mexicans always pronounce *kill* in Westerns. " 'Eeef one speaks to warn heem, I keel the other one, you see?' " [Louis L'Amour, *The Tall Stranger*, 1957]

keep it under your war bonnet Keep it a secret, keep it under your hat. " 'Listen,' I whispered to Junior to keep it a secret . . . 'Keep it under your war bonnet.' " [Sherman Alexie, "A Drug Called Tradition," 1993]

keep your eyes peeled; keep your eyes skinned To keep your eyes wide open, to keep a sharp lookout. The earliest known form of the frontier expression, recorded in 1833, was to *keep your eyes skinned* (presumably meaning with the lids drawn back). Originally Western slang, the expression is now commonly heard throughout the United States.

Keep your word good Always be honest. "I've kept my word good all my life."

Kelly's Excellent bits and spurs long made by the El Paso firm P. M. Kelly and Sons.

kept his private graveyard Said of a killer with many notches on his gun. "The deference that was paid to a desperado of wide reputation, and who 'kept his private graveyard,' as the phrase went, was marked, and cheerfully accorded." [Mark Twain, *Roughing It,* 1872]

kershaw An old name for a pumpkin; probably corrupted from *cashaw,* the Algonquian name for the pumpkin but possibly so named because a Texan by the name of Kerr grew them.

ketch dog A dog trained to hold down cattle by the nose until cowboys could tie them.

kicked into a funeral procession To be killed by a wild, kicking horse.

kicker Short for SHITKICKER.

kicking the jackrabbits off the trail Said of a horse galloping very fast.

kick like a bay steer To vigorously protect or resist or exert oneself. "He kicked like a bay steer when they tried to take him in." See also BAY STEER.

kill-fighter A deadly gunfighter. "He had the look of a kill-fighter, not a man who was happy to rough it up." [Walter Van Tilburg Clark, *The Ox-Bow Incident,* 1940]

kilt Killed. " 'Mommer, Popper, come out hyah. That man that kilt Mr. Hatch has come ter see yer!' " [Katherine Anne Porter, *Noon Wine,* 1937]

kindly noisy Kind of noisy. " 'It's fixin to get kindly noisy in here,' he said." [Cormac McCarthy, *All the Pretty Horses,* 1992]

King Ranch The biggest of cattle ranches. Started in 1851 by Irish immigrant Richard King who by the end of the 19th century owned over 1 million acres on the Texas Gulf Coast. Today it is over 1.25 million acres, half the area of Delaware. (See XIT.)

king salmon A large salmon of the northern Pacific Ocean; also called *Chinook salmon.*

king's ex A term for "time out" in tag and other children's games; it possibly derives from "king's excuse."

Kiowa A Plains Indian people of the Southwest, the name meaning "the principal ones" in their language.

kiss the ground To be thrown by a horse.

kit fox A small gray fox *(Vulpes velox* and *Vulpes macrotis)* of the Western plains and deserts.

ki-yi The bark or yelp of a coyote.

knockaway See ANAQUA.

know how to die standing up To be courageous and unafraid, especially in a fight.

know one's cans Cowboys on the range in the 19th century were usually starved for reading matter and often read the labels on the cook's tin cans, learning them by heart. A tenderfoot could always be distinguished because he didn't *know his cans.* The expression isn't recorded in the *Dictionary of Americanisms* but is given in Ray Allen Billington's *America's Frontier Culture* (1977). "The back and the side doors of the dwelling . . . littered with the empty tin cans that mark any new American settlement, and especially one whose drought is relieved by the thirst-quenching coolness of tinned tomatoes and peaches. Perhaps the canned tomato, as much as anything else, made possible the settling of the vast West and Southwest." [Edna Ferber, *Cimarron,* 1930]

krummkake Mainly an Upper Midwest term for a large, light thin cookie made from an egg-based batter and cooked in an iron similar to a waffle-iron. Formed into a cone while pliable, it is allowed to harden and then is filled with whipped cream. Scandanavian settlers introduced the dessert and the Norwegian word for it. Also *krumcake.*

L

ladies of the line Most people have heard of the self-explanatory *ladies of the night,* for prostitutes, but why *ladies of the line?* The expression comes to us from the American West, where prostitutes did business in tents and jerry-built shacks stretched out in lines at the outskirts of towns, mining camps or railroad yards.

ladrone A word used in the Southwest for a thief; from the Spanish *ladrón* meaning the same.

laid out Played hookey. " 'What are you doin' out of school today?' 'I laid out.' " [Cormac McCarthy, *All the Pretty Horses,* 1992]

Lamanite The name given to American Indians in the *Book of Mormon,* which represents them as descendants of the Jewish prophet Laman, who led them to America from Jerusalem in 600 B.C.

land in a shallow grave A cowboy expression meaning to be killed and buried without formal ceremony, as cowboys were often far out on the plains away from towns and churches.

land-office business Before the Civil War, the U.S. government established "land offices" for the allotment of government-owned land in western territories just opened to settlers. These offices registered applicants, and the rush of citizens lining up mornings long before the office opened made the expression *doing a land-office business* (a tremendous amount of business) part of the language by at least 1853. Adding to the queues were prospectors filing mining claims, which were also handled by land offices. After several decades, the phrase was applied figuratively to a great business in something other than land.

Land of Gold An old nickname for California.

Land of mañana See MAÑANA.

Land of Promise A nickname for the West in the mid-19th century.

Land of Red Apples An old nickname for Oregon.

Land of the Golden Hills A name given by Chinese to California at the time of the gold rush of 1849. "The carriage bumped its way down Dupont Gai, or Dupont Street, the main thoroughfare of the Chinese section of Gum San Ta Fow—Big City in the Land of the Golden Hills . . ." [Fred Mustard Stewart, *The Glitter and the Gold,* 1989]

Land of the Honeybee A nickname for Utah.

Land of the Redwoods A nickname for California.

Land of the Webfeet Another nickname for Oregon. A *webfoot* is someone from Oregon.

Land of Setting Suns A nickname for California.

Land of Silver A nickname for Nevada.

lands A common exclamation. "Why, lands, yes, we aim to be there first thing in the morning."

lapboard A device once used to kill wolves, coyotes and other carnivores. "A dozen auger-holes, bored almost through, were filled with lard, in which were a few grains of strychnine, and then the surface of the board was similarly smeared . . . Any carniverous animal that comes to a lapboard stays there—licking the lard from the board." [Charles F. Lummis, *A Tramp Across the Continent*, 1892]

la raza When used with a plural verb, *la raza* refers to Mexican-Americans collectively. With a singular verb, it means Mexican-American culture. It is a borrowing from Spanish.

lariat Deriving from the Spanish *la reata* (the rope), this Western term for a long-noosed rope used to catch cattle and horses is first recorded in 1831.

larrup To whip, thrash or beat. "He larruped him good for stealing the horse."

larrupin' Delicious. *Larrupin' truck* means "good food." " '. . . Jett says it's larrupin' and that what he has got in the barbecue sauce makes it taste different . . .' " [Edna Ferber, *Giant*, 1952]

lasso A long rope with a running noose at the end used for roping cattle, horses and the like; from the Spanish *lazo* for the same.

Last Roundup See GREAT ROUNDUP.

latigo (1) A leather strap securing and tightening the end of a cinch to the saddletree of a Western saddle; a borrowing of a Spanish word for the same. (2) The rawhide thong attached to a pistol holster and tied around the leg to keep the holster steady. Pronounced *lad-ih-goh*.

laverick An old, slightly contemptuous term for a man, usually a stranger.

law (1) Often used to mean sue. "She's going to law him." (2) Lord. " 'Law,' she said. 'Look at that face.' " [Benjamin Capps, *Tales of the Southwest*, 1990]

law-and-order A nickname for a lawman or someone who is a stickler for the letter of the law. "Take it easy, law-and-order,' Gil told me. 'This ain't our picnic.' " [Walter Van Tilburg Clark, *The Ox-Bow Incident,* 1940]

lawdog A sheriff or deputy. "Some lawdog tracked him down in Wyoming."

lawing Working as a law enforcement officer of any kind. "Lawing and medicine practiced jointly kept his life continually absorbing. Medicine led to crime or crime led to medicine." [Richard S. Wheeler, *Incident at Fort Keogh,* 1990]

law of the prairie Some people, by words and actions, insist that we still live by the *law of the jungle,* that is, like animals not governed by the rules of civilization. The term probably dates back to the late 19th century. *Law of the prairie,* a similar U.S. term, is first recorded in 1823.

Lawson's cyprus The name for an ornamental Western tree also called the *Port Orford cedar.* Named after the Edinburgh, Scotland, nurseryman who in 1854 began cultivating the tree from seeds collected in the United States.

law wrangler A lawyer.

laying fence-worm An old term for laying down the rails of a new fence.

lay out To cut or absent oneself from a class in school.

layout An outfit, a group or party of people. "They was a pretty sorry layout if you ask me."

lay the dust To take a drink; refers to clearing the dust of the trail from one's throat with a drink.

lazy Used for a brand lying on the side, as in the "Lazy W brand."

lead-pipe cinch A cinch, borrowed from the Spanish *cincha,* is a saddle-girth used on horses or a girth used on pack mules. Because a well-fastened cinch holds the saddle securely to the horse so that a saddle won't slip off, about a century ago the word *cinch* became a natural synonym for something sure and easy, a surefire certainty, something held in a grasp so firm that it cannot get away. *Cinches,* however, are usually made out of leather, canvas or braided horsehair, not lead pipe. So the expression a *lead-pipe cinch* is something of a mystery. One guess is that the phrase is from the underworld. Criminals using lead-pipe blackjacks, according to this theory, found it a cinch to dispatch their victims and a cinch to dispose of the blackjack should police near the scene of the crime stop them and frisk them for weapons.

league A measure of land of about three miles, the term often used in Southwestern areas when they were a part of Mexico.

leaky mouth A humorous expression for someone who talks too much, a big mouth who can't repress his or her mouth.

lean, mean hombre   See quote. ". . . a tall, gangling westerner had slouched in . . . He was what western writers call 'a lean mean hombre,' but he moved with an easy grace . . ." [James A. Michener, *Centennial*, 1974]

leather it   Put away or holster one's gun. "Hondo had started to turn away when Lowe went for his gun. 'Not in the back!' Buffalo shouted. 'Leather it!' " [Louis L'Amour, *Hondo*, 1953]

leather pounder   A cowboy; from pounding up and down in his leather saddle.

leather slapper   A gunfighter.

leave the reservation   To go off the limits of a RESERVATION to depart from any usual practice or idea. "Truman's sweeping demand for civil-rights legislation stampeded the Southerners right off the reservation . . ." [*Saturday Evening Post*, July 2, 1949]

leavin' Cheyenne   Going away; from the Western song "Goodbye, Old Paint, I'm leavin' Cheyenne," often played as the last song at cowboy dances.

left settin' on air way up in the sky   Thrown from a horse; the last line from an old Western song about a cowboy trying to break a horse and failing:

When my stirrips I lose and also my
    hat,
And I starts pullin' leather as blind as
    a bat,
And he makes one more jump, he is
    headed up high
Leaves me settin' on air way up in
    the sky.

leg   A professional gambler; from *blackleg*, meaning a swindler.

leg knife   A heavy knife Western hunters often carried in their boots.

lemita   A Western sumac whose acid fruits are used in making mock lemonade.

lepero   An old term for any low character or villain; a borrowing of the Spanish *lepero* meaning the same.

leppy; leppie   A term used in Nevada for a motherless lamb. Also called *bum, bummer* and *bummie*.

less   A common pronunciation of *let us*. "Less get going."

let her rip   Letting things go at full speed was called *let-her-rip-itiveness* in mid-19th century America. The Americanism derives from another American expression, *let her rip*, which apparently first referred to railroad locomotives. Americans were always obsessed with speed. Wrote one early train traveler out West: "Git up more steam—this ain't a funeral! Let her rip!"

let's see your color   Let's see the color of your money, how much money you've got. "I'll make it a hundred and a quarter and won't ask you where you got it,' said the judge. 'Let's see your color.' " [Cormac McCarthy, *Blood Meridian, or, The Evening Redness in the West,* 1985]

letter carrier An old term for a postman said to be commonly used in northern California; it is still occasionally heard in metropolitan New York and other areas as well.

Levis The word *Levis* has become more popular in the eastern United States recently as a synonym for jeans, denims or dungarees—probably due to the bright-colored styles that Levi Strauss and Company are manufacturing today. The trademarked name has been around since the gold rush days, though, when a pioneer San Francisco overall manufacturer began making denim pants. Levi Strauss reinforced his heavy blue denims with copper rivets at strain points such as the corners of pockets, this innovation making his product especially valuable to miners, who often loaded their pockets with ore samples. Within a few years, the pants were widely known throughout the West, where the name *Levis* has always been more common than any other for tight-fitting, heavy blue denims.

lick Cowboy slang for syrup. "Get the lick from the chuck box."

lickety-brindle Very fast, lickety-split. "He got there lickety brindle."

life's a twisting stream Possibly an old Western saying; used in Larry McMurtry's *Lonesome Dove* (1985).

lift the hair To scalp.

light Get down, alight, from a wagon; get out of a car. "He called, 'you-all light and come in this house.' " [Elmer Kelton, *The Time It Never Rained,* 1973]

light a rag See quote. " 'Light a rag, then . . . Get out. Vamoose. Drag it. Hit the grit. Get out of here.' " [Luke Short, *Hardcase,* 1941]

light a shuck Leave or depart quickly. The expression is said to have originated from the practice of men lighting a corn shuck as a crude torch just before leaving a campfire so that they could briefly see in the darkness and accustom their eyes to it. Since such corn shuck torches burnt quickly, a man had to light one and leave at once or its light would burn out. Thus he "lit a shuck and left."

light out Depart suddenly, leave in a hurry. "I'm going to light on out of here."

like a house on fire Although log cabins weren't the homes of the earliest American settlers—Swedes settling in Delaware introduced them in 1638—they became a common sight on the Western frontier in the 18th and 19th centuries. As practical as they were, these rude wooden structures were tinderboxes once they caught fire. So fast did they burn to the ground that pioneers began to compare the speed of a fast horse to a log cabin burning to the ground, saying he could go *like a house on fire.* By 1809 Washington Irving, under the pseudonym Diedrich Knickerbocker, had given the expression wide currency in his *History of New York from the Beginning of the World to the End of the Dutch Dynasty,* the first great book of comic literature by an American. The phrase soon came to mean "very quickly or energetically."

like a kerosened cat Very fast. "He was out of there like a kerosened cat." [Thomas McGuane, *Nothing but Blue Skies,* 1992]

like a steer, I can try This cowboy expression, meaning roughly "I'll do my best, even if it's futile," is said to derive from the habit of steers never losing their sexual drive, despite their castration, and often trying to mount each other.

like the devil beating tan bark Said of someone or something that is fast and furious.

limber pine A valuable pine, *Pinus flexilis,* of the Pacific Coast.

line Once used as a synonym for the frontier in the West, the dividing line between settled and unsettled territory. "We had crossed the line and were in Indian territory."

line rider A rider who patrols the boundaries of a ranch or herd.

lingo Language. " 'You oughta be doing your turn on the stage with the lingo that you've got.' " [Max Brand, *The Nighthawk Trail,* 1932]

Lion of the West (1) An old nickname for American statesman Henry Clay (1777–1852). (2) A frontier bully or ruffian.

lippin' Talking back to. "Stop lippin' me."

little Often attached to first names where the son has the same first name as the father. "In some parts of the world Little Joe would be called Joseph Twine II, but in Henrietta he's called Little Joe, to distinguish him from his father, Big Joe." [Larry McMurtry, *Cadillac Jack,* 1982]

little bitty Very small. "Hank Marlowe was a little bitty dried up fellow with a thin leathery face . . ." [Frank O'Rourke, *Diamond Hitch,* 1956]

little cow-and-calf deal A small ranch. " 'I've got a little cow-and-calf deal in Whiteface, Texas,' J. B. told this reporter." [*Countryside Magazine,* Summer 1993]

little old Little; "old" is often superfluously attached to "little," as it is in the South. "We saw this little old boat coming round the bend."

Little Sure Shot A nickname given to ANNIE OAKLEY by the Sioux chief Sitting Bull, who starred with her in Buffalo Bill's Wild West Show. "Sitting Bull is in love with Annie Oakley, he calls her his little sure shot. She had her picture made with him, he is very proud of it and shows it to anyone who will look." [Larry McMurtry, *Buffalo Girls*, 1990]

live dictionary An old cowboy term for a school marm or for a very talkative woman.

live oak A name for various evergreen oak species of the Pacific Coast, Texas and other states.

live on what a hungry coyote would leave Live very frugally. "He did not need much. He could, as the saying goes, live on what a hungry coyote would leave." [J. Frank Dobie, *Coronado's Children*, 1930]

livestock king A wealthy rancher. "He was the livestock king of Wyoming."

llano A Spanish term used in Texas and New Mexico for arid, treeless prairies like the vast Llano Estacado (Staked Plain), a high dry plateau of 40,000 square miles in Western Texas and New Mexico.

Llano Estacado See LLANO.

lluvia de oro A name, from the Spanish meaning "shower of gold," for the palo verde *(Parkinsonia Torreyana)*, a tree with a lemon-yellow bloom.

Lo

Hope springs eternal in the human breast;

Man never is, but always to be blessed.
The soul, uneasy, and confined from home,
Rests and expatiates in a life to come.

Lo, the poor Indian! whose untutored mind
Sees God in clouds, or hears him in the wind;
His soul proud sciences never taught to stray,
For as the solar walk, or milky way;
Yet simple nature to his hope has giv'n,
Behind the cloud-topped hill, an humbler heav'n.

Alexander Pope's well-known words *Lo, the poor Indian* in the above lines from his *Essay on Man* (1733–34) inspired the term *Lo* for an American Indian. The word isn't recorded in this sense until 1871 but must be considerably older. "Is it longer a matter of astonishment," someone wrote in 1873, referring to Indians in the West, "that the Lo's are passing so rapidly from the face of the earth?"

loafer The large gray mountain or timber wolf; a corruption of the Spanish word *lobo* for the wolf. Also *lofer*.

lobo Spanish for wolf. "Now wolves had come to them, great pale lobos with yellow eyes that trotted neat of foot or squatted in the shimmery heat to watch them . . ." [Cormac McCarthy, *Blood Meridian, or The Evening Redness in the West*, 1985]

loco A Spanish word meaning crazy that became common in the West and finally all the United States, the language needing as many words for "crazy" as it can get.

locoed Said of someone who acts crazy, as if he or she had eaten locoweed.

locoweed Various plants of the genera *Astragalus* and *Oxytropis* of the southwestern United States are called *locoweed* (from the Spanish *loco*, "insane," and *weed*) because when eaten by horses, cattle and sheep they cause irregular "crazy" behavior in the animals, including weakness, impaired vision, paralysis and finally death.

locust A migratory grasshopper *(Melanoplus spretus)* of the Rocky Mountains.

lodgepole pine A Western tree, *Pinus murrayan*, so named because it was used by Indians for poles to make lodges; also called the *white pine* in Colorado and Montana and the *tamarack pine* in California.

lofer The large gray mountain or timber wolf; also called *loafer*. " 'You never did have the sense God gave a lofer wolf, to run when you're outmanned and outgunned.' " [Loren D. Estleman, *Bloody Season*, 1987]

loganberry California Judge James Harvey Logan (1841–1921), who had been a Missouri schoolteacher before working his way West as the driver of an ox team, developed the *loganberry* in his experimental home orchard at Santa Cruz. Logan, formerly Santa Cruz district attorney, was serving on the superior court bench in 1880 when he raised the new berry from seed, breeding several generations of plants to do so. Though a respected amateur horticulturist, he never adequately explained how the berry was developed. One account claims that the *loganberry* originated "from self-grown seeds of the Aughinbaugh (a wild blackberry), the other parent supposed to be a raspberry of the Red Antwerp type." Several experts believe that it is a variety of the Western dewberry, or a hybrid of that species, crossed with the red raspberry. The dispute may never be resolved, but experiments in England have produced a plant similar to the loganberry by crossing certain blackberries and red raspberries. In any case, there is no doubt that the purplish-red *loganberry* is shaped like a blackberry, colored like a raspberry and combines the flavors of both—and that it was first grown by Judge Logan and named for him. Its scientific name is *Rubus loganbuccus*, and the trailing blackberry-like plant is grown commercially in large quantities, especially in California, Oregon, Washington and other places having fairly mild winters.

logrolling "You scratch my back and I'll scratch yourn" was the idea behind this term, which was invented by American pioneers on the Western frontier. Settlers clearing land and building their log cabins could always count on neighbors for help in rolling down logs, with the tacit understanding they'd do the same for their neighbors whenever asked. The good neighborly expression, with its associations of rum, food and fiddling, became tainted when politicians in many fields adopted it. Legislators are still well-known for *logrolling* with representatives from other states; that is, one congressman will support the pet project of another if he assists in passing a bill furthering the interests of the first. *Literary logrollers* form mutual admiration societies, favorably reviewing each other's books in order to promote sales and reputations. Commenting on one instance of such a practice, A. E. Housman said there had been nothing like it since the passage in Milton where Sin gave birth to Death.

loma The borrowing of a Spanish word meaning "small hill;" used in place names such as Yucca Loma.

the Lone Ranger The fictional masked rider of the plains who with his "faithful Indian companion Tonto" and his "great horse Silver" was a champion of justice to a generation of devoted followers on radio, in the movies and on television. This enduring symbol of the imaginary West was born in 1933 on Detroit radio station WXYZ. He shot pure silver bullets, never shot to kill and at the end of each program always shouted a hearty "Hi-ho, Silver!"

Lone Star A favorite beer of Texans, once advertised as "The National Beer of Texas."

Lone Star State A nickname for Texas, from the state flag with its one star.

long bit See SHORT BIT.

long country Vast, open country a long way from any settlement. " 'This is long country to be afoot in.' " [Larry McMurtry, *Lonesome Dove*, 1985]

long knife An Indian name for a frontiersman or settler, from the BOWIE KNIVES they often carried.

long longer'n A long time longer than. "She's goin' to be around a long longer'n me. I'd like to see you make up your differences." [Cormac McCarthy, *All the Pretty Horses*, 1992]

long rider An outlaw who spent most of his time riding in order to evade capture.

long socks A euphemistic Western term for stockings, which was considered an "indelicate" term in the mid-19th century.

long syphilis See quote. " ' . . . if a man lives long enough, he sees a lot of sons of bitches go down. Merc Marsh squeezed his heart dead squeezing for profits. Nick Brudd, I hear, has softening of the brain, which is short for paresis, which is short for long syphilis. There's more. So I count the good against the bad and come out maybe even.' " [A. B. Guthrie Jr., *Arfive*, 1970]

Long Tom A name for the long rifle or large-caliber rifle of the buffalo hunter.

lookathere Look over there. "'Well, lookathere,'" said Monte Walsh. 'One new shack and a frill on the store.'" [Jack Schaefer, *Monte Walsh*, 1958]

lookey: looky Look here. Also *lookahere*.

looking-glass prairie An old designation for a beautiful, often somewhat circular prairie.

look like 12 miles of corduroy road To look tired, disheveled, a mess, like a primitive corduroy road made of logs. "'You look like twelve miles of corduroy road. You ever sleep any more?'" [Elmer Kelton, *The Time It Never Rained*, 1973]

looks like he dove off a three-story building into a waffle iron Said of someone who has been injured and marked up many times, as in many rodeo events over the years. "A cowboy from Wolf, Wyoming, probably put it best. 'That hairy old son of a bitch looks like he dove off a three-story building into a waffle iron,' he said." [Larry McMurtry, *Cadillac Jack*, 1982]

looky there Look over there. "'Looky there,' Pea said. 'I reckon that's the new cook.'" [Larry McMurtry, *Lonesome Dove*, 1985]

looloo Apparently this was once a facetious poker term in the West.

One author tells this story: "'A looloo?' he repeated. 'What is a looloo, anyway?' 'Three clubs and two diamonds,' cooly replied the miner . . . He jerked his thumb toward a pasteboard sign which ornamented the wall of the saloon. It read: *A Looloo Beats Four Aces*." [John F. Lillard, *Poker Stories*, 1896]

loose the herd To turn cattle loose to run where they can after branding them.

Los Angeles A shortening of the California city's original name: *El Pueblo de Nuestra Señora la Reina de los Angeles de Porciúncula* (The town of Our Lady Queen of the Angels of Porciúncula). It is more often called *L.A.* Call it "L.A." and it loses 54 letters.

los muertos no hablan See DEAD MEN DON'T TALK.

lousy with This widespread term meaning "to have plenty of" possibly originated in the West.

low-neck clothes A cowboy's best clothes for special occasions.

lubber Any clumsy, stupid person, the expression an old one dating to the 15th century and used in other regions as well. "Great big lubbers sitting around whittling!" [Katherine Anne Porter, *Noon Wine*, 1937]

lucky dab A lucky throw of a lasso that catches something.

lug A crate or box used for shipping fruit, a fruit crate; the term is primarily used in The West.

luminaries Pueblo peoples in New Mexico build bonfires called luminaries outside their houses during the Christmas season, a custom deriving from the Mexican Christmas custom of setting votive candles called *luminarias* (Spanish for lamp or lantern) in sand inside small paper bags, often colorfully designed, through which light shines. The custom has spread in recent times throughout the Southwest, where neighborhoods are filled with luminarias lining driveways, sidewalks and rooftops. Luminarias are also called *farolitos*.

lumpy jaw A sometimes fatal, infectious disease among cattle that can be transmitted to humans and is found throughout the West; also called *big jaw* and *wooden tongue*.

lunger Someone suffering from lung fever. " 'I count that raw talk for a friend of that stage-robbing tinhorning whore's-son of a lunger, Doc Holliday.' " [Loren D. Estleman, *Bloody Season,* 1988]

lung fever A wasting disease for which there was no cure in the early West. "Into the winter his summer cough worsened, he had very little appetite, drank a lot of water, and finally had periods of irrationality during which he ran a high fever and his face shone red beneath an unseasonal sweat . . . [He dropped from 200 down to 75 pounds] . . . Henry was dying of lung fever." [Richard Clarke, *The Homesteaders,* 1986]

lunkhead A widespread term, first recorded in the California gold fields, for a stupid, thick-headed person.

M

ma'am A respectful form of address to a woman.

McCarthy; McCarty A hair rope used by cowboys in the West that took its name from a mispronunciation of the Spanish *mecate* meaning the same; also called a *McCarthy*.

machete A large heavy knife often used for cutting brush and as a weapon; from the borrowing of a Spanish word.

maclura Another name for the *Osage orange* or BODARK; from its scientific designation *Maclura pomifera*, honoring American geologist William Maclure.

mad as hops Very angry. ". . . Mr. Hatch safe in jail somewhere, mad as hops, maybe, but out of harm's way . . ." [Katherine Anne Porter, *Noon Wine,* 1937]

made a nine in his tail Said of a man or animal that departs quickly; possibly derives from cows lifting their tails in the shape of a figure nine when running in fright.

Madre de Dios! A Spanish exclamation meaning "Mother of God!" heard in the Southwest. "The first woman backed away, one hand at her mouth, as they pushed forward.

'Madre de dios!' she said." [Jack Schaefer, *Monte Walsh,* 1958]

madrina Spanish for the leading mare among horses. " '. . . they respected her. She was the leading mare—the madrina . . .' " [Edna Ferber, *Giant,* 1952]

maguey A rope made from fiber of the maguey plant *(Agave cantala.)*

Mahonia The evergreen shrub with small, blue, edible berries also known as the *Oregon grape;* from its genus designation *Mahonia,* named after American botanist Bertrand McMahon.

mail rider A rider carrying the U.S. mail during the early days of the West; a *mail party* was travelers journeying in a *mail coach,* that is, a stagecoach carrying mail.

make an outfit a hand Be a good worker, perform well as a cowboy. "I've never had much and never will. But like most of the breed, I've always had a good time and I've always tried to make an outfit a hand as long as I was drawin' wages." [Sam Brown, *The Crime of Coy Bell,* 1992]

make out like To pretend. "Make out like you're rich."

make the riffle To cross a riffle or rapid, to surmount any obstacle. "He couldn't quite make the riffle."

make tracks To leave quickly, travel. "Let's make tracks out of here!"

make yourself to home Make yourself at home. " 'Make yourself to home, Ladino. I'm going next door to Doc Tim's . . .' " [William Hopson, *The Last Shoot-out*, 1958]

makin' horse-hair bridles An old expression meaning to serve time in prison, where convicts often passed the time by making intricate bridles.

makin's The tobacco and paper needed for making roll-your-own cigarettes. "He took out his makin's and rolled a smoke."

malpais Bad country, badlands, a rugged tract of often volcanic land; from the Spanish *mal* (bad) and *pais* (country).

mamelle A rounded hill; from the French *mamelle* for a woman's breast. See also TETON RANGE.

mañana The Spanish word for tomorrow or sometime in the future. The *land* or *kingdom of mañana* was a term used to mean a place where time was often disregarded, a land of postponement, and was often applied to Mexico.

man at the pot! A cowboy camp cry that often goes up when a man rises to fill his coffee cup; such a man, upon hearing the cry, is obliged to fill up all the other cups in camp. "The nearest approach was an occasional cry of 'Man at the pot!' If in any cow camp a man rose to fill his coffee cup and that cry was given, it was his duty to go around with the pot and replenish all the cups held out to him." [Philip A. Rollins, *Gone Haywire*, 1939]

man for breakfast Lawlessness often went unpunished in the West, and people reading their morning newspapers had their *man for breakfast*, or murder, every day. The expression persisted from the late 19th century well into the 20th century. Another story eliminates the newspaper and claims the expression arose because there were so many killings at night in frontier towns that citizens would see bodies laid out in the street every morning before breakfast.

mangana A throw used in roping wild horses where the animal is roped by the forefeet and spilled; also called *forefooting*. A borrowing of a Spanish word meaning the same.

Manifest Destiny The 19th-century belief or doctrine that it was the divine destiny of the United States to expand its territory over the whole of North America. An 1845 editorial by John L. O'Sullivan supporting the U.S. annexation of Texas was the first to use the term: "[It is] our manifest destiny to overspread the continent allotted by Providence for the free development of our yearly multiplying millions."

maple bar A pastry in the shape of a bar with a maple-sugar frosting that is popular in the Northwest.

maquiladora city Cities in Mexico on the U.S. border that have *maquiladora programs* set up by the Mexican government. Under these programs, parts are shipped by, say, an American manufacturer in El Paso to a company in the nearby Mexican city of Juarez that assembles the parts, the finished products exported back to the United States duty free except for the value added in Mexico. The idea was born in about 1964. *Maquiladora* derives from the Spanish *maquila* (the portion received by a miller for milling someone's grain).

marijuana Apparently smoking the herb is a practice that goes back to the early West, as the testimony of a cowboy in J. Frank Dobie's *Coronado's Children* (1930) indicates: " 'Have I eaten some *raiz diabólica* [peyote] to be seeing things?' Otis asked himself aloud . . . 'No, I ain't, and I haven't been smoking marihuana weed either.' " *Cannabis sativa* takes its popular name *marijuana* from the Spanish prenomens *Maria* and *Juana,* translating as Maryjane, and no one knows why. George Washington is said to have grown it at Mount Vernon—for the rope produced from the hemp. One hundred years ago, according to the National Institute of Mental Health, "extracts of *Cannabis* were as commonly used for medicinal purposes in the U.S. as aspirin today."

markin A common pronunciation heard in the West for *American.*

Mark Twain Samuel Langhorn Clemens first used this name as a pseudonym in the Virginia City, Nevada *Territorial Enterprise* on February 2, 1863. He probably took it from the penname of a previous writer, who, in turn, got it from *"mark twain!",* a slurred mispronunciation of "mark on the twine, six fathoms!," called out when Mississippi riverboat leadsmen sounded the river with weighted twine. Or having been a riverboat pilot himself, Clemens may have coined the penname independently. But on February 24, 1866, the *Eastern Slope* newspaper in Washoe, Nevada, printed this possible origin: "When he came in there and took them on tick, he used to sing out to the barkeep, who carried a lump of chalk in his weskit pocket and kept the score, 'mark twain,' whereupon the barkeeper would score two drinks to Sam's account—and so it was, d'ye see, that he came to be called 'Mark Twain.' "

Marlboro man A rugged cowboy character in Marlboro cigarette advertisement that has become something of a symbol of the West. Both Wyoming and Texas claim him as their own, Texans saying the ads are filmed on a Texas ranch, according to James A. Michener in *Texas* (1985).

marshal The law enforcement *marshals* of the early West take their name ultimately from the Germanic word *marahskalk* (horse servant or groom). The word passed into English as *marshal* and was applied to high royal court officers and finally to law enforcement officers in England.

mash To iron. "I'm fixin to mash those clothes today."

matilija poppy A giant Southwestern poppy *(Romneya coulteri)* that takes its name from Matilija Canyon, California where it grows.

maul oak The California evergreen oak *Quercus chrysolepis.*

maverick An unbranded cow; a nonconformist. Texas lawyer Samuel Augustus Maverick (1803–70) reluctantly became a rancher in 1845 when he acquired a herd of cattle in payment for a debt. Maverick, a hero who was imprisoned twice in the war for independence from Mexico, eventually moved his cattle to the Conquistar Ranch on the Matagorda Peninsula, 150 miles from San Antonio. But he was too involved in other activities to prove much of a rancher. When in 1855 he sold out to A. Toutant de Beauregard, their contract included all the unbranded cattle on the ranch. Since careless hired hands had failed to brand any of Maverick's calves, Beauregard's cowboys claimed every unbranded animal they came upon as a *Maverick*. So apparently did some of Maverick's neighbors. Though Sam Maverick never owned another cow, his name soon meant any unbranded stock and later any person who holds himself apart from the herd, a nonconformist. *Maverick* is also used in West Texas for a motherless cow.

may can May be able to. "She may can go."

may you always ride a good horse Common parting words from a cowboy.

may you never get your spurs tangled An old Western good luck wish.

meadow An upland tract of grassland near the timberline.

mean as a tom turkey Very mean and irritable. " 'I'm mean as a tom turkey when I'm disappointed.' " [Larry McMurtry, *Lonesome Dove,* 1985]

mean as billy hell Very mean and nasty.

mean enough to kill his (her) grandmother A very mean, lowdown person without any principles.

mean enough to steal the pennies off his (her) grandmother's eyes In days past, the eyelids of dead people were weighted with coins; someone mean enough to steal these coins off his own dead grandmother's eyes was as lowdown as they came.

mean enough to take the fillings out of his (her) grandmother's teeth Another expression for someone beneath contempt.

Mearn's coyote A small, bright-colored coyote *(Canis mearnsi)* of southern Arizona named for American naturalist Dr. Edgar A. Mearns (1856–1916).

meat in the pot An endearing term for a trusty rifle, "old meat in the pot."

medicine See quote. "The word 'medicine' itself is a good example of the American Indian's dualism of theology and medicine . . . He employed the term not only for a drug or herb but also for some supernatural agency which may be invoked to cure disease or even insure the success of an undertaking." [Maurice B. Gordon, *Aesculapius Comes to the Colonies,* 1949]

medicine arrow A specially made arrow Indians believed had magical powers.

medicine bag A bag, often elaborately made, in which Indians carried charms, fetishes and remedies of many kinds. "The Chief then directed his wife to hand him his *medison* bag which he opened and showed us fourteen fingers . . . of his enemies he had taken in war." [*Journals of the Lewis and Clark Expedition,* 1805]

medicine man (1) A person Indians believed to possess supernatural or magical powers, a shaman. (2) A seller of patent medicines who ran a medicine show.

medicine show A traveling show selling fake medicines that were frequently said to be magical Indian cures.

medicine wolf The small COYOTE revered by Indians in the West.

medico An old-fashioned title for a doctor. "I'm going next door to Doc Tim's . . . You'll like our medico." [William Hopson, *The Last Shootout,* 1958]

meeching Cheap, petty. "Mr. Thompson . . . sometimes thought Mr. Helton was a pretty meeching type of fellow . . ." [Katherine Anne Porter, *Noon Wine,* 1937]

me-ma A word heard in Texas for grandmother. "Your me-ma is watching you today."

merry-go-round in high water A cowboy term for the milling of cattle in water, which is very difficult to control.

mesa A common Southwestern land formation having steep walls and a relatively flat top but less extensive than a plateau.

mescal (1) An intoxicating drink made from the fermented juices of certain agave species. (2) An agave yielding such juices.

mescal button A dried, buttonlike top of a mescal of the genus *Lophophora* long used as a hallucinogen by certain Southwestern Indians during religious ceremonies.

Mescalero A group of Apache Indians who once inhabited northern Mexico and the southwestern United States and now are situated in New Mexico.

meskin A derogatory term for a Mexican.

Mesmeriser Creek, Texas Over a century ago, a settler on the banks of this intermittent Texas waterway southeast of Dallas attempted to domesticate American bison by hypnosis, his colorful ways inspiring the colorful place-name *Mesmeriser Creek.*

mesquite (1) A spiny shrublike tree of the Southwest *(Prosopis juliflora* or *glandulosa)* that often forms dense thickets. (2) The wood of such a tree, used for barbecuing at least since the Indians used it in cooking buffalo meat.

Messiah craze An outgrowth of the ghost dance excitement that led to the GHOST DANCE War of 1890–91, the Indians involved believing that a messiah was coming.

mestizo A man of mixed Spanish or European and American Indian ancestry; from a Spanish word meaning "of mixed race." *Mestiza* is the feminine form.

metis Any person of mixed ancestry, especially someone of white and Indian ancestry; a borrowing of the French word meaning the same.

Mex A short and derogatory term for a Mexican; first recorded in 1853.

Mexican breakfast A derogatory expression meaning a cigarette and a glass of water. See also CALIFORNIA BREAKFAST.

Mexican hog Another name for the wild Texas peccary *(Pecari angulatus).*

Mexican peak A sombrero. " '[He wore] a Mexican peak, Lew.' " [Max Brand, *The Black Signal,* 1925]

Mexican persimmon See BLACK PERSIMMON.

Mexican promotion An offensive term meaning an impressive new title but no increase in pay.

Mexicans don't count See INDIANS DON'T COUNT.

Mexican standoff A stalemate, a confrontation that neither side can win. Originally an American cowboy expression describing a gun battle with no clear winner, the words date back to the mid-19th century. It is often used to describe a pitching duel in baseball today.

Mexican strawberries Beans. " 'I don't know where you keep finding these Mexican strawberries,' he said, referring to the beans." [Larry McMurtry, *Lonesome Dove,* 1985] (See ARIZONA STRAWBERRIES.)

might can May be able to. "I might can go."

might could Might. " 'I might could get by without the one, but I can't without both.' " [Larry McMurtry, *Lonesome Dove,* 1985]

might would May. "He might would catch cold dressed like that."

a Mike Fink In days past, *a Mike Fink* was used to mean a rough-and-ready hero given to exaggeration about his exploits. Mike Fink was a real American frontier hero (c. 1770–1822), a riverboatman and Indian fighter whose tall tales contributed greatly to the American folklore of exaggeration, a fact attested by the 12 or more different accounts of his death. According to one tale, he "once set his wife on fire in a pyre of leaves because she winked at another man."

a mile wide, a foot deep, too thick to drink and too thin to plow An old description of the muddy, shallow Platte River in Nebraska.

mill To stop a cattle stampede by directing the lead animals in a wide arc; from the resemblance of the cattle's circular motion to the circular movement of millstones.

milling The action of a cattle herd running around in a circle, which often results in their injury.

miners' court A court set up by miners, especially during the 1849 California gold rush, to dispense justice in areas far from settled regions.

Minié rifle An amusing historical term once used in the West, especially California, for a cheap potent whiskey with a kick like a Minié rifle. In the April 23, 1857, edition of the *Los Angeles Star*, it was described as

"Knock 'em stiff and flaming redeye—such as kills 'em at the counter, forty rods or any distance."

Mr. John An old name for Indians in general. "The evidence told us Mr. John was in the area."

mistook identity Mistaken identity. " 'Your honor, this is pretty clearly a case of mistook identity . . .' 'Yes it is,' he said. 'Bad mistook.' " [Cormac McCarthy, *All the Pretty Horses,* 1992]

Miz Usually used for Mrs., though *Miz-ziz* is also used.

monkey skull A curse. See usage example at SCUM OF THE RUN.

Monkey Ward cowboy An old term for someone who dresses up like a cowboy, or dresses up the way he thinks a cowboy dresses, sporting expensive boots, colorful shirts and so forth, as new and clean as those in the Montgomery Ward catalog.

Montana *Montana,* previously the *Montana Territory,* takes its name from the Spanish word for "mountainous." The Treasure State was admitted to the Union in 1889 as our 41st state.

Montana feathers Straw used in stuffing mattresses.

Montana peak A cowboy hat with a conical top.

Montany An old pronunciation of *Montana.* " 'I guess that's why you're ready to head off to Montany.' " [Larry McMurtry, *Lonesome Dove*, 1985]

monte A card game of Mexican origin that first became popular in the Southwest. Today, three-card monte is an always crooked "game of chance" practiced by card swindlers on street corners throughout the United States.

Moola A notable statue in Stephenville, Texas honoring a local cow who produced a record yield of milk annually.

mordido Graft, a bribe. "The most useful word on the border. Means *little bite*. And sometimes not so little. It's the oil that makes Mexico run. Payola. Graft." [James A. Michener, *Texas*, 1985]

more guts than you could hang on a fence Said by cowboys of someone with lots of courage. "He wasn't a big man, but he had more guts than you could hang on a fence."

more luck than a short-tailed cat in a roomful of rockers Very lucky. " 'You son of a bitch,' Jake Guthrie said . . . 'You got more luck than a short-tailed cat in a roomful of rockers.' " [Cathy Cash Spellman, *Paint the Wind*, 1989]

Mormon The name of members of the Church of Jesus Christ of Latter-day Saints, which is centered in Salt Lake City, Utah. *Mormon* derives from the name of the fourth-century prophet said to be the author of writings found by Joseph Smith and published in 1830 as the *Book of Mormon*. *Mormon Church* is a common but unofficial name for the Church of Jesus Christ of Latter-day Saints.

Mormon City An old name for Salt Lake City, Utah.

Mormon tea The small bush *Ephedra trifurca*, so named because it was used by the Mormons in Utah to make a medicinal tea. Also called *canatillo*.

morral A Spanish word used in Texas for a horse's feed bag.

mosey According to Webster's and most authorities, the Spanish *vamos* (let's go) became *vamoose* in American English, which begot the slang word *mosey*, "to stroll or saunter about leisurely." But it is possible, one theory holds, that the word instead takes its name "from the slouching manner of wandering Jewish peddlers in the West, many of whom were called Mose, or Moses." Neither explanation seems ideal, but nothing better has been offered.

mosshorn See OLD MOSSHORN.

motel Most sources credit West Coast motor lodge owner Oscar T. Tomerlin with coining the word *motel* in 1930, Tomerlin welding it together from *motor hotel*, which he had previously called his place. But in her book *Palaces of the Public, A History of American Hotels* (1983), Doris E. King says that the word originated in 1925 with a San Luis Obispo, California establishment that offered a garage with its roadside cottages and called itself a *Motel Inn.*

mother lode A term used in the West since at least the 1880s for a principal vein of ore in a mine; also, capitalized, the Mother Lode of the Sierra Nevada, a great California quartz vein running from Mariposa to Amador.

mott; motte A grove or clump of trees in prairie land; a term used mostly in the Southwest that derives from the Spanish *mata* meaning the same.

mountain antelope Another name for the Rocky Mountain goat.

mountain lion The North American panther or cougar, the name originating in the Colorado Rocky Mountains.

mountain man A man, much celebrated in song and story, with great skills in living in the mountains, usually a guide, trapper or trader in the Far West before the region was settled.

mountain oysters Sheep's, hog's or bull's testicles eaten as food. See also PRAIRIE OYSTER.

mountain time The standard time in the Rocky Mountain area, mean local time on the 105th meridian.

mouthy Very talkative, short on substance. "He's more mouthy than a politician."

mover A historical term for a settler moving west in the great migration of the 19th century. Lodgings for them were common along the way, bearing such names as "House for Movers," "Movers Accommodations" and so forth.

mozo An assistant, especially a man who assists on a pack train; the word is a borrowing of a Spanish word meaning the same.

much Very. "She's not much old."

muchacho A Spanish word for a boy or a male servant. *Muchacha* is the feminine form.

mucker See quote. "Within a week he found work [in the mines] as a mucker, shoveling ore into ore carts . . ." [Jack Cummings, *The Rough Rider,* 1988]

mud hen The American coot (*Fulica Americana*).

mud lark See SLOW BEAR.

muffle jaw The rocky Mountain freshwater fish *Cottus semiscaber.*

mug To hold a cow by putting an arm around its head and placing one hand on its nose and the other around its neck.

mule deer A small, long-eared, 3½-foot-high deer (*Odocoileus hemionus*) of western North America. Also called *burro deer.*

mule-ears Cowboy boots featuring straps on the top to pull them on with.

mule skinner A mule driver. Also called a *mule whacker*.

muley A cow without horns.

mush (1) Cooked oat or wheat breakfast cereal served with milk and sugar. (2) French trappers in the Northwest used to urge on the dogs pulling their sleds across the snow with *"marchons!"* (let's go!, hurry up!). This was corrupted to *mush on!* in English and by 1862 had become *mush!* "Dog French," one writer called it.

mustang (1) A small wild horse of the Southwest plains descended from horses introduced to the New World by the Spanish; the word derives from the Spanish word *mustengo* (stray beast). (2) A tough, hardy cow pony of this breed. (3) Any wild person unused to "civilization."

mustang cattle Wild lively cattle.

Mustang Colt The nickname of Republican presidential Freesoil candidate John C. Frémont (1813–90), whose campaign song went: "Do your best with the Old Gray Hack . . . The Mustang Colt will clear the track."

mustang court A KANGAROO COURT.

mustanger One who captures wild horses or mustangs to break to the saddle or harness.

mustang grapes Strong light-colored grapes *(Vitis candicans)* of the Southwest; similar to the muscadine, with vines growing rampant.

mutt Slang for a sorry horse. "Mouse-colored mutt, he was. An' mean." [Jack Schaefer, *Monte Walsh,* 1958]

my ownself Myself. "It's on canvas and I made it my ownself." [Louis L'Amour, *The Haunted Mesa,* 1987]

N

nachurally   A pronunciation of *naturally*. Also *nacherally*. "I'm a nachurally peace-lovin' man." [Max Brand, *The Fastest Draw,* 1925]

nail the coonskin to the wall   Complete something, finish it; an old Texas saying.

nairy; nary   None, never, neither.

nairy a one   Not one, nobody. "Nairy a one came to the party."

narrow at the equator   Very hungry, belt tightened to the last notch. "I got to get me some grub, I'm getting' narrow at the equator."

nation   A word once used in the West to describe an area or territory where Indians lived, the Indian Territory. "We went down to the nation to trade."

national bird of Texas   A humorous expression for a building crane, first used during the building boom in the 1980s.

Native American   In the last decade *Native American* has been much used as a synonym for Indian, American Indian or Amerindian. It is preferred by some though far from all "aboriginal people of the Western Hemisphere." *Indian* itself is of course a misnomer used since Columbus, believing he had found India on his first voyage, applied the name to the people he found living in the Americas. A Native American, however, can be anyone born in America, and the first people known to have settled in America weren't Native Americans, being Asians who crossed the Bering Strait sometime during the late glacial epoch. The term *Native American* was first applied not to Amerindians but to white Anglo-Saxon Protestants in about 1837 when the Native American Association was formed as an anti-Catholic and antiforeign movement. Thus, though the term *Native American* does avoid offensive stereotypes associated with the word "Indian" throughout American history, it has a certain negative connotation of its own.

Navajo   A name the Spanish gave c. 1630 to what is now the largest Indian tribe in the United States. The origin of *Navajo* is uncertain; some say it is from a Spanish word for a clasp knife, while others contend it is from the Spanish *tewa Navajo* (great planted fields) where they first encountered these Indians. The Navajo Tribal Council is considering a proposal to change the Southwestern tribe's name back to *Diné* (pronounced din-EH), which means "the people" and was originally used by the Navajo.

Navajo ruby See ARIZONA RUBY.

the nearer the bone the sweeter the meat See quote. " 'Whether I am thin or not is none of your business.' 'Sure ain't. But like I always say, the nearer the bone the sweeter the meat.' " [Edna Ferber, *Giant,* 1952]

Nebraska Nebraska, previously the Territory of Nebraska, takes its name from the Omaha Indian *ni-bthaska* (river in the flatness) for the Platte River. The Cornhusker State was admitted to the Union in 1867 as our 37th state.

neck oil Liquor of any kind.

necktie party An old humorous term for a hanging; also *necktie social* and *necktie frolic.*

nehkid A common pronunciation of *naked.*

neither hide nor hair *In hide and hair,* meaning "completely, wholly, every part," goes back to Chaucerian times, but its opposite, *neither hide nor hair,* is a 19th-century Americanism, probably arising on the frontier. A hungry predator devouring his prey "hide and hair" has been suggested as the source of the first metaphor, but that is hard to swallow for man or beast. Anyway, the reverse phrase means "nothing whatsoever," and its earliest record is in an 1858 book by Timothy Titcomb, the pseudonym of the American writer Josiah G. Holland, who founded *Scribners' Magazine:* "I haven't seen hide nor hair of the piece ever since."

nester A squatter, homesteader or farmer who settled in cattle country; the name may derive from the patches of brush such settlers stacked around their first vegetable patches to protect them, these resembling bird nests to cattlemen.

Nevada The Spanish for "snowed upon" or "snowy" is the basis for *Nevada.* The Silver State, which had first been part of the Washoe Territory, was admitted to the Union in 1864 as our 36th state.

nevermind Attention. "Don't pay him no nevermind."

never stand when you can sit A cowboy saying common throughout the West.

never-sweat An old derogatory name for a Mexican worker.

New Mexico Spanish explorers from Mexico named this area Nuevo Mexico (New Mexico) in 1562 because it was close to Mexico. The Land of Enchantment became our 47th state in 1912, previously having been called the New Mexico Territory.

Nez Percé French traders named this Indian tribe they encountered in western Idaho the Nez Percé (pierced nose), though there is no evidence that they practiced nose piercing. Why they were so named remains a mystery.

nick A superior or good hybrid produced in the cross-breeding of cattle. "This nick is better than any we've had in 10 years."

nickel-plated Anything good, excellent; the best. "That was some nickel-plated woman."

nigger (1) An offensive derogatory term applied by some to Indians as well as blacks in the early West and up until recent times. " 'The Delawares kept callin' halts and droppin' to the ground to give a listen. There was no place to run and no place to hide. I don't know what they wanted to hear. We knew the bloody niggers was out there and speakin' for myself that was already an abundance of information . . .' " [Cormac McCarthy, *Blood Meridian, or, The Evening Redness in the West*, 1985] (2) The derogatory objectionable word was applied to themselves by white mountain men in the early West. " 'This nigger's throat plumb shuts up at snake meat,' [Hornsbeck said]." [A. B. Guthrie Jr., *The Big Sky*, 1947]

nigh horse A term heard in northern California for the horse on the left side of a team.

nighthawk A cowboy who herds the camp's saddle horses at night, preventing them from straying far away.

night-herding Herding cattle at night. "When on night-herd the men usually keep singing all the time as they ride around, that the cattle may know what is going on and not be suddenly started by the sound or sight of a passing horseman." [Reginald Aldridge, *Life on a Ranch*, 1884]

night horse A horse that is especially sure-footed in the dark and is used at night, usually the clearest-sighted and most intelligent horse in a cowboy's string.

night mare A humorous name for the NIGHT HORSE.

nimble Will An old name for the slender American grass *Muhlengergia schreberi*, which grows wild in northern Texas and other parts of the West.

nip and tuck *Nip and tuck* pretty much means "neck and neck," but the latter phrase suggests, say, two runners racing at the same speed with neither one ahead of the other while *nip and tuck* describes a close race where the lead alternates. The earliest recorded form of the expression is found in James K. Pauling's *Westward Ho!* (1832): "There we were at rip and tuck, up one tree and down another." Maybe the *rip* originally came from "let 'er rip" and later became *nip* because of the expression "to nip someone out" (to barely beat him), and the *tuck* was simply an old slang word for "vim and vigor." Other guesses at the phrase's origins are even wilder.

no beans in the wheel No bullets in a gun's cylinder. "He drew on me when I had no beans in the wheel."

no bigger than a corn nubbin Little, a child. "Why, you are no bigger than a corn nubbin! What are you doing with that pistol?" [Charles Portis, *True Grit,* 1968]

no game, plenty of beef—what the hell, let's eat! An old cowboy saying, referring to the abundance of beef cattle on the range. " 'You can't eat any of that without permission . . .' Cory shrugged. 'There's an old cowboy saying': "No game, plenty of beef—what the hell, let's eat."—Write me up in your surveillance report if it'll make you feel better.' " [Sam Brown, *The Crime of Coy Bell,* 1992]

no how Anyhow. In one of Solomon Franklin Smith's books set in the Southwest in the 1850s, he tells of a woman who was offered condolences on the death of her husband. "Warn't of much account, no how!" she replied.

noise tool Old cowboy slang, no longer heard much, for the Colt revolver.

No-Man's-Land See CIMARRON.

none of one's funeral Of no concern to you, an expression that was probably used in the West long before its first appearance in print in the *Oregon Weekly Times* in 1854: "A boy said to an outsider who was making a great ado during some impressive mortuary ceremonies, 'What are you crying about? It's none of your funeral.' "

none-so-pretties A folk name for the flowers more commonly called pansies.

nonpariel A name for the painted bunting *(Passerina ciris),* a common bird of the Southwest.

noon A term used in the Southwest meaning to eat lunch, the noon meal. "We nooned with the U.S. mule train near Phoenix."

no one knows the luck of a lousy calf An old saying meaning no one knows the fate of an unpromising person, he or she may succeed beyond all expectations.

nopal A Nahuatl name used for both a cactus of the genus *Nopalea* and a prickly pear of the Southwest.

Norskie This mildly derogatory term for a Norwegian-American is mainly heard in the Northwest.

North Dakota; South Dakota These states are named for the Dakota tribes in the area, *Dakota* meaning roughly, "allies," from *da* (to think of as) and *koda* (friend). North Dakota entered the Union as the 39th state in 1889; South Dakota became the 40th state that same year.

norther (1) A furious cold winter gale from the north, often bringing heavy rains, formed by an outbreak of polar air behind a cold front;

chiefly used in Texas and Oklahoma. (2) Any wind or storm from the north.

no sabe Don't know, don't understand; the Spanish phrase has been common in the West since the mid-19th century and is often pronounced *no savvy.*

no savvy See NO SABE.

no say-so of No business of. " 'It's no say-so of his when I drink.' " [Larry McMurtry, *Lonesome Dove,* 1985]

nose bag A California term for a horse's feed bag.

no-see-ums A broken-English name Indians supposedly gave to the minute buffalo gnats.

nose like a blue tick An excellent sense of smell, like a blue tick hunting dog. "She's got a nose like a blue tick—smelled that fire before the flames."

nose paint Whiskey, because drinking a lot of it can turn the nose red.

notch To score or achieve. "He's notched a few aces in his time." It was originally a Western term deriving from the cowboy tradition of filing a notch in the handle of a gun for each man killed but is now used nationally.

notcher A gunfighter who notched each kill on the handle of his gun, though such gunmen are probably more fictional than real.

nothing to him (her) Worthless, unsubstantial. "There ain't nothin' to him. Never was." [Cormac McCarthy, *All the Pretty Horses,* 1992]

not worth a red piss Worthless. " 'They're not worth a red piss and neither are you,' Dan said." [Larry McMurtry, *Lonesome Dove,* 1985]

noway In no way, anyway. "I don't remember noway."

'nuf sed An old term short for "enough (has been) said." Can also mean "fine, agreed," depending on the context.

nutcrackers Teeth. "He knocked out three of his nutcrackers when he fell."

O

o-be-joyful A humorous historical term for hard liquor; used mainly in the West and South.

o-be-rich-an'-happy Another historical term for hard liquor.

obfusticated Bewildered, used in Utah.

obliged Thankful. " 'It ain't that I ain't obliged,' he said." [Larry McMurtry, *Lonesome Dove*, 1985] Also heard as *much obliged*, meaning "I'm grateful," or "thank you."

ocotillo The cactus *Fouquiera splendens* of the Southwest. "[He] led the way through low sandhills to a small adobe surrounded by a living barricade of what seemed to be tall spines of cactus. 'Ocotillo,' he explained, 'makes the best fence ever.' " [Louis L'Amour, *The Lonesome Gods*, 1983]

off-breed A horse with glaring defects, an inferior horse not up to standards. "The boy had never owned a horse, even in this territory where mustangs and off-breeds were a dollar or two a head." [Lauran Paine, *Bannon's Law*, 1982]

off his feed Looking poorly, feeling badly. "He's been off his feed for months now."

off'n Off of. "Keep your hands off'n it."

off one's cabeza Slightly crazy, off one's head, the Spanish word for head being *cabeza*.

oily Mean, tough. "He's a right oily hombre."

oker An old-fashioned pronunciation of *okra*.

Oklahoma *Oklahoma* takes its name from a Choctaw word meaning "red people," for the Indians who lived in the region. The Sooner State (so called after those "sooners" who jumped the gun sooner" and grabbed choice land there before they legally should have) was admitted to the Union in 1907 as our 46th state. " 'Okla-homa,' he explained to Cim. 'That's Choctaw. Okla-people. Humma-red. Red people. That's what they called it when the Indians came here to live.' " [Edna Ferber, *Cimarron*, 1930]

Oklahoma rain A humorous name for a dust storm.

Old Baldy See BALDY.

Old Betsy A pet name for a favorite gun, long used in the West, among other regions.

old biddy A gossipy old woman, a busybody; this term is common in the East as well as the West.

old cackler A derogatory name for an old man or woman. "If that old cackler who didn't have the facts straight could heat me up when I knew he was wrong, then a lot of these men must be fixed so that nothing could turn them off unless it could save their faces." [Walter Van Tilburg Clark, *The Ox-Bow Incident*, 1940]

old man The owner or boss of a cowboy outfit. "We'll have to ask the old man if it's all right."

old man cactus The nickname of the Southwestern cactus *Cephalocerus senilis*, which has long drooping hairs or "whiskers."

old mosshorn An old person, often one set in his ways, like an old cow with moss on his horns. " 'He's one of those old mosshorns who thinks he made it up by himself and he doesn't need anybody.' " [Elmer Kelton, *The Time It Never Rained*, 1973]

old poison slinger See SHARPS.

old thing The customary drink. " 'How're ye, Billy, old fel. Glad to see you. What'll you take—the old thing?' " [Mark Twain, *Roughing It*, 1872]

old-timey days Old-time days, the past. " 'Just like in the old-timey days, that's you, Bick.' " [Edna Ferber, *Giant*, 1952]

olla A large unglazed earthenware crock, the term heard mainly in South Texas; borrowed from the Spanish. "Now he [the waterman] went from house to house filling the ollas that hung in the shade of a porch." [Louis L'Amour, *The Lonesome Gods*, 1983]

one-gallused Poor, with only one functioning suspender to hold up one's trousers. "It seemed so simple in the beginning to run off a bunch of one-gallused farmers and squatters." [Louis L'Amour, *Showdown at Yellow Butte*, 1953]

one-horse outfit Any small ranch or other enterprise.

one-trough town A small town in the early West. "Last time I seen him was down at a little one-trough town in the handle." [Jack Schaefer, *Monte Walsh*, 1958]

on foot A term used for cattle on the hoof; one memoir of 1846 tells of beef that could be "purchased in Missouri on foot, at from one dollar to one dollar and fifty per hundred pounds."

the only good Indian is a dead Indian General Philip Henry Sheridan credited by *Bartlett's Familiar Quotations* with this prejudicial remark so often quoted in old Western movies. But Sheridan said, "The only good Indians I ever saw were dead," which is a condensation of the words of the originator of the slander, Montana Congressman James Cavanaugh, who earlier said: "I have never in my life seen a good Indian . . . except when I have seen a dead Indian." This kind of ruins the old story about Sheridan making the remark at Fort Cobb, Indian Territory in 1869 after the Comanche Chief Toch-a-way (Turtle Dove) was presented to him. Chief Toch-a-way reportedly said: "Me Toch-a-way, me good Indian." Sheridan reportedly replied: "The only good Indians I ever saw were dead"—this from the man whose duty was to oversee the so-called Indian Territory.

on the block   Cattle sold slaughtered and dressed. See also ON THE HOOF.

on the dodge   On the run from the law. "Frank [James] was still on the dodge." [J. Frank Dobie, *Coronado's Children*, 1930]

on the drift   Drifting, looking for work.

on the grass   Out in the country. "Cole Weston controlled the thinking of those who lived on the grass; Barry Madden [controlled] those who lived in town." [Wayne D. Overholser, *The Lone Deputy*, 1957]

on the hoof   (1) Cattle sold alive. See also ON THE BLOCK. (2) Said of cattle moving under their own power.

on the lift   Said of cows too weak from hunger to get on their feet, about to die, on the point of departure.

on the peck   Very angry; also *on the prod*.

on the prod   (1) Very angry. "Stay away from him today, he's on the prod." Also *on the peck*. (2) Said of an enraged animal. "That bull is on the prod."

on the ragged edge   On the verge of. "They were on the ragged edge of starvation."

on the shoot   Ready to fight. "On the shoot. On the shoulder. On the fight, you understand? He didn't give a continental for *any*body." [Mark Twain, "Buck Fanshaw's Funeral," 1872]

open-faced cattle   The famous breed of white-faced Hereford cattle.

op'ry house   The rail fence where cowboys sit watching horses being broken.

Oregon   *Oregon* may come from the Spanish *oregones,* meaning "big-earred men" and referring to Indians who lived there. Other possibilities are the Algonquian *Wauregan* (beautiful water) for the Colorado River and an unclear Indian name possibly meaning "place of the beaver" that was misspelled on an early French map. The Beaver State was admitted to the Union in 1850 as our 33rd state.

Oregon bedstead   The *Oregon Spectator* of May 8, 1851, explained this term: "[It] consisted of two cross-sticks run in between the logs of the houses; underneath the end of each was placed an upright stick by way of legs to the bed; length-wise on top then boards were laid, and on top of this a good straw bed."

Oregon grape An evergreen shrub *(Mahonia aquifolium)* of the West Coast with small, blue, edible berries.

Oregon jargon An early name for Chinook trading jargon.

Oregon Trail A 2000-mile-long route from Missouri to Oregon much used during the 1840–60 westward migrations and called "the longest unpaved highway in the world." Over half a million pioneers used it.

ornery Mean, nasty, obstinate, ill-tempered. "Then my dad says to me: 'Willy, men is ornery, good for nothin' critters, ain't they?'" [Max Brand, *The Making of a Gunman,* 1929]

oro The Spanish word for gold, used in the West for gold or money in general. "I plugged down $500 puro oro on the jack for an ace." [J. Frank Dobie, *A Vaquero of the Brush Country,* 1929]

oryide: orie-eyed Drunk; derives from "hoary-eyed." "[They] roared around the waterfronts orie-eyed with Napa-Valley red." [*Time,* March 9, 1942]

Osage The name of these Sioux Indians derives from their tribal name *Wazhazhe,* meaning "war people."

Osage orange See BODARK.

ought Often used instead of should. "Ought I come?"

ought to be bored for the hollow horn Said of a seemingly feeble-minded person, after the hollow-horn disease in cattle, which made cattle ill and feeble and was supposedly cured by drilling a hole in the horns.

ounce A term once used in California for an ounce of gold dust. "I have two ounces I'll bet on him."

Our Lord's candle See quote "The flowers of *Yucca Whipplei,* one of the most beautiful of all Yuccas, are of a lovely golden hue, glowing in the bright sunlight like lighted candles before the altar, and known as 'Our Lord's candle' . . . After they have blossomed the tall, white stalks remain standing for some time, so that the hills look like they have been planted with numbers of white wands." [Margaret Armstrong and John Thornbec, *Field Book of Western Wild Flowers,* 1915]

out among the willows An old term for an outlaw dodging the law. "He's out among the willows, haven't seen him for a year."

outfit A group of cowboys and their horses and equipment working a ranch. "He was foreman of the G-bar outfit."

outlaw (1) A badman or desperado. This word did not originate in the wild and wooly West, though it had much use there. It derives ultimately from an Old Norse word meaning "outlawed or banished." The Old Norse word became *utlaga* in Old English and was applied to criminals in general, *utlaga* eventually becoming *outlaw*. (2) A vicious, intractable horse that can't be broken because of initial brutal handling or a vicious temperament. (3) Any rogue animal.

out of pocket Used in the Southwest for "absent, unavailable." "I'll be out of a pocket awhile, but I'll call you as soon as I can."

out of snuff Very upset. "He's out of snuff since you done that."

overlander A name for the pioneers who began going west on the Oregon Trail in 1843.

overland stage A historical term for a stage operated on a route to the Far West.

P

pachucos A Spanish word for impudence or nerve heard in the Southwest; also *pachukes*.

pack To carry, to carry a gun, as in the popular old song "Pistol-Packin' Mama."

pack lead Carry a gun, the expression often heard in Western movies.

padre A Spanish word for a priest or monk used in the Southwest.

pail To milk a cow. "It took him an hour to pail that cow." Also *juice*.

paint A pied, calico or spotted pony or horse; also called a *calico horse*. See also PINTO.

painted cat An old name cowboys had for a prostitute.

painter Panther, mountain lion. "Painter meat, now, that's some. Painter meat, that's top now." [A. B. Guthrie Jr., *The Big Sky,* 1947]

paint horse (pony) See PAINT.

paint one's tonsils To drink liquor; also *to paint one's nose (red)*.

paisano (1) A Spanish word used in the Southwest meaning a fellow countryman. (2) The ROADRUNNER bird, often domesticated by Mexicans to rid homes of mice. "He watched a roadrunner as it darted from under a clump of prickly pear and trotted along a dusty cowtrail, its long black, white-tipped tail stretched out, its spindle legs carrying it at an incredible speed. Paisano, the Mexicans called it; chaparral was the name the Anglos gave." [Elmer Kelton, *The Time It Never Rained,* 1973] (3) Sometimes used as a derogatory term for a Mexican or Hispanic in the Southwest.

palaver Talk, inconsequential chatter. " 'Let's teach 'em a lesson, boss . . . To blazes with this palaver.' " [Louis L'Amour, *The Tall Stranger,* 1957]

palo duro The name of a common Texas bush, a borrowing from the Spanish, in which it means "hard wood." It gives its name to the Palo Duro Canyon.

palomino *Palomino* comes from the Spanish *paloma* (dove), the word first used to describe horses of a dove-like color. Palomino is the color of a horse, not a breed, and today describes a horse with a golden coat, white mane and tail and often white markings on the face and legs.

palooka An inferior prizefighter or dumb lout. Mencken in *The American Language* says this word may be related to the synonymous *palouser,* which may be derived from the name of the Palouse Indians of the Northwest. Others suggest that it may come from the Spanish *peluca,* (a severe reproof).

pan Apparently the parent of this verb is the expression *it didn't pan out.* American prospectors during the California gold rush were expert at using metal mining pans to separate gold from the sand and gravel they scooped from a stream bed. When gold wasn't found after the pan was shaken, miners would say that it hadn't *panned out.* Similarly, when any effort, for example, a stage play, didn't pan out, it didn't succeed. After enough literary critics had said plays or books didn't pan out, to criticize a production severely came to be known as *panning it.* Another suggestion is that *to pan* derives from the head, or "pan," of a tamping bar, which receives the blows of a sledgehammer, but the first recorded use of the word in this sense contains several allusions to mining processes, including panning.

panther piss Cheap liquor. " 'Why don't you have one more big old swaller of that panther piss and see if you don't want to forget the whole thing?' " [Sam Brown, *The Crime of Coy Bell,* 1992]

pan out See PAN.

pants rats A humorous term for body lice.

papoose An Algonquian word for a child or baby that was being used by colonists as early as 1633, long before the West was settled, although the word was used extensively in the West. "We had ridden into an Indian burial ground without knowing it. The [dead] papoose had been tied to a tree but the fastening had come loose and the body swung to and fro. It was a grisly sight with its face shriveled up and staring at us, looking very strange with all its beads and ornaments attached to it." [Richard Matheson, *Journal of the Gun Years,* 1991]

pard In the California gold rush during the 1850s prospectors shortened *pardner,* an American pronunciation of *partner,* to *pard.* " 'And you can say, pard, that he never shook his mother.' " [Mark Twain, "Buck Fanshaw's Funeral," 1872]

pardner A common pronunciation of *partner* throughout the West.

park A valley enclosed by mountains or high hills, especially in the Rocky Mountains of Wyoming and Colorado.

parking A term used in the West and Upper Midwest for the grass strip between street and sidewalk.

parlor gun A contemptuous expression for any small gun, such as a DERRINGER.

partial to Favor, like. " 'You like chicken and dumplins Mr. Cole?' 'Yessir I do. I been partial to 'em all my life.' " [Cormac McCarthy, *All the Pretty Horses*, 1992]

partida Spanish used in the Southwest for a party or a group of people or animals. "They rounded up a partida of bandits."

parts Places, a region. " 'I traded in them parts, you know.' " [Larry McMurtry, *Lonesome Dove*, 1985]

paseo A pleasure walk or ride; the borrowing of a Spanish word meaning the same.

passed in his checks Died. " 'You see, one of the boy's passed in his checks and we want to give him a good send-off.' " [Mark Twain, "Buck Fenshaw's Funeral," 1872]

passel Used mainly in the South and West for a group, many; a corruption of "parcel." " 'If [your daughters] take after you, you're in for a passel of old maids.' " [Larry McMurtry, *Lonesome Dove*, 1985]

pastor A Spanish word for a sheepherder. "There was a flock of sheep up there and pastor, along with a well-trained sheep dog."

pater An old term meaning to amble along. "He patered down the trail."

Pathfinder of the West A nickname for John C. Frémont (1813–90),

U.S. general explorer and first Republican presidential candidate.

patio An open inner court or garden; the word, borrowed from the Spanish, was first used in California and the Southwest before becoming popular throughout the United States.

patrón Boss. This word comes from the Spanish (meaning the same) and also from the French (meaning the master of a boat) through the early voyageurs and fur traders.

Paul Bunyan A legendary giant lumberjack, an American folk hero of the Northwest.

paw Kick. "The mare pawed him three or four times before Clara could reach him . . ." [Larry McMurtry, *Lonesome Dove*, 1985]

pawin' 'round for turmoil Looking for trouble; probably after an angry animal pawing at the ground.

paydirt One authority traces this expression to the Chinese *pei* (to give) used by Chinese miners in California, *pay dirt* thus meaning "dirt that gives gold." However, it more likely derives from the fact that it is dirt containing enough gold dust to pay for working it. The expression is first recorded in 1856.

peaceful place Heaven. " 'He's gone, don't worry about him. He's gone to the peaceful place.' " [Larry McMurtry, *Lonesome Dove*, 1985]

Peacemaker The nickname of one of the most famous weapons in American history, the Colt Revolver Model 1873, the name being adopted because it helped lawmen keep the peace in the American West. As an extra benefit, its .44 ammunition could be used in the 1873 Winchester rifle. "Cradled in his right hand in an unpleasantly purposeful fashion was a Peacemaker Colt." [Alistair MacLean, *Breakheart Pass,* 1974] Also called a HOGLEG.

peach and cane land A term used in Texas for good land or soil.

peacherino An old expression for someone or something excellent, especially a young woman.

pear Sometimes used in the Southwest as short for the prickly pear.

peart; peert; pert Cheerful, lively, bright. "He looked right peart."

peckerwood Woodpecker.

Pecos (1) An Indian tribe once occupying the town of Pecos near Santa Fe, New Mexico. (2) Western slang meaning to shoot someone and then roll his body into the river (at first the Pecos River in Texas.) "You better keep your mouth buttoned over in the territory. There is also good shots over there. I would advise you to get into Socorro below the Panhandle across the Grande, but down there you might get yourself Pecosed." [Charles O. Locke, *The Hell Bent Kid,* 1957]

Pecos Bill A legendary folk hero of the Southwest, whose range-riding cowboy exploits rival the exploits of Paul Bunyan in the Northwest lumber camps.

peculiar domestic institution A name given by non-Mormons to Mormon polygamy.

Pedernales The river's name is pronounced *Per-dnal-iss* by Texans.

peeler A cowboy; a BRONCO-BUSTER; a teamster, driver.

peel out of To take off. " 'Peel out of that shirt . . . I said peel out of that shirt or I'll rip it off you. *Now!* " [Lauran Paine, *Custer Meadow,* 1988]

peepstone (1) The magic glasses Joseph Smith is said to have used to read the golden plates containing the *Book of Mormon.* (2) Any stone with magical properties.

pelado First referring to any poor ignorant Mexican, this Southwestern word is now a contemptuous term for a Latin American or Hispanic.

pelter An inferior horse, a nag.

Pend d'Oreilles The name of the Indian tribe for which Pend d'Oreilles River in Idaho and Washington is named; their name is a shortening of the French *pendent d'oreille* (ear pendant or ear ring) after the earrings they wore.

pendejo See quote. " 'Anybody can be a pendejo,' said John Grady. 'That just means an asshole [in Spanish].' " [Cormac McCarthy, *All the Pretty Horses,* 1972]

penitentes Members of a religious order, chiefly Spanish-American in New Mexico, known for their practice of self-flagellation; short for *Los Hermanos Penitentes,* the penitent brothers.

peon (1) A Spanish word that is used as a derogatory term for a Mexican or Hispanic in the Southwest. (2) An unimportant person.

pepper-bellied son of a bitch An offensive term for a Mexican or Mexican-American. " 'And when I get through there won't be a piece of hide left on you bigger than a postage stamp. Do you understand me, you pepper-bellied son of a bitch?' " [Elmer Kelton, *The Time It Never Rained,* 1973]

pepperbox A revolver with five or six barrels revolving on a central axis that was a favorite of California 49ers.

perro enfermo See quote. "Frank was now what the Mexicans called a *perro enfermo,* a sick dog, something in his center not quite as it was supposed to be." [Thomas McGuane, *Nothing but Blue Skies,* 1992]

peso Used humorously for the American dollar or money in general. "I hope to make a heap of pesos."

peter out It seems unlikely that disappointed American miners during the 1849 gold rush derived the expression *to peter out,* meaning to taper off or come to an end, from the French *peter* (to break wind). This would indeed have been an expression of their disappointment when a mine failed to yield more gold, but there were ample American words available to express the same sentiment. Another guess is that the *peter* here refers to the apostle Peter, who first rushed to Christ's defense in the Garden of Gethsemane, sword in hand, and then before the cock crowed thrice denied that he even knew Him. Most likely the expression springs from the fact that veins of ore in mines frequently *petered out,* or turned to stone. The gunpowder mixture of saltpeter, sulphur and charcoal, commonly called *peter* by miners, was used as an explosive in mining operations, and when a vein of gold was exhausted, it was said to have been *petered* out.

pettish Bothered, annoyed by. "Although Roscoe said little, he felt very pettish about the citizens of Fort Smith." [Larry McMurtry, *Lonesome Dove,* 1985]

peyote (1) MESCAL. (2) MESCAL BUTTON.

Picketwire See quote. "At the end of the first full day in Colorado they came to the Picketwire, the western river with the most delicate name. It was properly El Rio de Las Animas Perdido en Purgatorie. In Coronado's time three difficult and greedy

Spanish soldiers had revolted and struck out on their own to find the cities of gold. Sometime later the main body of explorers came upon them, naked and riddled with arrows, and one of the priests explained solemnly, 'God struck them down, using Indians as his agents, and for their disobedience their souls remain in purgatory.' The River of the Souls Lost in Purgatory! French trappers had shortened it to Purgatoire, and practical men from Indiana and Tennessee, adapting the sound to their own tongue, called it Picketwire." [James Michener, *Centennial*, 1974]

picklement Predicament, (in a) pickle. " 'Reckon you're in a sort of picklement, Matt,' he said . . ." [Ray Hogan, *The Rawhiders*, 1985]

picnic pot A can. See also TIN.

piggin' string The short, thin rope cowboy calf ropers use to tie a calf's feet. You see it between their teeth when they ride out of the chute in rodeos.

piece A short distance. "It's down the road a piece."

pig sticker A jacknife or long-bladed pocketknife.

Piker A settler who migrated to California from Missouri's Pike Country during the 1849 gold rush. Like the Okies of the 20th century, the pikers' nickname, justly or not, became a synonym for poor, lazy good-for-nothings because they cre-

ated such an unfavorable impression. Their name appears to have combined with the older English word *piker*, meaning a tramp or vagrant, to give us *piker* in its present sense of cheapskate, which was first recorded in 1901. The English word derives from *turnpike*, because many tramps traveled by foot along turnpikes, toll roads that took their name from the rotating barriers made of pikes, or sharpened rods, at their entrances.

Pikes Peak A mountain peak in Colorado. Pikes Peak was discovered in 1806 by Zebulon Montgomery Pike, who had been chosen to map the northern part of the Louisiana Purchase, but his badly equipped party failed to reach its summit. The explorer and army officer seems to be irrevocably associated with rocks. During the War of 1812, he was killed while leading a charge against the British garrison at York (Toronto), Canada. The retreating British set fire to their powder magazine, which exploded and loosed a piece of rock that fell on his head. It was at the top of Pikes Peak in the Rockies, 14,100 feet high, that Katherine Lee Bates conceived the words for the song "America the Beautiful."

Pikes Peak or bust Long a Colorado landmark, Pikes Peak became a guidepost for traders in the early 19th century, and by the time of the California gold rush of 1849, Indians in the area had begun to tell of gold deposits on the mountain. Thousands of people headed West to answer the call "Pikes Peak or bust." However, gold wasn't found high in the hills until 1860, a year after the height of the Colorado gold rush. The fortunes made from the pockets of gold deposits found in the soft quartz and sandy fillings of what was called *paydirt* established Colorado as the successor to California in gold mining, but crime, violence, hardship and death proved to be the common lot of the prospector, and most headed back home bitterly disappointed—having experienced elation going up and grim desolation coming down the mountain. In fact, many of the '49ers returned home with the words "Busted, By Gosh!" scrawled on their wagons. See also PIKER.

piki A paper-thin bread made by the Southwestern Hopi Indians.

piled Said when a BRONCO throws his rider. "Veteran buckaroos whoop with delight when a bronco-buster gets 'piled.' " [*National Geographic,* December 1943]

pilgrim (1) A tenderfoot, someone new to the West; this term is first recorded in 1841 but is probably older. " 'Say, what's your name, pilgrim?' " [Jory Sherman, *The Medicine Horn,* 1991] (2) Cattle newly imported to an area. (3) An old term for a cow or bull brought West from the East.

pilon Something extra, a free gift, a lagniappe; chiefly used in Texas, the term derives from the Mexican Spanish *pilón* (mortar).

pin A stake driven into the ground for tying a horse to.

pinch The smallest medium of exchange among California 49ers: all the gold (dust) a person could pick up between the thumb and first finger.

pinny A common pronunciation of *penny.*

pinole A Mexican trail mix of parched corn, peanuts and brown sugar. "Four pinches of pinole keeps you moving for a whole day." [James A. Michener, *Texas,* 1985]

piñon The Southwestern pine tree *Pinus edulis,* also called the *nut tree* for its edible nutlike seeds, which are also called pinole nuts. "They followed him into a room where a piñon fire blazed in the corner." [Willa Cather, *Death Comes for the Archbishop,* 1927]

piñon nuts See PIÑON.

pint A common pronunciation of *point.*

pinto A spotted horse or pony; from the Spanish for spotted or painted, first recorded in 1860. A cowboy who rode such a horse often named him "Paint."

pipeline The first pipeline to convey oil were conceived in about 1862 and with them came the obvious word describing them, which has over the years become slang for a rich source of anything valuable.

One of the best-known oil pipeline of the millions of miles of them in America is The Big Inch, which is actually a 24-inch pipe that conveys oil 1,341 miles from eastern Texas to New Jersey. Another is the Alaska Pipeline.

piss-pot A commode, chamber pot.

pistolero Spanish for a gunman. " 'That old pistolero's been cleaning his gun on this towel.' " [Larry McMurtry, *Lonesome Dove*, 1985]

pistol-whip Originally a Western expression meaning to beat someone with the barrel, not the butt, of a gun—it took too long to get a grip on the barrel in a fight.

pita The fiber of agave plants used for making rope, mats and similar items.

pitch To buck; a horse that pitches is called a *pitcher*. "I worked many a year on the range where you rode pitching horses—they bucked on the northern ranges, but they pitched where I worked . . ." [Benjamin Capps, *Tales of the Southwest*, 1990]

pitcher See PITCH.

placer mine A mine from which particles of gold, or other minerals, are obtained by washing the sand, gravel and the like.

plainscraft The art of living in open country on the plains. "And though their plainscraft might not be of a very high order, it was an old maxim

among the Cheyenne that all white men shoot straight with a rifle." [Max Brand, *Fugitive's Fire*, 1928]

platoo A common pronunciation of *plateau*.

play A party or social gathering without dancing.

playa The sandy, salty or mud-caked floor of a desert basin, usually filled with water after heavy rains.

play cat's cradle with one's neck An old expression meaning to hang. "They'll end up playing cat's cradle with his neck."

play hell sowed in oats React violently, like fields of oats burning in hell. " 'What made you set out for Mexico?' said Rawlins . . . 'Cause you knowed they'd play hell sowed in oats findin' your ass down there.' " [Cormac McCarthy, *All the Pretty Horses*, 1992]

playing Texas See quote. "They're just vain,' Uncle Brawley said . . . 'Vain as peacocks and always making out like they're modest. Acting all the time, most of them. Playing Texas.' " [Edna Ferber, *Giant*, 1952]

play the sober Indian During drinking bouts, various Indians often chose one person to remain sober and look after their weapons, horses and goods; this practice led to the now obsolete expression *to play the sober Indian*, applied to one of a party of soldiers or settlers appointed to do the same.

plaza A word widely used throughout the United States for a public square or open space; first used in the Southwest, it is an American borrowing of a Spanish word meaning the same.

pled Pleaded. "She pled with him."

plews Beaver skins. "A man took chances, hunting small; Indians might happen on him any day. If he kept his scalp, though, he got plews." [A. B. Guthrie Jr., *The Big Sky*, 1947]

pliersman A contemptuous name rustlers gave to cowboys loyal to their employers; the loyal hands used pliers to fix wire fences on the ranch.

plow-chaser A contemptuous cowboy term for a farmer.

plug An old broken-down horse.

plumb Completely. Often used as a modifier in expressions like *plumb full* and *plumb loco*. "When he got into the war he went bad, plumb bad.' [Louis L'Amour, *Showdown at Yellow Butte*, 1953]

plunder room A storage room, an old term used in central Texas.

pocketbook Wallet. " 'You throw your pocketbook up in the air, I'll put a hole in it,' he said." [Cormac McCarthy, *All the Pretty Horses*, 1992]

pocket-miner See quote. "Old Slug was a pocket-miner. [He] always in-

sisted that these pockets of gold existed mainly in Nevada country. There the hills were dotted with pine and hemlock, and the underbrush is thickened with creeping vines. Beneath this covering of verdure are quartz ledges, gravel deposits, and pockets of gold." [Sam Davis, "The Pocket-Miner," 1886]

pogonip An icy winter fog that forms in Western mountain valleys, especially in Nevada, the heavy fog often blocking the sun for days and appearing like a fine snow; the Shoshonean word *pogonip* has been translated as "white death," the fog thought to cause pneumonia.

point man See RIDE POINT.

poke (1) A wallet or purse, a supply of money. ". . . I had me a little poke and got into a game of, uh, chance an' put a bit more into my poke." [Frank Roderus, *Hell Creek Cabin*, 1979] (2) An act of sexual intercourse. " 'I'm a woman, and I'm right here. You could have the pokes, if that's all it is.' " [Larry McMurtry, *Lonesome Dove*, 1985]

pokomoo An originally Indian name for the poisonous black widow spider that is now heard mainly in parts of California. In the past, California Indians sometimes dipped their arrowheads in the poison of this spider.

polecat The ornery *polecat* is not an invention of the American West. This close relative of the skunk was so-named five centuries ago; the *pole* in its name is a corruption of the French *poule* (chicken), making it a cat that likes chicken and likes to raid chicken coops to get them. In Western speech, a despicable person is often called a polecat. "Stand up on your legs, you polecat, and say you're a liar!" [Owen Wiser, *The Virginian*, 1902]

poncho A blanketlike coat with a slit in the middle for the head that cowboys borrowed from the Mexican vaqueros, who in turn took the word *poncho* from the South American Araucan Indians, the inventors of the garment.

pond monkey Lumberjack talk for a worker who guides logs down a river, leaping from one log to another breaking up logjams.

pony; pony express The *pony* is related to the young chicken, though only in language. Both words have their roots in the Latin word *pullus* (a young animal), which yielded the French *poulet* (a young fowl), this becoming the English *pullet* and the French *poulenet* (a young horse), which in turn became the Scottish *powney* and then the English *pony*. The *pony express*, more often called simply the *pony* at the time, was the common designation for the Central Overland Pony Express Company, which lasted only from April 3, 1860, to October 24, 1861, but is still operating in Western novels and films. It had 190 stations along its route between Missouri and California, riders, including Buffalo Bill Cody, changing swift Indian ponies

at each station and riding on with the mail—often through bad weather and Indian ambushes. The record for its 2,000-mile run was seven days, seventeen hours, but it couldn't beat the telegraph that connected East and West in 1861, and the pony express went out of business that year.

pook A word originally used by the Mojave Indians for a kind of wampum or money.

poor doe An old name for tough, lean venison.

poorly In poor health. " 'Truth is, I'm mighty poorly. Don't see how I'll get through the winter.' " [Fred Grove, *Search for the Breed*, 1986]

pop Commonly used for a carbonated soft drink.

porch More commonly used in the West than any synonym, such as *piazza*, though *veranda* is common in the Texas Panhandle.

portal A Spanish word used in the Southwest for a porch.

Portlander A native of Portland, Oregon or Portland, Maine.

Port Orford cedar A large Western evergreen tree (*Chamaecyparis lawsoniana*) named for Port Orford, Oregon, where it was first found.

possibles An old expression that means small personal property, guns, ammunitions, tobacco and the like.

"The hermit appeared darkly in the door. 'Just stay with me,' he said . . . 'Bring ye bed, bring ye possibles.' " [Cormac McCarthy, *Blood Meridian, or, The Evening Redness in the West,* 1985]

possum belly A cowhide slung underneath a chuck wagon to carry cooking utensils or wood or cowchips for fuel. Also called a *bitch,* a *cooney* and a *caboose.*

possum plum See BLACK PERSIMMON.

potlatch A ceremonial festival of American Indians of the Pacific Coast at which gifts are bestowed on the guests in a show of wealth that the guests later try to outdo.

potrero The borrowing of a Spanish word for pasture or meadow; sometimes also found in place names.

pourdown A term heard in California for a very heavy rain, a downpour.

powder-burnin' contest A long gunfight.

Powder River! Let 'er buck! A slogan of encouragement used since about 1893, when it was said to have originated as a joke by a cowboy who drove horses across the almost dry Powder River near Caspar, Wyoming. It later became a battle cry among Wyoming volunteers and then all troops in the Argonne during World War I. There is controversy about the phrase, some contending that it first applied to the Platte River, not the Powder River. As a character notes in James A. Michener's *Centennial* (1974): "The full challenge was 'Powder River, let 'er buck. A mile wide and an inch deep. Too thin to plow, too thick to drink. Runs uphill all the way from Texas.' Today, wherever rodeos are held, the cowboy who draws the toughest bronco shouts as he leaves the chute, 'Powder River! Let 'er buck!' So do drunks entering strange bars . . . Wyoming is divided across the middle on this one. Those in the north are sure that the phrase belongs to the Powder; those in the south claim it for their Platte, and each side is ready to fight. My own guess is that the words go far back in history and were probably applied to the Platte years before the Powder was discovered. But I am not brave enough to say so in print." " 'Powder River let 'er buck!' Blue used to say—I never did know what he meant by it but it sounded good at the time." [Larry McMurtry, *Buffalo Girls,* 1990]

power An old term meaning a large number of. "He got a power of hogs."

powerful sight of A great deal of. " 'Takes a powerful sight of work, ranching.' " [Edna Ferber, *Giant,* 1952]

pozo A well or spring; borrowed from Spanish and used mainly in the Southwest.

prairie beef A buffalo; buffalo meat.

prairie chicken Two birds of the Western prairies: (1) *Tympanuchus cupido* (the greater prairie chicken); (2) *Tympanuchus pallidicinctus* (the lesser prairie chicken).

prairie dog Any of several burrowing rodents with a barklike cry, especially *Cynomys ludovicianus,* of the Western prairies. *Prairie dog* was one of the some 1,528 names given to animals, plants and places observed on the Lewis and Clark Expedition into the Louisiana Territory in 1803—this said to be a record in vocabulary-making. Captain Meriwether Lewis had first called the animal a *barking squirrel,* but this probably more accurate description was changed to *prairie dog* by his friend William Clark.

prairie eel A joking name for any snake.

prairie lawyer An old humorous term for a grey wolf, regarded as a clever, impudent nuisance.

prairie oysters; mountain oysters In a country where the prudish have called the bull "a cow's father," "a cow creature," "a male cow," "a Jonathan," and "a gentleman cow," it is no wonder that there are so many euphemisms for bull's testicles. In French and Spanish restaurants, bull's balls are sometimes called just that on the menus, but in America, when they are offered, they're invariably labeled either "prairie oysters," "MOUNTAIN OYSTERS," "Rocky Mountain oysters" or "Spanish kidneys." Believed to be an elevating aphrodisiac dish despite their low origins, they are probably no more than a psychological aphrodisiac. But French neurologist Charles Brown-Dequard, who founded the much disputed "science" of organotherapy in 1889, thought differently. He claimed that both he and his patients had greatly enhanced their sexual prowess by eating bull's testicles. The 70-year-old scientist went so far as to transplant bull's testicles under the abdominal walls of patients, but it has since been established that testicles cannot store sex hormones such as testosterone and that when transplanted they wither and die.

prairie schooner A type of covered wagon, similar to but smaller than the Conestoga wagon, used by settlers on the way West. Also called FORE-AND-AFTER.

prairie shark An old term for a nondescript breed of hog.

prairie smoke See quote. "Ellen . . . began pulling up the russet pink flowers of prairie smoke . . ." [Thomas McGuane, *Keep The Change,* 1989]

prairie state (1) A state in the West's prairie region. (2) Often used, capitalized, as the nickname for Illinois and for North Dakota.

prairie tenor A humorous name for a coyote.

prairie wolf See quote. "Actually, a coyote was not the same as a wolf, but the Texas sheepman customarily called him that anyway. It was a natural shortening of the old term 'prairie wolf.' This part of the country hadn't seen a real wolf in fifty years." [Elmer Kelton, *The Time It Never Rained*, 1973]

predicamint A common pronunciation of *predicament*.

press the bricks Northwestern lumberjack slang for to spend time out of the woods loafing in town. "I was pressing the bricks for six months before I got the job."

pretty A pretty ornament or toy or clothes. "He leaned way down to kiss his mother's cheek. 'Bye, Mom. I'll bring you a pretty.'" [Elmer Kelton, *The Time It Never Rained*, 1973]

prickly pear (1) A cactus of the genus *Opuntia* with showy, usually yellow, flowers and edible fruit. (2) The fruit of the prickly pear cactus.

Pride of the West A nickname for Cincinnati, Ohio, coined at a time when the city was considered to be far west.

prime The best of its kind. "He chewed on it and swallowed . . . 'That's prime pie,' he said." [Jack Schaefer, *Shane*, 1949]

privy-pit An old term for any undesirable place. "'I'm supposed to drop everything and go to that privy-pit because you owe somebody a good turn?'" [Loren D. Estleman, *Stamping Ground*, 1980]

prod A common pronunciation of *proud*.

progressive A name given by whites to Indians who adopted white ways and did not resist change. "'[My father] avoids whites, mixed bloods, and even full-blooded progressives.'" [Don Worcester, *Man on Two Ponies*, 1992]

prong A branch or fork of a river or canyon.

pronghorn See GOAT.

pronto Spanish for quickly. "'Tell me when we are to start on the road.' 'Pronto,' said Tommy." [Max Brand, *The Making of a Gunman*, 1929]

pronunciamientos A proclamation, manifesto, edict; the borrowing of a Spanish word meaning the same.

prospector Someone who explores an area for gold, silver and other valuables or oil; the term is first recorded in the West in 1846.

pueblo (1) A communal multiple-dwelling structure used by certain agricultural Indians in the Southwest. (2) Capitalized, a member of a group of Indian peoples living in pueblo villages in the Southwest since prehistoric times. (3) A village, community; borrowed from a Spanish word meaning the same.

Puke Ravine A California gold field.

pull To draw a gun from a holster or belt. " 'Pull, you yellow dog, and be prepared for Hell!' the Cisco Kid cried."

pull freight for the tules According to J. Frank Dobie in *Coronado's Children* (1930), this means "to take the wilds or tall timber."

pulling the badger A common joke played mainly on ignorant Easterners. According to Ramon Adams in *The Old-Time Cowhand* (1961), "[Cowhands would gather round the greenhorn] and begin talkin' excitedly 'bout the comin' badger fight . . . Declarin' they'd have to have some disinterested party, they'd begin lookin' 'round and suddenly discover the greener . . . [Then] some cowhand would give the new referee some advice as to how to pull the badger . . . When they got to the place of the fight, there was the dog . . . Nearby was the tub the badger was supposed to be under, and there was a rope runnin' out some distance from beneath the tub . . . When he [the tenderfoot referee] was ordered to 'pull' he gave the rope a hard yank just as one cowhand tipped up the tub from the rear . . . There was no badger on the end of the rope at all . . . but . . . one of them vessels usually found under the bed at night [a 'piss-pot' or commode]." Also called *the badger fight* and *the badger season*.

pull in your horns Stop, desist from doing something.

pull leather To hold the saddle with both hands in order to stay aboard a bucking horse.

pull out of a jackpot To help someone out of big trouble. "Many a time he had pulled Tom Flagg out of a jackpot so easily that Tom never realized he had even been in trouble." [Elmer Kelton, *The Time It Never Rained*, 1973]

pulque A milky fermented drink made from the juice of certain species of agave.

pulqueria A place in Mexico and the Southwest where pulque is sold; in the past these bars had colorful signs with names like "The Little Hell" and "The Devil."

punch To drive cattle, prod them, to work as a cowboy.

puncher A cowboy, short for *cowpuncher*.

pune To act sick or be ill; this verb derives from *puny*.

pungle An old term for to pay money; from the Spanish *pongalo* meaning the same.

punkin' roller An old derogatory name for a farmer. " 'Them punkin' rollers,' Dan Suggs said contemptuously." [Larry McMurtry, *Lonesome Dove*, 1985]

pup An old word for a PRAIRIE DOG.

pure See COLD-BLOODED.

pureblood A word invented by whites for an Indian of "unmixed descent."

pure dee luck Pure unadulterated luck. "My second was a heart shot and pure dee luck. I'd tried for the heart, of course, but with him running like that it was a chancey thing." [Louis L'Amour, *Bendigo Shafter*, 1979]

puro A term once used in the Southwest for a cigar, the borrowing of a Spanish word meaning the same.

purp A humorous form of pup, referring to the PRAIRIE DOG.

purple fool An arrogant, conceited, full-fledged fool. " 'Then you're a fool, Captain . . . you're a purple fool.' " [Luke Short, *Ambush*, 1948]

purty Pretty. " 'He's standing in front of the barber shop all purtied up.' " [Wayne D. Overholser, *Buckaroo's Code*, 1947]

pussyfoot Teddy Roosevelt appears to have either coined or popularized *pussyfoot* in about 1905. Meaning crafty, cunning or moving in a cautious or timid manner, it refers to the way cats can walk stealthily by drawing in their claws and walking on the pads of their feet. It's possible, if unlikely, that the redoubtable William Eugene "Pussyfoot" Johnson, a crusading American do-gooder, has something to do with the expression. Johnson was nicknamed "Pussyfoot" because "of his catlike policies in pursuing lawbreakers" when he served as chief special officer in the Indian Territory, from 1908 to 1911. Later his nickname, in the form of *pussyfooters*, was applied to all advocates of Prohibition. While crusading in England, fresh from his triumph of securing the passing of Prohibition here, Johnson was blinded by a stone thrown by a crusading drunk.

put a big pot in a little one To outdo oneself entertaining. "She put a big pot in a little one when they came over."

put in bed with a pick and shovel To bury someone.

put up Put away. "Put up that gun."

Puyallup A Salish tribe of Indians residing in Washington.

puzzly-gutted Potbellied.

Q

quaker A popular name for the quaking aspen tree.

Quandary Peak A 14,265-foot-high mountain in the Park Range of the Rocky Mountains in central Colorado.

a Quantrill Any fabled gunfighter or guerrilla; after William Clark Quantrill (1837–65), who formed a pro-Confederate guerrilla band during the Civil War, more to serve his penchant for cruel bushwhacking, bloodletting and looting than out of any sympathy for the Confederacy. In 1863 he led 448 men into Lawrence, Kansas where they slaughtered 142 Jayhawkers, or pro-Union, citizens. Quantrill died two years later after being shot in the back while trying to escape from a detachment of Union soldiers.

Quapaw A member of a Southwestern tribe of Sioux Indians; from their native name *Uqakhpa* (downstream people).

quarter-breed A derogatory, offensive term for an American Indian with one white grandparent.

quarter horse This breed of strong saddle horses was developed in the West for herding livestock; they were so named because they competed in quarter-mile races.

quarter section The Americanism *quarter section* of land was popularized by the Homestead Act of 1862, which said that any settler in the West could have 160 acres of public land free if he could raise a crop on at least 40 acres of it for five years. The 160 acres equaled a quarter of a square mile and was commonly called a *quarter section* or *quarter*. The former term, however, had been used as early as 1804, and the latter as early as 1640.

Queen City of the Hills An old nickname for Houston, Texas.

Queen City of the Mountains A nickname for Helena, Montana; also called *Queen City of Montana*.

Queen City of the Plains A nickname for Denver, Colorado.

Queen City of the Rio Grande A nickname for Albuquerque, New Mexico.

queen of the prairie *Filipendula rubra,* a tall plant with pink flowers growing in meadows and prairies.

Queen of the West An old name for Cincinnati, Ohio; also called *Queen*

City of the West; from a time when Cincinnati was considered far west.

quick draw A contest in which the winner is the quickest person to draw a gun from a holster, fire it and hit a target. The term is now used throughout the United States.

quicker than hell could scorch a feather Very quickly, instantly. "I'll be in his hair quicker than hell could scorch a feather." [*Davy Crockett's Almanac,* 1840]

quién sabe Spanish for "who knows?" Often pronounced *kin savvy.* "Some say it would have been a whole lot easier on everybody if she had divorced him a mite earlier. *Quien sabe,* as the cowhands say." [Max McCoy, *The Sixth Rider,* 1991]

quinnat salmon A large salmon of the upper Pacific coast.

quirley An old cowboy term for a cigarette.

quirt (1) To hit with a quirt, a flexible leather riding whip with a lash of three or four thongs. (2) To hit with any whip or rope. "But Glanton called the dog to him and when it did not come he . . . leaned down and quirted it viciously with his hobble rope and drove it out before him." [Cormac McCarthy, *Blood Meridian, or, The Evening Redness in the West,* 1985]

quit off To stop. "I quit off smoking."

quit the flats To leave a place, to leave the country. "He quit the flats after he shot Curly."

R

rabbit bush See quote. "The sandy soil of the plain . . . was splotched with masses of blooming rabbit brush,—that olive-coloured plant that grows in high waves like a tossing sea, at this season covered with a thatch of bloom, yellow as gorse, or orange like marigolds." [Willa Cather, *Death Comes for the Archbishop,* 1927]

rabbit roundup A hunt for jackrabbits in an area overrun with them.

rackabone An old-fashioned word meaning a very skinny person, a rack of bones.

rag city A name prospectors gave to the tent cities that sprang up in the West during the gold rush years.

rag house A historical Western term for an early Western shanty or house fashioned in large part from rags; also a *rag shanty.*

rag-tag-and-bobtail Poor, disheveled. " 'The Army has never made a practice of letting every rag-tag-and-bobtail frontier loafer dictate its policies.' " [Luke Short, *Ambush,* 1948]

rain belt theory An old theory that the arid regions of the West would receive adequate rainfall as soon as extensive agriculture was begun there.

rainbow cactus The colorful Southwestern red-and-white-spined cactus *Echinocerus rigidissimus.*

raining pitchforks and bull yearlings A term used in Texas for raining very heavily.

raise billy hell Make a big fuss or commotion. "She raised all billy hell about the ruined curtains."

raise Cain To indulge in noisy disorder, raise hell; often heard in the West but national in usage.

raised on sour milk Said of someone with a nasty, cranky disposition.

raise hair An old expression from frontier times meaning to scalp, a practice of both whites and Indians.

raise the fog To celebrate boisterously, noisily. "We really raised the fog last night."

raising Breeding, manners. "Don't you forget your raisin'."

ramada An open shelter with a thatched, dome-shaped roof; from the borrowing of a Spanish word meaning "an arbor."

rambling Leaving, moving on. " 'No, I'll be rambling,' said Joe." [Max Brand, *Shotgun Law,* 1931]

ramrod A boss, the cowboy in charge of a herd on the trail.

ranch (1) A place maintained for raising livestock under range conditions. (2) In the western U.S., a large farm used to raise one kind of crop or animal, such as a fish ranch or an avocado ranch. (3) A dude ranch. (4) A ranch house. From the Spanish *rancho,* which originally meant a soldier's messhall.

ranch brand See ROAD BRAND.

ranch egg A Western term for a fresh egg.

rancher Someone who owns and operates a RANCH.

ranchero A Spanish word used in the Southwest for a cowboy.

ranchette This recent term, dating only to the 1950s, means a small ranch of a few acres.

ranch hand A cowboy on a RANCH.

ranch house The place where a ranch owner lives.

rancho Mexican-Spanish for a ranch. "The *rancho* was like a little town, with all its stables, corrals, and stake fences." [Willa Cather, *Death Comes for the Archbishop,* 1927]

rangeland Grazing land for cattle. "Sometimes the rangeland's lonesome an' sometimes it's kind o' green." [S. Omar Barker, "Draggin' in the Tree" in *Buckaroo Ballads,* 1928]

ranger Short for a TEXAS RANGER.

range rider Cowboy, first recorded in 1890.

range wars Armed encounters common in the 19th-century West over conflicting claims to the ownership or use of cattle ranges.

ranikaboo A term for a caper or prank heard in the Southwest.

ranny A top cowhand, short for *ranahan* meaning the same. "Roy was a mighty tough ranny who'd been ramrodden' a big spread down thataway . . ." [Louis L'Amour, *Showdown at Yellow Butte,* 1958]

ransation An old term for spiritual excitement at a revival meeting.

Rapaho A shortening of "Arapaho Indian," a tribe of American Indians of the Colorado plains now residing in Colorado and Wyoming.

rattler Short for a rattlesnake; a term that originated in the West, where the snake is abundant.

rattler-mean As mean and dangerous as a rattlesnake. " 'You watch that Dornie . . . he's rattler-mean.' " [Louis L'Amour, *Showdown at Yellow Butte,* 1953]

Rattlesnake Buttes A landmark in Colorado infested with myriad poisonous snakes. "Rattlesnake Buttes! A thousand westward travelers would remark about them in their diaries: 'Yesterday from a grate distance we seen the Rattlesnake Butes they was like everybody said tall like castels in Yurope and you could see them all day and wundered who will be bit by the snakes like them folks from Missuri?' " [James A. Michener, *Centennial*, 1974] See WATER-MILLION.

rattlesnake killer A nickname for the ROADRUNNER.

raw-heels A name old hands gave to new arrivals during the California gold rush of 1849 because these *tenderfeet* weren't used to wearing boots, which chafed their heels. See also TENDERFOOT.

rawhide (1) Tease. "He really rawhided him." (2) To gather cattle alone on the range. (3) Another name for a cowboy.

rawhide artist A cowboy especially skilled in using a branding iron.

Rawhide State A nickname for Texas.

rawhide Texan A very tough, rough Texan.

raw land Uncleared or uncultivated land.

raw one An untamed or green pony.

reach Go for the revolver holstered at one's side. "Each man 'reached'. Musset drew a fraction quicker and Grumble was a dead man. This was in 1857." [J. Frank Dobie, *Coronado's Children*, 1930]

the real McCoy Livestock trader Joe McCoy bought most of Abilene, Kansas for $4,250 in 1867 after a railroad spur was put into the town and became the first cattle king, running long horns from Texas to the railhead and shipping them East. He has been suggested as the McCoy of the expression the real McCoy, meaning the real thing, though this derivation is far from certain and there are other more likely candidates.

rebel yell; Texas yell A leading expert believes that the *rebel yell*, or *yalo*, originally used in combat in the Civil War and intended to strike terror into the hearts of the enemy, came from the Creek Indians, loosely combining "the turkey gobbler's cry with a series of yelps." The high-pitched, blood-chilling yell was borrowed by Texans and adopted for their *Texas yell*, but others say the Texans got their yell from the Comanche Indians. In any case, everyone agrees that the "Yah-hoo" or "Yaaaaaheee" of fiction writers sounds nothing like the rebel yell. Several experts believe it is a corruption of the Old English foxhunting cry *"tally ho!"*

rebozo The Spanish word for a woman's long woven scarf or shawl worn over the head and shoulders.

"Her straight back outlined itself strongly under her clean bright blue cotton rebozo." [Katherine Anne Porter, "Maria Concepción," 1922]

reckon Think, suppose, guess, believe. "I reckon he's gone to Houston."

red assed Cowboy talk for being in a bad mood. "He's real red-assed today."

red brothers; red brethren; red men; red children Names given to American Indians by Western settlers. See also REDSKIN.

red devil See REDSKIN.

red dog (1) A historical name for unreliable, frequently worthless Western banks that often failed. (2) A mixed alcoholic drink made with tomato juice. " 'If you're the bartender, make me a red dog,' Karla said." [Larry McMurtry, *Texasville*, 1987]

redeye Cheap, potent whiskey.

Red River country The area around the Red River in northeast Texas.

redskin A term invented by white men, who are not really white, for all Indians, who are not really red, in about 1699, long before whites went West. *Red man* is first recorded in 1725 and the derogatory *red devil* in 1834, all before the West was "won."

redwood The giant tree species *Sequoia sempervirens* of California and Oregon; one specimen growing in California's Redwood National Park is the tallest tree in the world at 373 feet.

reefin' Raking a horse's sides with one's spurs.

refried beans See FRIJOLES REFRITOS.

relocation center A place to which Japanese-American citizens on the West Coast were unjustly removed by the U.S. government during World War II because they were thought at the time to be security risks.

remblings An old-fashioned word for *remnants*.

remember the Alamo! The rallying cry of the troops under Sam Houston at the Battle of San Jacinto. The ALAMO itself, in San Antonio, Texas, took its name from the Spanish *alamo* (cottonwood tree), the fortress situated in a grove of alamo trees.

Remington A popular Western revolver introduced in the West in about 1870 by the Remington Arms Company.

remuda A group of corralled saddle horses from which cowboys choose their mounts for the day; from the Spanish *remudar* (to change). "The remuda became restless, and Newt drove over to help . . ." [Larry McMurtry, *Lonesome Dove*, 1985]

rendezvous (1) To bring cattle together in one place. "We rendezvoused the cattle near Newton." (2) An annual summer get-together held in the 19th century by mountain men to sell furs, buy supplies and generally have a good time.

rep A representative of a ranch at events such as a round-up or rodeo.

reservation A tract of land set aside for the use of an Indian tribe; the word was first used in this sense in the East.

reserve Reservation, used especially among Indians in Canada and the Northwest. "It was a common enough theme in novels and movies. Indian leaves the traditional world of the reserve, goes to the city, and is destroyed. Indian leaves the traditional world of the reserve, is exposed to white culture, and becomes trapped between two worlds. Indian leaves the traditional world of the reserve, gets an education, and is shunned by his tribe." [Thomas King, *Green Grass, Running Water,* 1993]

return address Cowboy slang for a cow's or horse's brand.

riata; reata A lariat or rope; from the Spanish *reata* meaning the same.

ribbons Reins. "Take the ribbons on a main-line [stagecoach] run and remember every mile what's in the coach is more important than you . . ." [Jack Schaefer, *First Blood,* 1953]

ricos Used in the Southwest for rich or wealthy, the borrowing of a Spanish word meaning the same.

ride a line To ride a prescribed boundary, preventing cattle from straying over it.

ridden hard and put away A person who looks like he has lived a hard life.

ride close herd on To *close herd* literally means to keep cattle close together, compact; thus *to ride close herd on something* is to pay close attention to it, not to let it get far out of your sight or out of hand. "He rode close herd on that plan from the start."

ride herd (1) To guard cattle in the open or on the trail. "He rode herd on 3,000 cattle." (2) To court a woman. (3) To keep close watch on anything.

ride him, cowboy! A cheer commonly given to cowboys riding a bucking horse, especially in rodeos. " 'Ten thousand damnations!' roared Pendleton. 'Get his head up. Stick your spurs into him! Ride him like a man!' 'Ride him, cowboy!' screeched the child in the street." [Max Brand, *Rogue Mustang,* 1932]

ride mail A historical term meaning to carry the mail from one place to another.

ride over that trail again To explain something again, make it clearer.

ride point To ride at the head of a herd, directing the cattle and setting the pace; these riders were called *point men.*

ride shotgun See SIT SHOTGUN.

ride the chuck line Said of a cowboy riding from camp to camp when out of work, getting a meal (chuck) or a few meals at each and then riding on.

ride the fence To patrol the fence surrounding a cattle ranch, keeping it in good repair.

ride the long trail See   GREAT ROUNDUP

ride the owlhoot trail To be an outlaw, to ride at night as an outlaw. Also *ride the hoot-owl trail.*

ride the skin off To ride fast. "You better start riding the skin off that horse of yours before them Indians get here."

ride to the last roundup To die. "I'll be ninety-five soon, I'm getting ready to ride to the last roundup."

ride trail To drive cattle; also called *to ride on trail.*

ridge-runner A wild horse that stations itself on a high ridge to watch for danger and warn the herd.

ridiculous Ridiculously, outrageously. "Those girls behaved ridiculous."

riding out of town with nothing but a head Having a bad hangover from the night before.

riffle (1) A rapid in a stream caused by a shoal or reef. (2) A shoal or reef.

right Very. "It's right interesting."

right around About. "Papa had right around two hundred and fifty dollars in his purse . . ." [Charles Portis, *True Grit,* 1968]

right good time A very good time. " 'Why, sure,' says Stubby. 'I had me a right good time.' " [Jack Schaefer, "Stubby Pringle's Christmas," 1990]

rightly Really. See usage example at SPREAD.

right on the goose According to Bartlett's *Dictionary of Americanisms* (1858), this is an expression of unknown origin used to describe those favoring slavery in Kansas in the 1850s.

right on your drag See quote. " 'The two men at [the rear end of the herd], they're the drag . . . You know we've got a saying here in Texas if you owe money or somebody is after you hot on your trail we say, 'He's right on your drag.' " [Edna Ferber, *Giant,* 1952]

right smart (1) A great deal, large number, many, much. "Mohair's one of the finest filies [fibers] in the world, and it's outsellin' wool by a right smart here lately." [Elmer Kelton, *The Time It Never Rained*, 1973] (2) Very well. " 'We used to have an old accordion, and Mr. Thompson could play it right smart . . .' " [Katherine Anne Porter, *Noon Wine*, 1937]

riled up Angry. From *roil* (to stir up, disturb, irritate). "He was all riled up."

rincón (1) A Spanish word used in the Southwest for an out-of-the-way place or for a bend in the river. (2) A piece of land, especially a small round valley. "He crossed the rincon, heading for the mouth of the canyon that led to the sacred mountain . . ." [Richard S. Wheeler, *Beneath the Blue Mountain*, 1979]

ring-tailed snorter An expression dating back to the 1800s for a very energetic, impressive person; perhaps patterned on the fierce wildcat called the ringtailed painter. Also a *ring-tailed roarer*.

ringtum ditty A Western dish of cheese cooked with bacon, onions, tomatoes, corn and other ingredients. Its origin is unknown.

ripgut A colorful synonym for very coarse grass.

ripsniptious An early term for smart, lively, attractive, grand. "That's a ripsniptious horse he has there." Also *sniptious*.

rip-snorting Wild and violent. " 'We're gon' out, by God, to a brand-new, two-fisted, rip-snorting country, full of Injuns and rattlesnakes and two-gun toters and gyp water and des-per-*ah*-dos! Whoop-*ee!*" [Edna Ferber, *Cimarron*, 1930]

rise An old term for "get along," as in "How do you rise?", that is, "How do you get along; how are you doing?"

riz Rose. "The whole bunch of them riz up after him."

road agent A highwayman, the term first recorded in 1863.

road agent's spin A technique that involves spinning a revolver backward instead of forward; also called the *Curly Bill spin*.

road brand See quote. "The slight brand put on the stock at the time (that is, when the herd is started to market over the trail) is called a road brand, in contradistinction to the ranch brand, which is usually put on the animal when young." [Joseph G. McCoy, *Historic Sketches of the Cattle Trade of the West and Southwest*, 1874]

roadrunner The long-legged bird (*Geococcyx Californianus*), popular in cartoons and so common in the deserts of the Southwest, was once widely eaten and used as a remedy for boils and snakebite. It is also called the *paisano*, the *chaparral bird* or *cock*, the *snake killer*, the *ground cuckoo*, the *prairie runner*, the *prairie* *cock,* the *runner,* the *lizard killer,* and the *rattlesnake killer.*

roaring camp A wild mining camp where there were few restraints regarding drinking, gambling, prostitution or any behavior.

roasting ear Corn grown for human consumption as opposed to corn grown for feeding stock.

Rockies Short for the ROCKY MOUNTAINS since the early 1800s.

rocky ford An excellent net-veined muskmelon originally grown only around Rocky Ford, Colorado.

Rocky Mountain canary A humorous term for a burro.

Rocky Mountain cedar A Western juniper *(Juniperus scopulorum)* yielding a soft reddish wood used for building fences and also called the *Rocky Mountain red cedar* and the *Colorado red cedar.*

Rocky Mountain goat A long-haired, short-horned, white antelopelike animal *(Oreamnos montanus)* of Western mountainous regions, especially the Rocky Mountains.

Rocky Mountain locust A migratory locust *(Melanoplus spretus)* that causes great danger to crops. Also called *Rocky Mountain grasshopper.*

Rocky Mountain oysters See *prairie oyster.*

Rocky Mountains North America's chief mountain system, ranging from Central New Mexico to northern Alaska with its highest peak being Mount McKinley (Alaska) at 20,300 feet. Also called the *Rockies.*

Rocky Mountain spotted fever An infectious disease transmitted by ticks that was first reported in the Rocky Mountain area.

Rocky Mountain states The Western states in the Rocky Mountain region, which have traditionally been Arizona, Colorado, Idaho, Montana, Nevada, New Mexico, Utah and Wyoming,

rod Short for RAMROD.

rodeo A *rodeo,* from the Spanish *rodear* (to surround), was originally a roundup of cattle held once a year on Western ranches. Cowboys often challenged each other at these roundups to see who could throw a cow fastest, break a horse, etc., and *rodeo* came to mean a public contest or tournament of cowboy skills, the word first recorded in this sense in 1889.

rodeoing Participating as a contestant in rodeo events. " 'Why hell, Jack, I don't even thank you *like* rodeoin'!' he exclaimed, some thirty miles later." [Larry McMurtry, *Cadillac Jack,* 1982]

roll Used in the West and other regions for a bankroll. " 'I gotta find a low hound that picked my pocket of a thousand-dollar roll!' " [Max Brand, *Three on the Trail,* 1928]

rolled out flatter than a blue corn tortilla To be cheated badly. " 'Did Monte get took that time? Ye-as, I should up and say he did. Rolled out flatter'n a blue corn tortilla.' " [Jack Schaefer, *Monte Walsh,* 1958]

roll one's tail To travel rapidly, to leave on the run. "They rolled their tails for Yuma."

rope A lasso. "He whirled his rope in the air."

roper A cowboy who is expert with a lasso.

roping rope A rope or lariat used in roping animals.

rough as a cob Very rough and tough. "He looked rough as a cob, like a coarse corn cob, and no one messed with him."

roughneck A worker in the oilfields. "Despite his awkwardness, he had been a popular hand, often taking shifts for older roughnecks if they turned up too drunk to work." [Larry McMurtry, *Texasville,* 1987]

roughrider A term for a Western cowboy often used to describe Theodore Roosevelt, whose Rough Rider cavalry unit, many of whom were cowboys, fought in the Spanish-American War. See also THAT DAMNED COWBOY.

round ass A cowboy who has lost his nerve and won't ride bucking horses.

roundup (1) The driving together of cattle, horses or other animals for inspecting, branding and shipping to market, as practiced in the West. (2) A party.

roust out Turn out for work quickly. " 'Go roust out Sam and Farney, Jim.' " [Luke Short, *The Guns of Hanging Lake,* 1968]

rub out To *rub someone out,* "to kill someone," isn't gangster talk from the Prohibition era, as is so often assumed. The term dates back to the early 19th-century American Far West and has its origins in Plains Indian sign language, which expresses "to kill" with a rubbing motion. The term is first recorded in George Ruxton's *Life in the Far West* (1848), and it is he who gives the sign language source.

ruinatious An old-fashioned word meaning ruinous, disastrous. "The war was ruinatious to our business."

run (1) A stampede of cattle. "We hadn't a run on the whole trip." (2) To chase and shoot buffalo while on horseback. "The Kiowa were good at running buffalo." (3) Used to describe the action of settlers rushing to claim land in areas opened for settlement. "He and his family made a run for their homesteads." (4) Often said for *ran.* "They run after them all week and never caught 'em."

run a blazer To bluff or deceive, especially in a card game. "He had run a blazer on Hadley and won the pot."

run into the ground To overdo something, the phrase first used by cowboys in the late 19th century. "You've already told us twice, don't run it into the ground."

runnin'est See quote. " 'She was the trailin'est dog I ever had, and the smartest. And there was Old Rip; he was the runnin'est dog I ever had . . . Now here's Old Rip, the fightin'est dog I ever had. . .'" [Benjamin Capps, *Tales of the Southwest,* 1990]

running cattle Gathering cattle on a ranch.

run off To stampede or drive off cattle.

runt Run. " 'Better men than you have runt from him,' Boog said." [Larry McMurtry, *Cadillac Jack,* 1982]

run wild as outhouse rats See quote. ". . . their parents were occupied with many different wonders, and they proceeded to invent their own amusements and to run as wild as outhouse rats, as the Kansas wheat farmers used to say." [Max Evans, *Orange County Cowboys,* 1987]

rusher A historical term for a settler rushing to an area recently opened to settlers.

rustic siding Heard in northern California for clapboard used on the exterior of houses.

rustle (1) To steal livestock, especially cattle. (2) To hustle, be active. (3) To hunt or find, as in, "He rustled up some grub."

rustler A cattle thief. This usage is first recorded in the West in 1882. At first the word meant an energetic person, one who rustled up stray cattle for his boss. The word appears to have evolved from "hustler," as this quote from Owen Wister's *The Virginian* (1902) indicates: "It ('rustler') was not in any dictionary, and current translations of it were inconsistent. A man at Hossie Falls said that he had passed through Cheyenne, and heard the term applied in a complimentary way to people who were alive and pushing. Another man had always supposed it meant some kind of horse. But the most alarming version of all was that a rustler was a cattle thief. Now the truth is that all these meanings were right. The word ran a sort of progress in the cattle country, gathering many meanings as it went." Of course, the common meaning of the word came to be "a cattle or horse thief." As a matter of fact, Texas state legislator Bubba London was convicted of cattle rustling as recently as 1983.

rustle up some grub To prepare food for a meal. "I'm gonna rustle us up some grub."

S

sabbey A common pronunciation of sabe. "The Mex looked at him, too quick and narrow for not understanding, but then all he did was shake his head and say, 'No sabbey,' again." [Walter Van Tilburg Clark, *The Ox-Bow Incident,* 1940]

sabe (1) Know-how, understanding. (2) To understand. A borrowing of the Spanish *saber* (to know). Also savvy.

sack Bag.

sacred fire A ceremonial fire kept burning by American Indians, especially New Mexico's Pueblo tribes.

saddle tramp buckaroo A cowboy who rides from place to place, always working temporarily. "You'll be a saddle tramp buckaroo—if I put out the word that I fired you." [Jack Cummings, *The Rough Rider,* 1988]

sad enough to bring tears to a glass eye Very sad.

sadiron A word used mainly in the western and northern United States for a flatiron pointed at both ends with a detachable handle; from *sad* in the obsolete sense of "solid, heavy" and *iron*.

sage. Short for sagebrush.

sagebrush *Artemisia tridentata* and several similar *Artemisia* species that grow wild on the Western plains and deserts and are a symbol of the West. ". . . the air had quite lost that lightness, that dry, aromatic odour. The moisture of plowed land, the heaviness of labour and growth and grain-bearing, utterly destroyed it; one could breathe that only on the bright edges of the world, on the great grass plains or the sage-brush desert." [Willa Cather, *Death Comes For The Archbishop,* 1927] In *Roughing It* (1872), Mark Twain wrote, ". . . if the reader can imagine a gnarled and venerable live oak tree reduced to a little scrub two feet high, with its rough bark, its foliage, its twisted boughs, all complete, he an picture the 'sage-brush' exactly."

Sagebrush State A nickname for Nevada.

Sage Hen State Another nickname for Nevada.

saguaro *Carnegiea gigantea,* a large branching cactus of the Southwest, the genus named after millionaire-philanthropist Andrew Carnegie (1835–1919). One specimen found near Madrona, New Mexico in 1950 had candelabra-like branches rising to 53 feet.

saint A contemptuous name rustlers gave a cowboy loyal to his employer.

sala See quote. "He strode angrily across the sala, the large main room of the house . . ." [F. M. Parker, *The Shadow Man,* 1988] From the Spanish for "large room."

salt a mine To secretly stock a gold, silver or diamond mine with ore or precious stones to make it appear valuable. The expression is said to derive from the practice of dishonest miners scattering a handful of salt, which is the color of gold dust, through mines they wished to sell to unwary investors.

salty Descriptive of an animal that acts up, is a handful of trouble. " 'How about that big red steer today. He sure was salty.' " [Frank O'Rourke, *Diamond Hitch,* 1956]

same old six and seven Same as usual. "He asked, 'Any news in town?' 'Same old six and seven.' " [Elmer Kelton, *The Time It Never Rained,* 1973]

sand (1) The only reference I've found to one meaning of this expression is in Pulitzer Prize winner A. B. Guthrie's *Arfive* (1970), part of his four-novel series about the West: "There came to mind a time long ago when he had been riding with some young, randy harum-scarums . . . [who] had flushed a lone Indian girl from a chokecherry patch [intending to rape her] . . . Their old, their young cries sounded again.

'Catch her! Catch her, Jake, before she sands!' Watching, he saw the girl run, saw her, before Jake ran her down, snatch up a handful of soil, hoist her skirt and jam the dirt into herself. Dismounted, Jake slapped the girl to the ground and got back on his horse, but before they rode on he asked as if nobody in his senses could answer, 'What do they want to do that for? Goddam!' They went away grumbling but agreed on one point: as a book might put it, sex and sand were not compatible." (2)Grit, courage. "He was still full of sand after losing ten times."

sand eel A humorous term for a snake; also *desert eel.*

sand painting This Navaho and Pueblo Indian ceremonial practice consists of creating symbolic designs on a flat surface with varicolored and sand and other materials.

sandstorm A phenomenon of the Southwestern desert. "A man caught in a sandstorm cannot see his hand . . . The yarn goes that a cowboy awoke one morning to find his horse standing on top of a mesquite tree instead of under it where he had staked him." [J. Frank Dobie, *Coronado's Children,* 1930]

sand whirl A sand spout.

sandy Any crooked scheme. " 'They're runnin' a pretty cagey sandy on Bruce McFee, and it's sewed up tight.' " [Luke Short, *Hardcase,* 1941]

San Jose scale A fruit tree disease of Asian origin first introduced into the United States in the San Jose, California area.

Santa Anna Strong, hot, dusty winds that descend from inland desert regions to the Pacific Coast in the area of Los Angeles. Named for Mexico General Antonio Lopez de Santa Anna (1795–1876) who commanded Mexican forces at the Alamo and who, legend has it, later introduced chewing gum to the United States when he brought chicle here from Central America.

Santa Fe Trail An important trade route between Independence, Missouri and Santa Fe, New Mexico from about 1821 to 1880.

santo A carved figure of a saint; from the Spanish *santo* (saint).

sashay To glide, move or proceed easily or nonchalantly. "She sashayed across the room."

save A historical term meaning to kill. "The boys were anxious to lose no chance in saving an Indian." [J. S. Campion, *On the Frontier*, 1877]

savvy (1) To know or understand. (2) Practical understanding, common sense. (3) Shrewdly informed, canny. Also *sabe*.

sawbuck American slang for a $10 bill that originated on the Western frontier. The sawbuck was originally a sawhorse with legs that formed an X at each end, X being the Roman numeral for ten.

sawchips Sawdust. "He walked away through the sawchips spread over the ground to keep the dust down." [Sherman Alexie, "Because My Father Always Said He Was the Only Indian Who Saw Jimi Hendrix Play the Star-Spangled Banner at Woodstock," 1993]

sawed-off Short, less than average height or stature; the term is now widely used throughout the United States in terms such as *sawed-off runt*.

sawed-off shotgun A shot gun with its barrels sawed off short; the gun was first used by express messengers in the West.

say it pretty Say it nicely. " 'Mister,' he said, quiet, deadly. 'Out here in this godforsakin [sic] hole we don't talk to a lady like that. You'll say you're sorry and you'll say it pretty.' " [Jack Schaefer, *Monte Walsh*, 1958]

says which Often used in place of "what" in answer to an unheard question. "Says which?"

scabland An elevated area of rough, rocky, barren volcanic topography, with thin soil, if any, and very little vegetation. "We explored the scablands of eastern Washington."

scalawag Undersized, lean, undeveloped cattle that were of little use were called *scalawags* by American ranchers and farmers in the West toward the middle of the 19th century. The term then came to be applied to disreputable people, rogues, scoundrels, rascals, those who refused to work, and it had a special use in the South after the Civil War to describe anyone willing to accept Reconstruction. As for *scalawag* itself, the word remains something of a mystery. It may derive from the Gaelic *sgalag* (a lowly servant or rustic) but more likely comes from *Scalloway,* one of the Shetland Islands that is known for its dwarf ponies and cattle, which could have been considered worthless. Other suggestions are the Scottish *scurryvaig* (a vagabond), the Latin *scurra vagas* (a wandering buffoon) and the English dialect *scall* (skin-disease). No one seems to know why the word, with so many possible derivations, is first recorded in America.

scalp To remove the scalp of the head, along with the accompanying hair, from the heads of enemies as a sign of victory, a practice of some Indians and whites during the colonial and frontier periods of U.S. history.

Scandahoovian A humorous, mildly derogatory name for a Scandanavian. " 'That's a kind of Scandahoovian song,' said Mr. Hatch." [Katherine Anne Porter, *Noon Wine,* 1937]

scattered from here to breakfast Scattered over a great distance. "The kids are all grown . . . Scattered from here to breakfast and all doing all right." [Jack Schaefer, *The Kean Land,* 1953]

schoolmarm A humorous logging term for the inverted crotch formed by two tree trunks growing together.

scrambled eggs See GOLD FIELDS.

screaming fantods Extreme nervousness. "The girl was halfway between a sweat and the screaming fantods . . ." [Charles O. Locke, *The Hell Bent Kid,* 1957]

scum of the run An early curse not much heard today. "His eyes were like two sword blades flashing in the sun: 'Greasers! Scum of the run! Monkey skulls!' " [Edna Ferber, *Cimarron,* 1930]

sea lion Old cowhands called Texas longhorns raised near the Gulf Coast sea lions, joking that their range was the Gulf of Mexico and that they could swim like ducks. They were also called *coasters.*

sech Such. "I've hearn tell of sech."

seed (1) Testicle. "Charlie split the scrotum. The horse flinched as the seed popped out. Charlie used an emasculator to pinch off and crimp the cord to minimize the bleeding." [Elmer Kelton, *The Time It Never Rained,* 1973](2) Often used instead of *saw.* "She seed the accident."

seegar A common pronunciation of *cigar.*

seen Saw. "If you don't care I'd like to tell it from the beginning. From the first time ever I seen the horse." [Cormac Mccarthy, *All the Pretty Horses,* 1992]

seeps See quote. "There are seeps [in the desert] where in a week or more a few quarts of water may collect. I would go to one of these places, drink a little . . ." [Louis L'Amour, *The Lonely Gods,* 1983]

seepweed A shrub *(Suaeda intermedia)* of Western alkali regions thought to be an indication of water in an area.

see the elephant (1) To see the world, the town, to gain experience in general; the expression suggests someone seeing an elephant at the circus for the first time. (2) An imaginary portent, a warning of bad things to come said to have been experienced by some settlers going West. "Levi went into the darkness to check his four remaining oxen, and out of the shadows rose the elephant. It was gigantic, thirty or forty feet tall, with wild, curving tusks and beady eyes that glowed. It seemed to Levi to represent all the terror they had experienced and all that might lie ahead on the way to Oregon . . . Levi knew he was destined to turn back. He returned to camp, wakened Elly and said 'I saw the elephant' . . . On this trail, when a man saw the elephant, clear and overwhelming, rising out of the darkness with those beady, flaming eyes, he must heed its warning . . ." [James Michener, *Centennial,* 1974]

see the elephant and hear the owl hoot Have a good time deep into the night. " 'Hullo, Hal,' he greeted. 'See the elephant and hear the owl hoot up in Denver?' " [Conrad Richter, *The Sea of Grass,* 1937]

sego A name borrowed from the Shoshonean Indians for the showy perennial plant *Calochortus muttali;* the *sego lily* is the state flower of Utah.

segundo Spanish for second. "During the two years . . . Gault had worked for Axe, he had become a *segundo,* assistant and righthand man to Lew, who ramrodded the spread . . ." [Jack Cummings, *The Rough Rider,* 1988]

seldom Different, unusual. " 'There's something mighty seldom about Piggy,' declared Bud . . . 'I never yet see anything on the hoof that he exactly grades up with.' " [O. Henry, "The Passing of Black Eagle" in *The Best Short Stories of O. Henry,* 1945]

send up Green River An expression used in the Southwest meaning to kill or to die. See also UP TO GREENRIVER.

Señor A Spanish title of respect equivalent to Mr.

Señora A Spanish title of respect equivalent to Mrs.

Señorita A Spanish title of respect similar to Miss.

sequoia The largest and tallest living things on earth, the giant *sequoias* of California and Oregon are named for the exalted Indian leader Sequoyah, who invented the Cherokee syllabary, which not only made a whole people literate practically overnight but formed the basis for many Indian languages. Sequoyah (also Sequoya or Sikwayi) was born about 1770, the son of a white trader named Nathaniel Gist and an Indian woman related to the great Cherokee King Oconostota. Though he used the name George Guess, he had few contacts with whites, working as a silversmith and trader in Georgia's Cherokee country until a hunting accident left him lame. With more time on his hands, Sequoyah turned his attention to the "talking leaves," or written pages, of the white man and set out to discover this secret for his own people. Over a period of 12 years, ridiculed by family and friends, he listened to the speech of those around him, finally completing a table of characters representing all 86 sounds in the Cherokee spoken language. His system, which he devised by taking letters of the alphabet from an English spelling book and making them into a series of symbols, was adopted by the Cherokee council in 1821, one story claiming that Sequoyah's little daughter won over the council chiefs by reading aloud a message that they had secretly instructed her father to write down. Thousands of Indians would learn to read and write thanks to Sequoyah's "catching a wild animal and taming it," in his own words. The redwood tree (*Sequoia sempervirens*) was named for him not long after his death in 1847.

Sequoyah A name proposed in 1905 for a U.S. state to be created from the Indian Territory in the Oklahoma Territory; it was to be named in honor of the Indian leader Sequoyah. See also preceding entry.

serape An American borrowing of the Spanish word *serape* for a shawl or blanket first worn by Spanish-Americans and Indians in the Southwest.

serviceberry Another name for the *juneberry (amelanchie* species). "The blueberry of the northern plains" was dubbed the *serviceberry* as far back as the 18th century, and the name has a touching story behind it. Since its white blossoms appeared almost as soon as the ground thawed in spring, American pioneer families that had kept a body through winter to bury in workable ground used these first flowers to cover the grave.

set To sit; sat. "We set around and talked."

Seven Cities Ancient towns in New Mexico that inspired the Spaniards to explore the Southwest because of their reputed wealth; now thought to be pueblos of Zuni, they are also known as the *Seven Cities of Cibola*.

seven-sided son of a bitch The Western U.S. variant of the expression *seven-sided animal,* both meaning a one-eyed man or woman, "each having a right side and a left side, a fore side and a back side, an inside and an outside, and a blind side." The expression originated in the late

17th century and lasted until the early 20th.

Seventy A name, capitalized, for an elder of the Mormon church ordained as a missionary.

severe An old expression meaning vicious, wild, powerful, headstrong, applied to both men and animals. "He managed that severe colt."

shack Another cowboy term for the bunkhouse. One theory has this word for a small, dilapidated dwelling deriving from the Aztec *xacalli* (a wooden hut), which came into English via the West from the Spanish *jacal,* pronounced *shacle.* Another theory derives *shack* from *ramshackle.*

shanghai The old expression *to ship a man to Shanghai* is the original version of this term. Sailors first used the words to describe how San Francisco press gangs got them drunk, drugged them or blackjacked them and forced them in service aboard a ship in need of a crew. Shanghai, a long way from America, was a leading Chinese shipping port, and many a shanghaied sailor did wind up there. Shanghai became so common in the 19th century that it was applied to anyone seized or forced to work unwillingly.

shank of the day Late afternoon.

Sharps The Sharps rifle "could be fired today and kill tomorrow," said quipsters, in reference to the story that one model could hit a target at five miles. This wasn't true, but the rifle—40 different models were made by the Sharps Company between 1840 and 1880—did have remarkable range, power and accuracy. Hunters called it the "Old Poison Slinger," and it was used extensively in slaughtering the buffalo of America. "Christian Sharps obliged the buffalo hunters by producing a heavy rifle with an octagonal barrel that could stand great pressure. The gun's rear sight was calibrated to one thousand yards. The rifle could drop a full-grown buffalo at six hundred yards, and a good marksman could kill 250 animals a day with it." [Lucia St. Clair Robson, *Ride The Wind,* 1982]

shaving Dealing a card dishonestly off the bottom of the deck. " 'Miner caught him shaving the ace of clubs and carved him up with a pocketknife.' " [Loren D. Estleman, *Murdock's Law,* 1982]

sheep dipper A contemptuous name rustlers gave to a cowboy loyal to his employer. Also called *saint.* See also BUCKET MAN.

sheep-eaters A name for a band of Shoshoni Indians who once lived in west-central Idaho.

sheepherder's delight. An old term for potent whiskey.

sheep off To graze a region out with sheep. " 'But what if you throwed your sheep round my range and sheeped off the grass so my cattle would hev to move or starve?' " [Zane Grey, *To the Last Man,* 1922]

shenanigans Though now it is always used in the plural, this Americanism for "mischief" or "trickery" was first recorded as *shenanigan* in 1855 in California. There have been several suggestions as to its ancestors, including the Spanish *chanada* (trick) and the argot German *schinaglen* meaning the same. More likely it comes from the Irish *sionnachuighim* ("I play the fox" or "I play tricks").

sherry-vallies An old, perhaps obsolete term for thick cloth riding leggings worn by old-time cowboys.

she-stuff A cowboy term for the females of cattle, sheep, horses and other species.

shet Shut. " 'Shet yer trap,' said the man, 'and keep it shet'r I'll shet it fer ye.' " [Katherine Anne Porter, *Noon Wine*, 1937]

shindig A big dance or party that lasted long into the night; perhaps from "shin scraper," in reference to the many dancers accidentally kicking each other.

shine (1) To radiate sexual appeal. " 'That's Dolly Ellender. Sure does shine, don't she?' " [Elmer Kelton, *The Time It Never Rained*, 1973] (2) To excel. "They can't ride for nothin'. Can't shine with Comanches, or even Crows." [A. B. Guthrie Jr., *The Big Sky*, 1947]

Shining Mountains A name the first explorers gave to the Rocky Mountains.

shinnery Any dense growth of small or dwarf trees, especially *shin oaks*.

Shiprock See quote. "And north of the canyon de Chelly [in New Mexico] was the Shiprock, a slender crag rising to a dizzy height, all alone out on a flat desert. Seen at a distance of fifty miles or so, that crag presents the figure of a one-masted fishing boat under full sail, and the white man named it accordingly. But the Indian has another name; he believes the rock was once a ship of the air. Ages ago . . . that crag had moved through the air, bearing upon its summit the parents of the Navaho race from the place in the far north where all peoples were made—and wherever it sank to earth was to be their land." [Willa Cather, *Death Comes for the Archbishop*, 1927]

shitkicker A Texan culture, according to Molly Ivins in *Molly Ivins Can't Say That, Can She?* (1991): "Shitkicker is pickup trucks with guns slung across the racks on the back and chicken-fried steaks and machismo and 'D-I-V-O-R-C-E' on the radio and cheap, pink nylon slips, and gettin' drunk on Saturday night and goin' to church on Sunday morning, and drivin' down the highway throwin' beer cans out the window, and Rastus-an'-Liza jokes and high school football, and family reunions where the in-laws of your second cousins show up . . ." And much more and, with a few minor changes, a culture in many places. *Shitkicker* has also been used in the West to mean a cowboy and as a synonym for boots.

shivaree A noisy wedding reception or celebration usually held late at night at the home of the bride and groom complete with a mock serenade with pots, pans and other noisemakers and good-natured pranks on the newlyweds; from the French *charivari,* meaning the same, though the French word, appropriately, comes from a Medieval Latin word meaning "headache."

shock A pile of hay, haycock.

shoot A euphemism for *shit.*

shoot a mile Common exclamation. "Well, shoot a mile, ma'am, we sure will be there!"

shootin' iron A handgun. This term dates back to 18th century America and did not originate in the West, despite its constant use in Hollywood Westerns. " 'If I was you, son, I'd put that shooting iron away while I was still able to do it.' " [Larry D. Names, *Boomtown,* 1981]

shootist A marksman, one known for his skill in shooting a gun.

shoot-out A gunfight, used in the West since the "Lead Age" of the gunfighter in the late 19th century.

shoot plumb Shoot straight. "Shoot plumb, too. Noise don't kill Injuns." [A. B. Guthrie Jr., *The Big Sky,* 1947]

shoot today kill tomorrow rifle A colorful Indian name for the Sharps large-caliber buffalo rifle, which had a range of one mile.

shore A common pronunciation of *sure.* " 'You shore do, Jack,' Goat said, pulling at a tuft of hair . . ." [Larry McMurtry, *Cadillac Jack,* 1982]

short bit In the old West, the *short bit* was a dime, being 2½ cents short of a bit (12½¢). According to the *Dictionary of Americanisms,* "In the West, when small coins, except the dime and the quarter (2 bits), were scarce, a dime was accepted in payment for anything priced at one bit. A *long* bit was the equivalent of 15¢, being the price paid when a dime was returned as change from a quarter tendered for a purchase priced at one bit."

shorten his (her) stake rope Keep him or her under better control, the comparison being to a horse tied to a stake in the ground.

shorthorn Someone new to the West, a tenderfoot, the comparison being to a young steer.

shot Slang used in the West and South not for whiskey but for a lunch-counter glass of Coca-Cola.

shoulder draw The draw of a revolver from out of a shoulder holster.

shoulder strap A historical term for a U.S. soldier.

shove in the steel To rake a horse with one's spurs.

show a feather A variation on to *show a white feather,* to be cowardly (based on the belief that white fighting cocks were supposed to be cowardly). " 'In this country you must never show a feather. Give up to them once and you're beaten.' " [Lee McElroy, *Eyes of the Hawk*, 1981]

Show Me State A nickname for Missouri since the early 20th century.

Show out To show off or brag. "He's been showing out all night."

shuck (1) Take off. "Sitting down I shucked my small pack from my shoulders and carefully removed my guns . . ." [Louis L'Amour, *Jubal Sackett*, 1985](2) A cigarette wrapped in corn shuck. (3) An early slang name for a Mexican.

shucks! A mild exclamation of disgust or regret.

sh-yit A common pronunciation of *shit* in Texas.

sibley A historical term for a bell-shaped tent used by the U.S. Army in the West; named after General Henry Hastings Sibley (1811–94) and probably based on Sioux tepees.

sick Often used instead of *ill*.

side Ride alongside. " 'Which way you ridin'?' the sheriff asked. 'South.' 'Good. I'll side you.' " [Luke Short, *The Man on the Blue*, 1936]

sidewinder (1) A rattlesnake. (2) A dangerous, treacherous man, from

the sidewinder rattlesnake, so called for its lateral locomotion.

sierra Hill or mountain ranges, such as the Sierra Nevada, rising in peaks that resemble the teeth of a saw; an American borrowing of a Spanish word meaning the same.

siesta The afternoon nap as taken in Spain and Latin America.

sign Tracks, broken sticks and the like indicating the presence of men (usually Indians) or game. "We didn't see any fresh sign of the Sioux." See also CUT A SIGN.

sign rider A LINE RIDER.

Silicon Valley Silicon semiconductors and microelelectric chips are the backbone of the modern electronics industry. Their manufacture is the primary industry on the plain between San Francisco and San Jose, California, which is called *Silicon Valley*.

silk popper A historical term for a stagecoach driver, who popped his whip.

silver baron A rich silver mine owner.

silver bloc The congressional group of senators from the silver-producing states of Idaho, Utah, Montana, Nevada, Colorado and Arizona.

silver king A rich, prominent person in the silver mining industry.

Silver Knight of the West　William Jennings Bryan of Nebraska, who fought for the silver standard and was famous for his Cross of Gold speech at the 1897 Democratic National Convention.

silverland　This was an old nickname for Nevada and sometimes Colorado because of the silver found there. ". . . all the peoples of the earth had representative adventurers in the Silverland . . ." [Mark Twain, *Roughing it,* 1872]

Silver State　A nickname for Nevada, after the silver mines there.

silver thaw　A rain that freezes on hitting the ground.

since Adam was a cowboy　A long time. "I haven't seen him since Adam was a cowboy."

since I was frog-high　Since childhood. " 'Been huntin' my own meat since I was frog-high,' he told me." [Louis L'Amour, *The Lonesome Gods,* 1983]

singer　See CATTLE SINGER.

sing Indian　Indians under torture or in great peril often courageously defied death by singing or chanting; this inspired the now historical expression *to sing Indian,* to act courageously in the face of death. "Sing Indian when Death has the draw on you."

singin' with one's tail up　Being happy, carefree. "He's a rare one, always singin' with his tail up."

Single Star State　An old, obsolete nickname for Texas, referring to the single star on its flag.

sinker　A humorous term for a doughnut or a biscuit, often a heavy one.

sint　A common pronunciation of *sent.* "He sint for the catalog."

a sin to Davy Crockett　A historical expression meaning something exceptional or extraordinary, referring of course to Davy Crockett (1786–1836), legendary frontiersman and hero at the Alamo. "The way we used 'em up [killed them] was a sin to Davy Crockett."

Sioux　This Indian tribal group takes its name ultimately from the Chippewa *Nadowessi* (little smoke, enemy).

sire　A euphemism for a bull.

sisters　An old term for Mormon wives under polygamy.

sit for a spell　Sit for a while. " 'Let me take them horses . . . then we can sit for a spell in the shade.' " [Lauran Paine, *Bannon's Law,* 1982]

sit in the shade of the wagon　Relax, take it easy. "After a hard day a man's entitled to sit in the shade of the wagon."

sit shotgun This expression, now general slang for riding as the passenger in a car, originated in the early West, where stagecoach drivers often had a guard with a shotgun sitting beside them. Often *ride shotgun.*

Siwash Chinook jargon for an Indian of the northern Pacific Coast; considered an offensive term by many.

6666, The A famous cattle ranch once owned by S. Burke Burnett, a Texan who won it in a poker game with a hand of four sixes.

six-gun See SIXSHOOTER. " 'Even a kid like you could be a killer with a six-gun.' " [Max Brand, *Riders of the Silences,* 1919]

six-shooter A popular name for the Colt revolver, patented by Samuel Colt in 1835 and also known as the *Colt* in the West. The revolver held six cartridges.

16-shooting liquor An old term for cheap, potent liquor; based on the *16-shooter rifle,* which fired 16 shots without reloading.

69er A participant in the Montana gold rush of 1869.

skedaddle Run away hurriedly; first recorded in about 1860, it may have been suggested by a similar Scotch dialect word. "You skedaddle back to your Pa."

skeered A common pronunciation of *scared.* "You got nerve, boy? You easy skeered?" [Louis L'Amour, *The Haunted Mesa,* 1987]

skeert Scared. " 'I bet them boys . . . are good and skeert . . .' " [Larry McMurtry, *Lonesome Dove,* 1985]

skeeters Mosquitoes. "Texas even has the biggest skeeters."

skid row The expression, common in all regions now, originated in the early Northwest, where roads were made of debarked small logs called skids. *Skid row* then came to mean a town with these skid roads and finally a disreputable part of town.

skirt scat A mountain man's term for women's talk. "I can stand to men's talk but not to skirt scat." [A. B. Guthrie Jr., *The Big Sky,* 1947]

skite An old contemptuous term for a cross, disagreeable man unliked by all.

skunk in the churchhouse A very delicate situation. See usage example at HAIR IN THE BUTTER.

skunk wagon A colorful cowboy term for a car.

skunt A word used for *skinned.* "He skunt his leg on the tree."

sky pilot A preacher. "Maybe he's one a them walking sky pilots." [Mari Sandoz, *Son of the Gamblin' Man,* 1960]

slab A term used in Oklahoma and elsewhere for a concrete or cement road or highway.

slapping leather Drawing a pistol in a gun fight. " 'I'm waiting, Wilson. Do I have to crowd you into slapping leather?' " [Jack Schaefer, *Shane*, 1949]

slash Flat clayey land that retains water after rain.

slattin' his sails Said of a horse that starts to buck.

sleepers A euphemism for the dead. " 'You need to rest your mind,' he said. 'Don't worry about the sleepers.' " [Larry McMurtry, *Lonesome Dove*, 1985]

slick (1) An unbranded cow or other animal. (2) A wild horse; also called *slick ears*.

slicker (1) A Texas name for a dumpling in chicken and dumplings. (2) A tool used for weeding. (3) A long oilskin waterproof coat; a *slicker roll* is a cowboy roll wrapped in a slicker. (4) A dude, as in *city slicker*.

slime in the ice machine A recent popular expression or catch phrase in the Houston, Texas area for anything dirty, icky, gooey, nasty, distasteful. Apparently the expression originated with Houston news broadcaster Marvin Zindler, who uses the words to denounce health violations in local restaurants: "Sliiii-ime in the ice machines!" According to the *New York Times* (3/9/94), a

Texas governor used the same expression publicly when "served a dessert slathered with gooey peach syrup," lending it more prestige. The president may be next.

Slope Country An old name for the broken country in eastern Wyoming and Montana.

slope out To leave quickly. " 'All the more reason to slope out of here,' I told him. 'You heard what he said. You've got one hour.' " [Wayne D. Overholser, *Gunlock*, 1956]

sloppin' good gravy Good food, a good meal.

slow bear According to an issue of *Overland Monthly* in 1869, "a hog clandestinely killed outside of camp and smuggled in under cover of darkness was called a 'slow bear' . . . 'Mud lark' signified the same thing."

slow brand See quote. "The law further required that every brand should be recorded in the county of its origin. A man who had blotted out a brand and put another in its place was naturally chary of putting his new brand on record. He simply ran it, trusting to get the cattle out of the county at the first opportunity. Such an unrecorded brand was called a 'slow brand.' " [Frank J. Dobie, *A Vaquero of the Brush Country*, 1929]

slow country Cowboy talk for a steep rocky trail.

slow elk Any stolen animal slaughtered and eaten was called *slow elk* in the early days of the West.

slug An old word from Gold Rush days for a lump of gold or for any of several large, odd-shaped gold coins.

slumgullion This slang word for a thick stew was applied by Western miners to the thick red-colored mud of their sluice boxes. It was also applied in the West to a kind of bread pudding and to a cup of tea. *Slungullion* (with an *n*) is heard in Texas for a stew.

small life Lice. "With his thumb he had been routing small life from the folds of his hairless skin . . ." [Cormac McCarthy, *Blood Meridian, or, the Evening Redness in the West,* 1985]

smearcase A German-derived term used in central Texas and elsewhere for cottage cheese.

smechin An old term for a little bit, a smidgen.

smell A glandular substance from a beaver that trappers used to bait beaver traps. "Bear showed me how to bait traps . . . Bear used a liquid he called 'smell.' It was named correctly, for it was the worst smelling stuff I'd ever come across." [G. Clifton Wisler, *My Brother, the Wind,* 1979]

smile A drink of liquor. "We had a few smiles together."

smiler A drinker.

smile when you say that! See WHEN YOU CALL ME THAT, SMILE!

Smith and Wesson A popular seven-shot pistol manufactured by Smith and Wesson and first used in the West in about 1860. See also SIX-SHOOTER.

smoke Shoot. " 'You don't smoke me and I don't smoke you." [Mark Twain, "Buck Fanshaw's Funeral," 1872]

smoked Angry. " '. . . he ain't never been smoked yet. You know, Cactus, we ain't had a row since he's been with us.' " [O. Henry, "The Passing of Black Eagle" in *The Best Short Stories of O. Henry,* 1945]

smooth as goose grease Anything or anyone very slippery or slimy. "He was a con man, as slick as goose grease."

smooth mouth A cowboy term for an old horse.

snake blood Downright meanness. "His veins is filled with snake blood."

snake dance An American Indian ceremonial dance in which snakes or representations of snakes are handled or imitated by the dancers; the Hopi Indians use it as a dance in which they pray for rain.

snake doctor See EAR SEWER.

snake-head whiskey Cheap rotgut liquor; once said to be brewed with snake heads added to the mixture for potency.

snake killer   The ROADRUNNER.

the snakes   Delirium tremens, alcoholism. " 'He died of the snakes four months ago.' " [A. B. Guthrie Jr., *Arfive,* 1970]

snap shooting   Shooting quickly, apparently without aiming. ". . . only two or three of those nearest to the boy saw his hand flash up, with a gun in it . . . and saw the crow, high above them, stagger . . . toward the ground. This was no miracle. It was simply a case of snap shooting that made their eyes start in their hearts." [Max Brand, *Mountain Guns,* 1930]

snatch (or jerk) baldheaded   An old expression meaning to manhandle. "Just let me get hold of him, I'll snatch him baldheaded!"

sneakin' by   Getting by. "We ain't got much money, but we're sneakin' by."

sniptious   See RIPSNIPTIOUS.

snoose   Snuff, finely powdered tobacco; from the Norwegian *snuse* for the same. "They're all like Jarrell—drunken, wife-beating, snoose-chewing geeks with big belt buckles and catfish mustaches." [Thomas McGuane, *Nothing but Blue Skies,* 1992]

snowshoe dance   A dance American Indians, especially the Ojibways, did wearing snowshoes when the first snow came.

snuffed out   Killed, like candles were extinguished by expert marksman in the West. "To be snuffed out by a kid like Tommy Mayo!" [Max Brand, *The Making of a Gunman,* 1929]

snuffing the candle   It hasn't been depicted in a Western film, but *snuffing the candle* was a genuine entertainment on the American frontier. The term is recorded as early as 1838 and referred to a frontier amusement in which incredibly accurate riflemen snuffed candles with bullets as a test of marksmanship. Some (using either rifles or pistols) were said to be so good that they could shoot through the flames *without* putting the candle out.

soapball   The flower head of a Yucca species. " 'Soap-balls,' said Squirreleyes, who had been raised in Texas. And so they were. There was a soaproot growing profusely in all this region, with which Mexicans washed their clothes. From the top of its stalk grew a round fuzzy ball about four inches in diameter, which would ignite at the touch of a burning match." [John R. Cook, *The Border and the Buffalo,* 1938]

soapstone son-of-a-bitch   I've found this derogatory expression only in Richard Ford's novel *Wildlife* (1990), set in Montana around 1960, but believe it is a Western regionalism. Soapstone has a greasy slippery feel to it and is thus an appropriate name for an unctuous character, just as "Soapy Sam" was a century ago. The pertinent quote from Ford is " 'You can't choose who your old man is,' he said to me . . . 'Mine was a son-of-a-bitch. A soapstone son-of-a-bitch.' "

sob To soak, become soaked. "That field is water-sobbed."

sobby Soaked.

sock feet Stockinged feet. "If it hadn't been for Specs I'd have come up in sock feet and killed you." [William Hopson, *The Last Shoot-out*, 1958]

soda fountain An old name for a mineral water spring containing soda.

sodbuster An old word for a farmer.

soddy A prairie sodhouse. "The [collapsed] soddy had been dug into a hillside . . . The other three sides were made of large sod bricks laid in double rows. Grass and flowers grew thickly on the partially caved-in-roof . . . The canvas door still hung askew from the broken cottonwood pole that served as a lintel. With charcoal someone had written on the stained, grey canvas:

250 miles to post office.
100 miles to wood.
20 miles to water.
6 inches to hell."

[Lucia St. Clair Robson, *Ride The Wind*, 1982]

sodhouse A house built of sod. See SODDY.

so drunk he couldn't hit the ground with his hat in three throws Very drunk.

springing heifer A cow about to give birth to her first calf.

sody A common pronunciation of *soda*.

soft as a young calf's ears Very soft, velvety.

so hot we're spittin' cotton So hot all one's spit has dried up. " 'We're so hot we're spittin' cotton.' " Edna Ferber, *Giant*, 1952]

sombrero Spanish for a large straw or felt hat with a broad brim and tall crown but long used in the West to mean any similar hat. Derived from the Spanish *Sombra* (shade). ". . . Gil took off his sombrero, pushed his sweaty hair back . . . and returned the sombrero." [Walter Van Tilburg Clark, *The Ox-Bow Incident*, 1940]

some better A little better. " 'My oh my,' murmured Monte. 'I feel some better.' " [Jack Schaefer, *Monte Walsh*, 1958]

somewheres Somewhere. "He's out there somewheres."

son-of-a-bitch-in-a-sack An old dish made of dough-covered dry fruit sewed in a sack and steamed; perhaps so named because of the cook's impatient cries of "son-of-a-bitch" as he made it.

son-of-a-bitch stew You use everything but "the hair, horns and holler," according to one recipe for *son of a bitch stew,* commonly made on chuck wagons in the old West. All the innards of a steer, including heart, brains and kidneys, had to be included in the stew, but the most indispensable ingredient was guts (tripe). This inspired the old saying: "A son of a bitch might not have any brains and no heart, but if he ain't got guts he ain't a son of a bitch." Sometimes the stew is called simply *son-of-a-bitch.* See also DISTRICT ATTORNEY.

son of a bug-eater See BUG-EATER.

son-of-a-gun Another name for SON-OF-A-BITCH-STEW.

son of a so-and-which A so-and-so, a son of a bitch. "He's a son of a so-and-which."

sonora A term used in California for a winter rain coming from the South, alluding to the state of Sonora in northwestern Mexico.

sons Short for *sons-of-bitches.* " 'Hell, them ornery sons ain't nothing but professional gunslingers.' " [Wayne D. Overholser, *Buckaroo's Code,* 1947]

sooner (1) Someone who entered what is now Oklahoma before it was officially opened to settlement on April 22, 1889. (2) Someone who entered any Western public land for settlement before the official settlement date in order to gain a choice location. (3) A native or inhabitant of Oklahoma, the *Sooner State.*

Sooner State A nickname for Oklahoma.

so poor his shadow has holes in it Someone very ragged and poor.

sopranner A pronunciation of *soprano.*

so ugly that when he was a little boy his momma had to tie a pork chop around his neck so the dog would play with him A saying heard in Texas.

sour belly; sour bosum An old term for bacon in east Texas; called *sow belly* elsewhere. See also SOW BOSUM.

sourdough bread Now known in commercial forms throughout the United States, *sourdough bread,* made from sour or fermented dough, was first a mainstay of miners in the early West, who were called *sourdoughs* because they carried some of the fermented dough with them from place to place to start new batches of bread.

South Dakota. See NORTH DAKOTA.

southwest spurs See quote. "Ladino eased in dulled, four-prong 'southwest spurs' and loped Pete, the chestnut, toward where Buster had topped the spot for equine investigation." [William Hopson, *The Last Shoot-Out,* 1958]

sow bosum   Salt pork. " 'Sow bosum,' even of the saltiest variety, was a rare luxury.' " [J. Frank Dobie, *Coronado's Children,* 1930]See also SOUR BELLY.

spaghetti western   A cheap Western movie, first made in Italy in the 1960s, usually featuring bloody violence rather than plot or character. See also HORSE OPERA.

Spanish-American   A word used since at least 1811 for a U.S. citizen of Spanish descent.

Spanish bayonet   One of several *Yucca* species, especially *Yucca aloifolia,* whose leaves resemble bayonets. "Everything was dry, prickly, sharp; Spanish bayonet, juniper, greasewood, cactus; the lizard, the rattlesnake—and man made cruel by a cruel life." [Willa Cather, *Death Comes for the Archbishop,* 1927]

Spanish dagger   Any of several *Yucca* species, especially *Yucca gloriosa.*

Spanish kidneys   See PRAIRIE OYSTER.

Spanish trail   A road or way used in the West since early times.

spice and tang   Flavor, joi de vivre. "The two of them hammered away at each other . . . thinking up arguments and throwing them at each other . . . I was near full grown

before I understood that was how they liked it, how they kept some spice and tang in a hard life." [Jack Schaefer, *The Kean Land,* 1953]

spike   A name hunters used for a buffalo.

spindletop   The first big Texas oil gusher, drilled in 1901.

spint   A common pronunciation of *spent.*

spit of   The spitting image of. "He's the spit of his father."

spizorinkum   Born on the American frontier, *spizorinkum* was originally used during the 1850s as the term for "good," hard money, as opposed to greenbacks or paper currency but soon came to have many diverse meanings, including "tireless energy." It was possibly used so much just because people liked the sound of the word! In any case, *spizorinkum* is what one etymologist calls "an impossible combination" of the Latin *specie* (kind) and *rectum* (right)—that is, "the right kind."

splindid   A common pronunciation of *splendid.*

split the log   According to Everett Dick in *The Dixie Frontier* (1948), a peculiar way of "banking" gold and silver on the frontier was "to bore holes in large blocks of wood, fill the holes with coins, and drive tightly fitting pegs in them. Then the pegs were sawed off short. This left no way to remove the money except by splitting the log."

spook To frighten or become frightened, especially said of cattle and horses. "That shot spooked the herd."

spooky Said of a horse easily frightened. "My horse was real spooky and bolted off."

sporting woman A prostitute, loose woman. " 'I don't suppose there's a sporting woman in this town, is there?' " [Larry McMurtry, *Lonesome Dove*, 1985].

spread A ranch. " 'I don't rightly know,' Cotton said finally, 'why a man would stay on a spread where he don't like the owner and hates the ramrod.' " [Wayne D. Overholser, *Buckaroo's Code*, 1947]

spring holster A holster worn under a loose coat and situated near the armpit, enabling a gunman to fire faster and more accurately. " '. . . spring holsters are hard to keep in order, working easily, and . . . it's not very comfortable . . . to have a pair of big guns rubbing between your arms and ribs every step you take.' " [Max Brand, *The Galloping Broncos*, 1929]

so dry the bushes follow the dogs around Very dry weather, a drought.

spring poor Said of cattle that are lean in spring after a hard winter.

spud A white potato.

spuds Money. "He's got enough spuds saved up to buy a car."

square up Make right. " 'Come over to see if I couldn't square up whatever's wrong between us.' " [Elmer Kelton, *The Time It Never Rained*, 1973]

squat A bit of land; a claim.

squaw An Algonquian word meaning "woman" that is recorded in the East as early as 1634, long before the West was settled by whites, but is used in many Western terms (including those that follow).

squaw ax A small ax like those used by Indian squaws.

squaw dance An Indian dance in which the women chose partners.

squaw hitch A hitch or knot used in the Old West by trappers.

squaw man (1) A white man with an Indian wife. (2) An Indian who does "woman's work." (3) A derogatory name for an Indian who adopts white ways.

squaw talk Gossip, irrelevant talk, chatter.

squaw winter An early cold spell in autumn just before Indian summer.

squaw wood Gathered firewood that doesn't have to be chopped or sawed.

squeech owl An occasional name of the screech owl.

stag dance A dance that apparently originated on the frontier in forts or mining camps, where there were few women, in which only men participated. The terms *stag dinner, stag smoker* and *stag film* probably all derive from this term.

stake (1) To mark off a land or mining claim with stakes. (2) To furnish money or supplies for a mining venture or any undertaking.

stake horse A horse tied to a stake in the ground, a common practice in Western mining camps.

stampede Cowboys borrowed the Spanish word for a sudden frenzied flight of a herd of animals. It derives from the Spanish *estampida* (stamp, rush, uproar) and is first recorded in 1843, though it was probably used 20 years earlier. A *stampede* is also an annual celebration combining a rodeo, contests and exhibitions.

stamper A synonym for a broncbuster, a cowboy who breaks horses.

stamping ground The home range.

stand dayherd To watch cattle during the day while they graze and drink.

standing dead A name given by firefighters in the West to trees left standing in a forest fire. " 'Do you know what they call the trees that're left up when the fire goes by?' 'No,' I said. 'The standing dead,' my mother said. 'Don't they have an interesting terminology for things?' " [Richard Ford, *Wildlife*, 1990]

standing pat Not changing one's position, refusing to shift. ". . . gambling terms of the West and the Southwest had slowly been incorporated into the language of daily use. In *keeping cases on him . . . standing pat . . . bluffing . . . bucking the tiger.* Terms filched from the gaming table; poker and faro and keno." [Edna Ferber, *Cimarron,* 1930]

stand like a post Stand quietly without moving, do nothing. " 'Just stand there like a post,' Buf said." [Larry McMurtry, *Lonesome Dove,* 1985]

starved rat Another name for the Rocky Mountain little chief hare *(Ochotoma princeps)*; also known as the *rock rabbit.*

stationhouse A place where stagecoaches stopped to change horses in the early West.

stay in the tree! Stay in the saddle!; a cry of encouragement to bronc busters, and by extension, to anyone.

stay until the last dog is hung An old expression meaning to stay until the very last.

Steamer Day The day before mail steamers sailed to the states from early San Francisco; occurring bimonthly, Steamer Day was an important date on the calendar when businessmen and all citizens readied things for the mail.

Stetson After poor health forced John Batterson Stetson (1830–1906) to travel west at the time of the Civil War, it occurred to him that no one was manufacturing hats suited to the practical needs of the Western cowboy, and on his return to Philadelphia in 1865, he went into the hat business, specializing in Western-style headgear. The wide-brimmed, 10-gallon felt hats he manufactured immediately became popular with cowboys and have been called *Stetsons,* or *John B.'s,* ever since.

a stiff rope and a short drop A hanging. "He's headed for a stiff rope and a short drop."

stinger See quote. " 'The black patch [down below] is brush. The little thing moving along [cutting it] is the stinger, it's a kind of tank with great knives and arms and head like a steel monster. It's called a tree dozer, too.' " [Edna Ferber, *Giant,* 1952]

stingy (cheap) enough to skin a flea fer its hide and taller (tallow) See quote. "He ranched on the Frio, and, as the saying goes, was 'stingy enough to skin a flea for its hide and taller.' " [J. Frank Dobie, *Coronado's Children,* 1930]

stob A stake, sharp stick; used mainly in the South and West. ". . . Po was trying to pull a stob of some kind out of his body . . . but the stob wouldn't come out." [Larry McMurtry, *Lonesome Dove,* 1985]

stock ranch A ranch on which cattle are raised for the market.

stock saddle A heavy saddle of 30 to 40 pounds with a strong tree and horn used for roping stock.

stogy; stogie A heavy boot made in the East; named after the Conestoga wagon manufactured in Conestoga, Pa., just as *stogy cigars* were.

stomp dance An Indian war dance.

stoneboat A sled or wheelless vehicle for dragging stones in from a field.

straddle bug Three boards nailed together in a tripod form and used to mark occupied claims by prospectors in the early West.

straight arrow A decent, upstanding person; after an archtypical upright Indian brave. Also *straight shooter.*

straight grain clear through Descriptive of an honest, upright, straightforward person. "He's a special brand we sometimes get out here in the grass country. I've come across a few. A bad one's poison. A good one's straight grain clear through." [Jack Schaefer, *Shane,* 1949]

straight shooter A decent, honest person. Also *straight arrow.*

straight through hell and out the other side Through the most difficult situation. " 'Hat Herrickson . . . Best damn trail boss I ever knew. He could take a herd straight through hell and come out the other side . . . [he'd] walk up to a grizzly and spit in its eye if that come along in the line of work.' " [Jack Schaefer, *Monte Walsh*, 1958]

strapped on his horse, toes down Dead; in reference to riders killed in range wars who were sent home strapped on their horses.

strengthy Strong. "He is a strengthy man though he don't look it."

stretching the blanket Stretching the truth, lying. " 'I think you are stretching the blanket.' " [Charles Portis, *True Grit*, 1968]

strike A sudden stroke of luck or success; the term is first recorded during the California gold rush in reference to a find of gold and was often called a *lucky strike* or a *big strike*.

strike it rich This common expression originated in the California gold fields. See also STRIKE.

string (1) A cowboy's rope. (2) A man's personal horses. (3) A line of fence.

stripper An oil well in Texas and other states that produces only 10 barrels of oil a day or less. All such wells together, however, make up one-fifth of the nation's oil output.

strong arm Physical violence; used in the early West since about 1850;

the term is first recorded as a verb meaning "to use physical force" some 50 years later.

strung up Hanged. See usage example at SWING.

stubborn as a government mule Very stubborn. "At any rate, he claimed that someone had tried to poison him, became as stubborn as a government mule and refused to go a step farther." [J. Frank Dobie, *Coronado's Children*, 1930]

studhorse An old name for stud poker.

study A common pronunciation of *steady*.

stump sucker See quote. "Some horses are called stump-suckers because they have a penchant for chewing wood. Once they get the taste they'll gnaw on stumps, fence posts, boards, and the corners of feed sheds. This neurotic habit is more apt to manifest itself in highly strung, overbred animals than in your common plug. Cowboys universally distrust the stump-sucking horse as being a beast with a mental disorder that renders them unfit for the long-term, trust-laden relationships they like to maintain with their mounts." [Larry McMurtry, *Cadillac Jack*, 1982]

stupid water A Comanche name for whiskey, because it made people act stupidly. ". . . the men of God [on the reservation] stripped the warriors of their very reason for living, war.

They no longer had any way to attain status within their tribe. Whiskey, the 'stupid water' that the People had always scorned, became their solace." [Lucia St. Clair Robson, *Ride the Wind,* 1982]

such a much   Such an important thing or big deal. "Didn't seem like such a much at the time." [Frank Roderus, *Hell Creek Cabin,* 1979]

sugan; sugin; soogan; sougan   A Scotch-Irish word for a coarse blanket or comforter made of patches of material; used by sheepherders, lumberjacks and others in the West.

suicide gun   Cowboys early in this century called the Colt .32 (and similar guns) a *suicide gun* because it lacked the power to stop an assailant dead in his tracks and thus often led to the death of the man who fired it. It was no match for the .44-caliber gun most gunfighters carried.

suit one's tooth   Appeal to one's taste. " 'They eat catfish down there. It got where it kinda suited my tooth.' " [Larry McMurtry, *Lonesome Dove,* 1985]

sull   To sulk; the word is a backformation from *sullen.* "There he is sullin' over something or other."

sull up   Get sullen or moody, uncommunicative. " 'Don't sull up on me. Let's get it aired.' " [Cormac McCarthy, *All the Pretty Horses,* 1992]

sumbitch   Son of a bitch. " 'That sumbitch must be harder than hell

to steer.' " [Thomas McGuane, *Keep the Change,* 1989]

sum buck   Son of a buck, a euphemism for son of a bitch. " 'Sum buck,' he said. 'Sum buck.' " [Cormac McCarthy, *All the Pretty Horses,* 1992]

summer name   An alias or pseudonym adopted by a man trying to hide his past.

the sun don't shine on the same dog's ass all day   Every dog has his day, or moment; the expression is used in Loren D. Estleman's Western novel *Bloody Season* (1987) and may be a Western regionalism.

sundown   A term used to indicate the Far West. Also *beyond sundown.* "They were seeking a new home beyond sundown."

sunfishing   The action of a horse bucking by dropping and raising its shoulders.

Sunshine State   A nickname for New Mexico.

sure as shootin'   An expression meaning "for certain" that is first recorded in the West in the mid-19th century.

sure as the world   For certain. " 'We're fixin' to get the horses snakebit sure as the world,' said Rawlins." [Cormac McCarthy, *All the Pretty Horses,* 1992]

surly A word used in Texas for a bull; perhaps from a bull's mean, surly expression.

surround An Indian hunting method in which animals were surrounded and driven off a cliff into a deep ravine from which they couldn't escape.

suspicion Sometimes used instead of the verb "suspect" in Southern and Western speech. "I suspicioned they were going to do that."

Swainson's hawk A Western hawk with a reddish breast-band and white under-plumage; named after English naturalist William Swainson.

swallow-and-get-out trough An old name for a fast-food place like the restaurants in railroad stations.

swallow the puppy Swallow one's pride. "They asked us was we ready to respect the Government in Washington City . . . We said yes . . . we swallowed the puppy . . ." [Charles Portis, *True Grit,* 1968]

swamper (1) A menial worker, such as a cook's helper, a janitor, a cleaner. (2) A low-level worker on a ranch.

swan Swear. " 'I'll swan!' Myrtle said . . . 'What could have done it, Buck?' " [Benjamin Capps, *Tales of the Southwest,*1990] Also heard as *swanny*.

sweet rolls A roll or pastry made of sweet dough, often with nuts, fruits and icing. "June brought him some sweet rolls and coffee and a carton of orange juice." [Thomas McGuane, *Nothing but Blue Skies,* 1992]

sweet tea Sweetened iced tea. " 'You boys want some sweet tea or something?' " [Philip Lee Williams, *All the Western Stars,* 1988]

swing Hang. "As they were about to be strung up, Red Curly begged to be shot instead of hanged. He was refused . . . and so, with handcuffs on, he and Russian Bill had to swing." [J. Frank Dobie, *Coronado's Children,* 1930]

swing a wide loop To have a free-wheeling lifestyle, do what one wants to do; to be unconfined, cover a large area.

swing rider A rider who guards the main body of the herd.

T

Tabasco The condiment sauce's name, which is a trademark, was apparently first applied to a potent liquor once popular in the Southwest. The liquor, in turn, took its name from the state of Tabasco in Mexico.

tabernacle A Mormon place of worship, especially the Grand Tabernacle in Salt Lake City, Utah.

tail (1) To throw a bull by grabbing its tail and tripping it. (2) To catch a disabled deer by the tail and hold it while killing it with a knife, a practice of hunters in the early West.

tailings The remains or debris left from the washing of gold ore.

tail rider A cowboy who rode in the rear of a cattle herd to handle stragglers.

take the bull by the horns Since the earliest quotation yet found for this expression is from 1873, it seems unlikely that it has its roots in bull-running, a brutal English sport popular from the day of King John until it was outlawed in the mid-19th century. (Bull-running consisted of a mob with clubs and dogs chasing a bull loosed in the streets and eventually beating it to death, a favorite trick for the braver bull chasers being to grab the poor beast by the horns and wrestle it to the ground.) More likely the expression originated in Spain or America. In bullfights Spanish banderilleros plant darts in the neck of the bull and tire him more by waving cloaks in his face and seizing him by the horns, trying to hold his head down. Rawboned early ranchers in the American Southwest also wrestled bulls, or steers, in a popular sport called bulldogging that is still seen in rodeos—the object being to grab the animal's horns and throw him. Either of these practices could have prompted the saying *take the bull by the horns,* "screw up your courage and cope with a dangerous or unpleasant situation decisively, head on."

take the hair To scalp. "The common expression now in use is that they proceeded to 'take the hair of their victims.' " [De Witt C. Peters, *The Life and Adventures of Kit Carson,* 1858]

take the rag off the bush If that doesn't beat everything. The expression, used in the South as well as the West, may have originated with Western hunters who fired at rags that were targets tied on bushes. " 'I made a lot of mistakes in my day but this does take the rag off the bush.' " [Edna Ferber, *Giant,* 1952] Often heard as *if that don't take the rag off the bush!*

take the town See quote. ". . . it was a common feat for him and his friends to 'take the town.' He and a couple of his friends might often be seen on one horse, galloping through the streets, shouting and yelling, firing revolvers, etc. On many occasions he would ride his horse into stores, break up bars . . ." [Mark Twain, *Roughing It,* 1872]

take the long trail for To leave or depart for. "He took the long trail for Mexico."

take to the tall timber To depart suddenly and unceremoniously, a variation on the 19th century *to break for the high timber,* which meant to escape into the high woods at the edge of civilization in order to make pursuit by the law difficult.

take up books To begin the school day. "Am I late? Has books been taken up?"

talking Texas See quote. ". . . these two were talking Texas . . . their conversation sounded like the dialogue in a third-rate parody of Texans. This was due partly to habit and partly to affectation born of a mixture of superiority and inferiority, as a certain type of Englishman becomes excessively Oxford or a Southern politician intensifies his drawl. Each was playing a role, deliberately. It was part of the Texas ritual. We're rich as son-of-a-bitch stew but look how homely we are, just as plain-folksy as Grandpappy back in 1836. We know about champagne and caviar but we talk hog and hominy." [Edna Ferber, *Giant,* 1952]

Talking Water River See quote. "The Comanche called the Colorado Talking Water River for good reason. The racing, leaping rapids tumbling over its rock-strewn bed drowned out conversation." [Lucia St. Clair Robson, *Ride the Wind,* 1982]

talk the bark off a tree To talk forcefully, vehemently, excessively. "He kept going on about it, talking the bark off a tree."

tall country The mountains. "We made for the tall country."

tamale A dish made of minced seasoned meat packed in cornmeal dough, wrapped in corn husks and steamed; from the Nahuatl Indian *tamalli* for the same.

tame Indian An offensive term once used for a friendly Indian who had adopted the ways of the white man, at a time when offensive things like this were done: " 'You get a puppy and hire a tame Indian. Then cut a willow switch and four or five times a day you have the Indian beat the puppy with the switch, and all the rest of his life he'll signal when an Indian comes close.' " [Louis L'Amour, *Hondo,* 1953]

tanglefoot rye; tanglefoot whiskey Cheap, potent whiskey that causes one to stumble. "It was unlike the white whiskey; not so bad, but still pretty bad—low grade, frontier tanglefoot rye, dear at a dollar a bottle." [Oliver LaFarge, *Laughing Boy*, 1929] "He could . . . hold more tanglefoot whiskey without spilling it than any man in seventeen counties." [Mark Twain, "Buck Fanshaw's Funeral," 1872] Also called simply *tanglefoot*.

tank (1) See quote. "There are places in the desert called tanks, where water collects in natural rock basins. Sometimes it's a large amount of water, sometimes only a little." [Louis L'Amour, *The Lonesome Gods*, 1983](2) Not a metal container that holds water but a facility up to an acre or more in size that holds water for cattle; called a *farm pond* in other regions. See also TUB.

Taos Indian   A New Mexican pueblo Indian tribe of the upper Rio Grande region; the name derives from the native name of their chief pueblo.

Taos Lightning   A potent liquor made from corn or wheat in New Mexico. "According to local legend, a sudden jolt of Ol' Towse had been known to stop the drinker's watch and snap his suspenders." [Matt Braun, *The Brannocks*, 1986]

tarantula juice   Cheap, potent liquor. ". . . the Comanches brought in a jug of fire water—regular old tarantula juice . . ." [J. Frank Dobie, *Coronado's Children*, 1930]

tarpoleon   A pronunciation of *tarpaulin*.

tarvia   A term used in central Texas for a paved or "tarviated" road, from the name of an old U.S. company called Tarvia that paved roads.

tata   A title of respect once used in the Southwest for any important man; from the Spanish *tata* meaning the same. "The mescaleros called the president the Tata Grande."

Taxas   A pronunciation of *Texas* often heard in Texas.

taxel   A name for the badger *(Taxidea taxus)*.

teacherage   A historical term for a cottage built near the schoolhouse for a school's teacher; patterned on *vicarage* and *parsonage*.

tears of the sun   An old Apache Indian term for gold, which the Apaches held sacred and not to be touched.

techy as a cook   Very touchy about the smallest things, like a chuckwagon cook. " 'My, you're techy, Bick,' he said. 'You're techy as a cook.' "   [Edna Ferber, *Giant*, 1952]

teeter-totter   Another word for seesaw.

Tejano   Spanish for a Texan, the word often used in the old Southwest. " 'Yessiree, knowed ol' Sam Houston, Bigfoot Wallace, an' all them early Tejanos.' " [Marquis James, *Cherokee Strip*, 1945]

temblo Spanish for an earthquake.

temple A Mormon place of worship.

tender Inexperienced. "He's new and tender at the job."

tenderfoot As early as the 17th century the British applied this word to horses that needed breaking-in before they could handle heavy loads. Next they used *tenderfoot* as a derogatory term for a vagrant. It wasn't until the California gold rush of 1849 that Americans applied the word to footsore people unused to the hardships of pioneer life as they traveled in search of gold. Soon *tenderfoot* was a Western term for any greenhorn, not only one with sore feet. "In my tenderfoot ignorance," Owen Wister wrote in *The Virginian* (1902), "I was looking indoors for the washing arrangements." Westerners also used *tenderfeet* as a synonym for imported cattle. See also RAW-HEELS.

10-gallon hat Although the name is usually thought to be an indication of its liquid holding capacity, the Americanism *10-gallon hat* has its origin in the Spanish word for braid, *galón*—the wide-brimmed hats worn by cowboys were originally decorated with a number of braids at the base of the crown. Vaqueros, in fact, called the hat the *sombrero galón*.

tepee A Plains Indian lodge made of skins and poles in a cone shape; from the Siouan *ti* (to dwell) and *pi* (used for).

tepee on wheels Indians gave this name to the covered wagons of settlers on the Oregon Trail.

Teton Range A mountain range in northwestern Wyoming that takes its name from the French *teton* (breast) because the mountains somewhat resemble women's breasts.

texas The roof of a covered wagon fixed to avoid water damage. "The old wagons blended into the gloominess. There was a waterproofed texas someone had made by raising a pole underneath the cloth, high in the center so water would run downward instead of accumulating in the center of the top, causing a hazardous sag . . . Everything seasoned rangemen could do to mitigate dampness had been done . . ." [Lauran Paine, *The Open Range Men*, 1990]

Texas The state of Texas takes its name from a Caddo Indian word meaning "friends or allies" (written *texas, texios, tejas, teyas*) applied to the Caddos by the Spanish in eastern Texas, who regarded them as friends and allies against the Apaches. Westerners, especially Texans, vary in their pronunciation of *Texas*. The leading contenders among Texans are *Tex-siz* and *Tex-sis*, with the Yankee *Tex-suhs* a distant third. Texas was admitted to the Union in 1845 as our 28th state.

Texas bluebonnet See BLUE-
BONNET.

Texas blueweed The Southwestern
sunflower *Helianthus ciliaris.*

Texas brag See quote. " 'He'll tell
you everything was originally made
in Texas. Texas brag. Worse than the
Russians.' " [Edna Ferber, *Giant*,
1952]

Texas butter An old term for a
gravy made of flour and animal fat.

Texas coaster See COASTER.

Texas fandango A variation on the
FANDANGO. "Jack Omohundro
danced a Texas fandango with her."
[Larry McMurtry, *Buffalo Girls*, 1990]

Texas fever (1) A fever of cattle
transmitted by a cattle tick *(Margera-
pees annulatus)* much feared in the
early West; also called *Texas mur-
rain, Spanish fever* and *fever.* (2) The
extreme desire to emigrate to Texas,
an expression common in the late
19th century.

Texas Independence Day March 2,
the anniversary of the independence
of Texas from Mexico in 1836 and
the birthday of Texan hero Sam
Houston as well.

Texasism Any expression peculiar
to Texas; the term has been used
since the mid-19th century.

Texas leaguer A cheap hit that falls
between the infield and the outfield
in baseball is called a Texas leaguer

because back in 1886 three players
who had been traded up to the ma-
jors from a Texas league team enabled Toledo to beat Syracuse by
repeatedly getting such hits. After
the game, the disgusted Syracuse
pitcher described the hits as just "little old dinky Texas leaguers" and the
name stuck.

Texas longhorn A once-common
breed of Southwestern beef cattle developed from cattle introduced from
Spain and noted for their fecundity
and resistance to disease. Also
called *coaster.*

Texas pony A cow pony.

Texas r "But there was another heritage that marked Texans far from
home, their Texas way of speaking;
the way they used a soft *r*, the way
they flavored their speech with Spanish words or Spanish curses, the way
they had of rarely raising their
voices, and this latter characteristic
had filled many an unmarked cow-
camp grave, because in a land of
violent, vociferous men, that soft-
spoken Texas drawl just didn't seem
to register deadliness." [Lauran
Paine, *Frontier Steel*, 1981]

Texas Ranger (1) A member of the
Texas state police force. (2) In days
past, a member of the mounted state
police. (3) A member of a group of
Texas settlers organized to maintain
order.

Texas sage A scarlet-flowered hairy
plant *(Salvia coccinea)* of the mint
family native to the Southwest.

Texas-size Large, big. "I've got a Texas-size headache."

Texas-star boots High-heeled leather boots with stars at the top for decoration.

Texas tea Another name for MARIJUANA. (2) A humorous name for oil.

Texas turkey A humorous name for the common armadillo.

Texas twist An intricate twist in the horns of Texas longhorn cattle, whose "rocking chair" horns can often measure over 77 inches. "And what made this bull additionally attractive were the cows and steers sired by him, their horns showing the Texas twist, some to such an exaggerated degree that they were museum pieces." [James A. Michener, *Texas*, 1985]

Texas wedge A humorous golfing term not for a wedge club but for a putter "when it can be used for a short approach shot over very flat rather bare ground, as might be found in Texas," according to Stuart Berg Flexner in *Listening to America* (1982).

Texian; Texican Old term for a Texan.

Tex-Mex This word, dating back to about 1945, means of or pertaining to aspects of culture developed in Texas but based on or strongly influenced by Mexican elements, such as Tex-Mex cooking.

thang cue A common pronunciation of *thank you.*

thank A pronunciation of *think.* See usage example at TOLT.

thankee An old-fashioned form of *thank you.* " 'Thankee. Sure feels better by this fire, I'll tell you.' " [Frank Roderus, *Hell Creek Cabin,* 1979]

thank you much Thanks a lot. "Joe got the money out of his shirt and reached it to him. 'Thank you much,' said the old man." [Thomas McGuane, *Keep the Change,* 1989]

that Sometimes used redundantly in phrases such as "Because that I couldn't go."

thataway That way. " 'Take half of the men and make a big circle thataway.' He indicated with a sweep of his hand a circle that would start toward the south, swing west, then come in from the north." [Sam Brown, *The Crime of Coy Bell,* 1992]

that damned cowboy Vice-President Theodore Roosevelt, who had been a North Dakota rancher from 1884 to 1886 and formed a cowboy "Rough Riders" unit during the Spanish-American War, became president of the United States in 1901 when William McKinley was assassinated. Political boss Senator Mark Hanna's comment was "Now look, that damned cowboy is president."

that don't mean pig pee That means nothing at all; an expression heard by the writer in an Austin, Texas bar.

that's all she wrote There's no more, that's all there is. Possibly referring to a "Dear John letter," this phrase became popular in the West during or just after World War II and is now used nationally.

that's where the West begins An expression from Arthur Chapman's poem "Out Where the West Begins," the refrain of which goes: "Out where the handclasp's a little stronger,/ Out where the smile dwells a little longer,/ That's where the West begins."

that there That. "That there horse is mine."

them The; those. "He took one of them horses."

them there Those. "Where are them there horses?"

there ain't no horse that can't be rode,/ there ain't no man that can't be throwed An old Western saying.

there's a one-eyed man in the game Watch out for a cheat. The expression had its origins in poker, from an old superstition that it was unlucky to play cards with a one-eyed gambler.

there's more difference within the breeds than between them See quote. "But hell, they were cows. Breed was a small matter . . . Char-lie always remembered what old-time cattle buyer E. W. Nicodemus had told him: 'There's more difference *within* the breeds than ever there was *between* them.' " [Elmer Kelton, *The Time It Never Rained,* 1973]

there's nothing in the middle of the road but yellow stripes and dead armadillos A warning against excessive moderation; attributed to Texas politician Jim Hightower.

these yere These. "These yere horses are mine."

the three B's A proverb once taught in Western schoolrooms: "Be kind, be thoughtful and be yourself."

thisaway This way. "We come 10 miles thisaway."

this child Used by a speaker to mean himself or herself. "This child's not going to be there no matter how many people come."

thish-yer This here. " 'Well, this-yer Smiley had a yaller one-eyed cow that didn't have no tail, only just a short stump like a bannanner . . .'" [Mark Twain, "The Celebrated Jumping Frog of Calaveras County," 1865]

this'n This one. " 'You ever eat a jackrabbit?' said Rawlins . . . 'You better rustle some more wood if you aim to eat this'n.' " [Cormac McCarthy, *All the Pretty Horses,* 1992]

thoughty Thoughtful. "That was mighty thoughty of you."

'thout (1) A contraction of *without* commonly heard in the West. "He wouldn't go 'thout his dog." (2) Unless. "I wouldn't go 'thout he came and got me."

thowed Common pronunciation of *throwed*. " 'You ain't ridin' with us,' said Rawlins. 'You'll get us thowed in the jailhouse.' " [Cormac McCarthy, *All the Pretty Horses*, 1992]

3-7-77 The numerals 3-7-77, accompanied by a skull and crossbones, were first used by Montana vigilantes to warn a man to leave the county; the measurement three feet wide, seven feet long and 77 inches deep is roughly that of a grave.

throwed (1) Often used instead of *throw* in a past tense usage and instead of *threw*. "When did you throwed it away?" "I throwed it away yesterday." (2) Shocked, disturbed, knocked off balance like a roped steer or horse. " 'Well say, Bick, I sure was throwed when I heard the news.' " [Edna Ferber, *Giant*, 1952]

throws a big loop A man who throws a big loop is a cattle thief or rustler, the "big loop" referring of course to his lasso roping in more than it should.

thumb See THUMBER.

thumb-buster An outdated, inefficient gun. " 'What did you bring to shoot?' said Rawlins. 'Just Grandad's old thumb-buster.' " [Cormac McCarthy, *All the Pretty Horses*, 1992]

thumber A shooter, opting for speed rather than accuracy, who thumbs or fans his gun by pulling back and releasing the hammer with his thumb instead of pulling the trigger.

thundermug A bedpan. "May laughed and picked the dreadful thing up . . . 'What's wrong, Prof? Never saw a thundermug in your life?' " [A. B. Guthrie Jr., *Arfive*, 1970]

Thu'sday A pronunciation of *Thursday*.

tidies Protective coverings for the backs of chairs. "There were fresh doilies on the marble-top tables and clean tidies on the chair backs." [Conrad Richter, *The Sea Of Grass*, 1937]

tienda A Spanish word used in the Southwest for a store or shop.

tie one to that! Beat that one if you can!, an expression mainly used after someone has told a wild tale or recited an improbable fact.

tiger shits Cowboy slang for very rough country like the South Dakota badlands. "We rode through the tiger shits yesterday."

tigers of the desert A nickname for the Apaches.

tighter than the bark on a tree An old expression applied to a very cheap person. "If you wasn't tighter than the bark on a tree, your wife wouldn't have to do her own washing." [*American Magazine*, November 1913]

till rattlers get tame Forever. " 'You could try till rattlers got tame, but it'd take ten like you to make one like Hal." [Max Brand, *Riders of the Silences*, 1919]

timber beast A colorful term for a logger or lumberjack that was once common in Oregon and Washington.

times, ver' quiet, ver' soft, like summer night, but when she mad she blaze A poetic term said to be "the Indian equivalent for firefly" by Mark Twain in his short story "A Horse's Tale" (1906).

time to whistle up the dogs and piss on the fire Time to leave. " 'Well, son,' he said, 'it's time to whistle up the dogs and piss on the fire. Have a good summer . . .' " [Thomas McGuane, *Keep the Change*, 1989]

tin (1) Synonymous with *can* since the early days of the West, when the country was already littered with them, as this quote from Owen Wister's *The Virginian* (1902) shows: "These picnic pots and cans were the first of her trophies that Civilization dropped upon Wyoming's virgin soil. The cowboy is now gone to worlds invisible: the wind has blown away the white ashes of his campfires; but the empty sardine box lies rusting on the face of the Western earth." (2) A pronunciation of *ten*.

tinhorn gambler In chuck-a-luck, an ancient dice game very popular during the California gold rush, gamblers bet against the house that all three dice used would read the same when rolled or that the sum of all three dice would equal a certain number or that one of the three dice would turn up a specified number. It is a monotonous game and was looked down upon by players of faro, a more complicated and costly pastime. Faro operators coined the name *tinhorn gamblers* for *chuck-a-luck* players, giving us the expression for any cheap gambler. Pulitzer Prize winner George Williston explained how in his book *Here They Found Gold* (1931): "Chuck-a-luck operators shake their dice in a 'small churn-like affair of metal'—hence the expression 'tinhorn gambler,' for the game is rather looked down upon as one for 'chubbers' (fools) and chuck-a-luck gamblers are never admitted within the aristocratic circles of faro dealers." The expression is commonly used throughout the United States today.

tinnis A pronunciation of *tennis*.

Tio Taco A recent slang expression for a Mexican-American who is accused of being servile to whites by other Mexican-Americans. It literally translates as "Uncle Taco." See also *Uncle Tomahawk*.

tiswin An intoxicating drink brewed and drunk by Apache Indians.

ti yi yee, ti yi yi yay A cowboy cry, as in this old folk song stanza quoted by Kerry Newcomb in *Morning Star* (1983):

So come on you dogies
It's late in the day
Sing ti yi yee
Ti yi yi yay.

tobacker A pronunciation of *tobacco.*

tol'able well Tolerably. "We're doin' tol'able well. How's things out your way?"

tolerable Tolerably; rather. "It's tolerable wet today."

tolt A pronunciation of *told.* " 'I tolt you,' he said. 'It's all you thank about.' " [Larry McMurtry, *Cadillac Jack,* 1982]

tongue oil In a continuing quest for synonyms for whiskey and other strong drink, I've come upon *tongue oil* several times. It's a Western expression dating back perhaps to the mid-19th century and obviously refers to the way spirits loosen one's tongue.

tonsil varnish An old cowboy name for cheap whiskey.

Tonto (1) Tonto, the name of the fabled Lone Ranger's sidekick, was a name indiscriminately given by the Spanish to several Indian tribes, including the Tonto Apaches. Tonto is the Spanish word meaning "fool" but reflects the ignorance and foolishness of the namers rather than the named. (2) An old term for Indians who have broken with traditions and are looked down upon by their tribes. ". . . Glanton and his men were host to a motley collection of citizens and soldiers and reduced Indians or tontos as their brothers outside the gates." [Cormac McCarthy, *Blood Meridian, or, The Evening Redness in the West,* 1985]

too brittle to bend Not adaptable to change; unable to bend with the wind. "I'm too old . . . and too brittle to bend." [Elmer Kelton, *The Time It Never Rained,* 1973]

too lazy to work and too nervous to steal Said of any totally useless no-account person.

toolhouse A tool shed.

too much mustard Used to describe someone very disagreeable and contentious. "He's got too much mustard."

too thick to drink and too thin to plow Muddy, unpalatable water.

toothpick Another name for the BOWIE KNIFE, also called an *Arkansas toothpick* and a *California toothpick.*

top screw An assistant ranch foreman.

tore Torn. "It was all tore up."

toro The Spanish word for bull; commonly used in the Southwest.

tortilla Spanish for a thin, round unleavened bread made from corn or wheat flour and baked on a flat iron plate or the like.

tote To carry. "He toted the sack up the hill."

trade rat Another name for the packrat or wood rat of the genus *Neatoma* that collect in or near their nests a great variety of small objects.

trail (1) A road made by the repeated passage of animals or people. (2) A cattle trail. (3) A specific trail, such as the Santa Fe Trail.

trail broken Cows used to walking on the trail.

trailin'est See usage example at RUNNIN'EST.

Trail of Tears See quote. "Tears came to his own eyes when he spoke of that blot on southern civilization, The Trail of Tears, in which the Cherokees, a peaceful and home-loving Indian tribe, were torn (1838–39) from the land which a government had given them by sworn treaty to be sent far away on a marsh which, from cold, hunger, exposure, and heartbreak, was marked by bleaching bones from Georgia to Oklahoma." [Edna Ferber, *Cimarron*, 1930]

trail waddy A cowboy. See also WADDY.

trap a squaw An old humorous expression meaning to get married.

trapper One who trapped animals, especially beaver, in the early West. "Your hunter is a man of temperament. He is an artist. He lives under a tension. But your trapper is a strategist." [Max Brand, *The Fastest Draw*, 1925]

traveler's friend Another name for the COMPASS CACTUS.

travois An Indian conveyance for goods and belongings pulled by a horse or dog. "Sam Joseph returned with two neatly trimmed travois poles. Dolan took the ax from him and cut several smaller trees to use for crosspieces. He got blankets from behind his saddle. Now, with Frank's rope, with the poles and blankets, with leather strips cut from the rear cinch of his own double-rigged saddle, he made a travois. After saddling Dunklee's horse, he lashed it in place." [Lewis B. Patten, *Posse From Poison Creek*, 1969]

Treasure State A nickname for Montana.

tree dozer See STINGER.

tree yucca See JOSHUA TREE.

true grit Unflinching courage or determination in a person.

T.T.T. Initials often seen on temperance wagons in the early West meaning the owner is a "tea-totaller."

tub A metal container that holds water. See also TANK.

tuckered out Very tired; an expression heard in other regions as well. " 'Is he dead?' Newt asked . . . 'No, just tuckered out,' Cal said." [Larry McMurtry, *Lonesome Dove,* 1985]

tule land A term used in Northern California for marshy, swampy land, from the Nahuatl *tollin* (bulrush), which grows in such low swampy areas. A Western region overgrown with these bulrushes is also called a *tule* and *tule swamp*.

tumbadore The Spanish name for cowboys or vacqueros who throw or tumble calves to be branded. " 'The men who are throwing the calves— they're called tumbadores . . . It looks like a feat of strength but they're not really lifting those calves. You squeeze the calf's ear, it jumps, you pull him sideways and he falls flat on his right side with his left side up, ready for branding.' " [Edna Ferber, *Giant,* 1952]

tumbleweed Any of several plants, including the *Amaranthus* genus and Russian thistle *(Salsola kali),* whose branching upper parts come loose from the roots and are driven by the wind across the prairie. The plant, like sagebrush, has become a symbol of the West, as in song lyrics such as "tumbling along with the tumbling tumble weed." One old belief has it that God put tumbleweed here to show cowboys which way the wind is blowing. More amusing perhaps is the "tumbleweed stampede" in Larry McMurtry's novel *Texasville* (1987), where he describes a field of marathon runners attacked by the "killer weeds" after an extraordinary wind breaks "thousands and thousands of them . . . loose from the thin soil . . ." and they cover "the whole plain solidly, as the herds of buffalo had once been said to cover it."

turd-floater A very heavy rain. "Unfortunately a rare downpour had occurred . . . It had been a real turd-floater . . ." [Larry McMurtry, *Lonesome Dove,* 1985]

turnaround A pioneer who, out of fear or hardship, turned back home after heading west. "McKeag said, 'I never figured you for a turnaround.' " [James Michener, *Centennial,* 1974]

turn loose To fire a gun. "He turned loose his gun on them."

turrible A pronunciation of *terrible*.

two-gun toter See usage example at RIP-SNORTING.

two whoops and a holler A short distance, not far, "within spitting range." The phrase probably dates back to the late 19th century.

tyee Chinook jargon used in the early Northwest for chief, boss, king.

U

ugh! There is no record of an American Indian ever uttering the sound ugh! when he or she meant "yes" or "hello." The term can be traced to dime romances about the American West popular at the turn of the century, its use perpetuated by early American motion pictures. As a sound of contempt and disgust, *ugh* is first recorded in 1837 but is probably much older. See also **a.**

ugly stick See WORKED OVER WITH THE UGLY STICK.

Uncle Tomahawk Recent slang for an American Indian who is accused of being servile to whites by other Indians; patterned on the older familiar term "Uncle Tom." See also TIO TACO.

uncombed Unkempt, dirty, disheveled. " 'He's a big, uncombed man, a brute.' " [Louis L'Amour, *Comstock Lode* 1981]

under a flag Said of someone living under an assumed name or alias.

until the last dog is hung Until the end, usually heard in reference to someone staying at a party until the very last. "We were there until the last dog was hung." The expression is first recorded in Stewart Edward White's Western novel *The Blazed Trail* (1902), and the hanged "dogs" in it probably referred to hanged men.

unwind To buck; said of a horse. "The horse unwound and threw her."

up To act suddenly, impulsively. "She up and run off with him."

up and down as a cow's tail Honest and forthright. "He's as up and down as a cow's tail."

up Green River When American mountain men killed a man a century ago, they sent him *up Green River,* this referring not directly to Wyoming's Green River but to the common Green River knives used in many a fight. They were called that because they were made at the Green River works and stamped with that designation. See also UP TO GREEN RIVER.

up Shit Creek without a bullboat An early Western expression for a futile situation, conveying the same idea as the better-known *up shit creek without a paddle.* A bullboat was a lightweight boat used by fur traders.

up to Green River Anything effective was once said to be *up to Green River* in the West because excellent knives used by hunters and trappers were made at the Green River works in the Western Territory. See also UP GREEN RIVER.

used to Formerly. "Used to, we'd stay out in the field till sundown."

used to could Used to be able to. "I used to could get around better'n I do now."

Utah Utah takes its name from the fierce proud Indian tribe called the Utes that resided there and whose name meant "hill dwellers." In 1850 the area encompassing present-day Utah constituted the Utah Territory, the colorful Mormon name for it, *Deseret*, or "honeybee," being rejected by Congress. Utah became our 45th State in 1896.

Utahan A native of Utah; also *Utahian, Utahn*.

V

vaca The Spanish word for cow, sometimes used by cowboys in the early Southwest.

vag To arrest for vagrancy. "They vagged him last night and threw him in the hoosegow."

vámonos Let's go; borrowed from the Spanish.

vamoose Leave quickly. "He vamoosed out of there." From the Spanish vamos, (let's go).

vaquero A direct borrowing of the Spanish word for a ranch hand or cowboy that Westerners were using as early as 1800. Buckaroo, meaning the same, is an English corruption of vaquero also used in the West, though in Texas the buckaroo is a roaming bachelor cowboy, and in California a buckaroo is a cowboy born or raised on a ranch and living there with his family.

variable hare See quote. "A rabbit as large as a spaniel flushed from a clump of grass . . . The variable hare . . . The jack rabbit of the high plains." [A. B. Guthrie Jr., Arfive, 1970]

varmint Though used in the West, varmint is not an Americanism, as one would think from scores of Westerns. The word for an animal pest or a despicable person is a corruption of vermin and of British origin. Vermin comes from the Latin vermis (worm).

varmint stew A stew made from animals usually not used for food. " 'This is my varmint stew,' Captain Maude said. '[Made from] whatever the dogs catch . . . or the dogs themselves, if they don't manage to catch nothing.' " [Larry McMurtry, Lonesome Dove, 1985]

vaya con Dios Go with God, a Spanish term commonly heard in the Southwest.

vecino A Spanish word that is used in the Southwest as a derogatory term for a Mexican or Hispanic.

vega An old word for a large plain, valley or meadow; from a Spanish word meaning the same.

veranda See PORCH.

verbena See quote. ". . . that low-growing purple verbena which mats over the hills of New Mexico. It was like a great violet velvet mantle thrown down in the sun . . . the violet that is full of rose colour and is yet not lavender; the blue that becomes almost pink and then re-

treats again into sea-dark purple
. . ." [Willa Cather, *Death Comes for the Archbishop,* 1927]

verdin A small yellow-headed bird *(Auriparus flaviceps)* of the Southwestern desert.

very dinky, the Something, usually something inanimate, that is the height of perfection. "Boy, that new saw is the very dinky." Also *the very dinkum.*

vinegaroon A large nonpoisonous whip scorpion of the Southwest that emits a fluid with a vinegary odor when disturbed.

visit with you Speak to or with on the phone. "Ah need to visit with you."

vittles An old term for food.

vomito A Southwestern term, from a Spanish word meaning the same, for a virulent form of yellow fever often accompanied by black vomit.

vouchers See quote. "Indian fighters with 'vouchers,' as they called the scalps dangling from their belts, paraded the streets [of San Antonio c. 1876]." [J. Frank Dobie, *Coronado's Children,* 1930]

voyageur An expert boatsman, woodsman and guide, often French Canadian, who transported people or goods in the early Northwest.

W

waddy Any honest cowhand, though *waddy* originally meant a cattle rustler; the word's origin is unknown. " 'This is how it was with the old waddies, ain't it?' " [Cormac McCarthy, *All the Pretty Horses,* 1992]

wagon boss The person in charge of a WAGON TRAIN.

wagon mound A hill that resembles the top of a covered wagon; used as a place name in the past.

wagon train A historical term for wagons traveling together in transporting settlers and goods West.

wait on (1) Wait for, await. "What are you waiting on?" (2) Said of a doctor who attends his patients. "The doc's waitin' on him."

wal A very common pronunciation of *well.* "Wal, I got to get going now."

Walker Colt See quote. "[Captain Sam Walker] sketched a picture of the battle of Pedernales, with himself on a black horse and El Diablo Hays on a white one. He sent the drawing to Samuel Colt, who had a die made of it. The scene became part of the cylinder on each nine-inch long, four-and-a-half-pound six-shooter, the Walker Colt." [Lucia St. Clair Robson, *Ride the Wind,* 1982]

walkin'-around longhorns A name given to prize Texas longhorns (whose "rocking chair" horns can measure more than 77 inches from tip to tip) kept as "pets" by rich Texans. " 'We call them 'walkin'-around Longhorns,' the man said. 'We buy them to adorn our ranches so women can "Oh!" and "Ah!" when they come out to see us from Houston or Dallas.' " [James A. Michener, *Texas,* 1985]

walking-stick cholla See CANE CHOLLA.

walking treaty A treaty in which the land granted was measured by the time it took to walk across it; Indians often sold land this way.

waltz through handsome Take especially good care of. " '. . . we want to give him a good send-off, and so the thing I'm on now is to roust somebody to jerk a little chin-music fer us and waltz him through handsome.' " [Mark Twain, "Buck Fanshaw's Funeral," 1872]

wa'n't A pronunciation of *wasn't.* "He wa'n't there."

want no truck with To want nothing to do with. " 'No wild animal wants no truck with a man.' " [Louis L'Amour, *Hondo*, 1953]

war A pronunciation of *was*. "It war too damp in East Texas."

warn't Wasn't. " 'I remember the big flume warn't finished when he first come to the camp.' " [Mark Twain, "The Celebrated Jumping Frog of Calaveras County," 1865]

warsh A pronunciation of *wash*.

Washoe The former name of the territory that became Nevada; from the name of the Washoe Indians of the region. "Washoe is a pet nickname for Nevada." [Mark Twain, *Roughing It*, 1872]

Washoeites A name for the miners who rushed to Nevada silver mines when the Comstock lode was discovered in 1859. See also WASHOE.

watch your hair A humorous farewell in the early west, referring of course to scalping by Indians. " 'See you around, John Selman. Watch your hair.' " [Gene Shelton, *Last Gun*, 1991]

watermillion Sometimes heard as a pronunciation of *watermelon*. "When men reached this area [Rattlesnake Buttes in Colorado] . . . they would sometimes in autumn stumble upon such a ball of writhing snakes [twisted together]—'they was as big as a watermillion'—and they would

be horrified . . ." [James A. Michener, *Centennial*, 1974]

water-shy Said of a person who doesn't wash much and looks and smells it.

water witcher One who divines water with a forked stick.

wawa A historical term for talk, speech; from Chinook jargon.

wax Chewing gum, especially in East Texas. "You got any wax?"

weaner A word used in the Rocky Mountains for a newly weaned animal such as a calf or pig; the term possibly originated in Australia.

wear Endurance. " 'If there's enough wear in you, you'll be the man for me.' " [Max Brand, *War Party*, 1934]

wearing calluses on his elbows Spending time in a saloon, according to *Western Words* (1961 edition) by Ramon F. Adams. Similarly, an *elbow bender*, another term from the Old West, means a "drinking man," because he bends his elbow to convey his glass to his lips.

wear the blanket See BLANKET INDIAN.

webfoot A humorous name for anyone from Oregon, because of the state's long winter rains, perfect for web-footed ducks.

well-greased Well thought out, planned. " 'A well-greased idea,' says the sheriff, admiring, 'to slip off down here and buy a little sheepranch where the hand of men is seldom heard. It was the slickest hideout I ever see.' " [O. Henry, "The Hiding of Black Bill" in *The Best Short Stories of O. Henry,* 1945]

well-heeled See HEEL.

well, I'm a hollow-horn A common exclamation. " 'Well, I'm a hollow horn! I sure didn't go fer to hurt your feelings.' " [Edna Ferber, *Giant,* 1952]

went Often used instead of gone. "She's went home."

West Generally used in the United States today to mean the region west of the Mississippi River. The term Westerner for someone who lives in the region west of the Mississippi is first recorded in 1835.

Westering A term used by pioneers meaning to travel West.

Western A term used since about 1929 for a movie or novel about the West, especially one featuring cowboys and Indians.

westerner See WEST.

Westernism A word or expression peculiar to the West; first recorded in 1837.

Western omelet See DENVER OMELET.

Western saddle See COWBOY SADDLE.

Western sandwich A sandwich made of an omelet with onions, green peppers and chopped ham between slices of bread or toast; also called a *Denver sandwich.*

wetback A Mexican immigrant or worker who illegally crosses the Rio Grande into the United States, sometimes swimming to get across; the term is a relatively recent one, first recorded in 1948.

wet bars and dry trails I've heard it said that many a cowboy's life was wet bars and dry trails. This may be a Western folk saying, or it may have been coined by Conrad Richter in his *The Sea of Grass* (1936), the only place I can find it recorded.

wet Chinook See CHINOOK.

wet stock Rustled horses that were smuggled across the Rio Grande in one direction or another. *Wet pony* is a similar expression.

whaleback See BALDHEAD.

Wham The fictional "explosive" town in which is set the classic Western *Destry Rides Again.* " 'Lil' ol' town, you don't amount to much,' said Harry Destry. 'You never done nothin' an' you ain't gunna come to no good. Doggone me if you ain't pretty much like me!' " [Max Brand, *Destry Rides Again,* 1930]

wham bam, thank you, ma'am An act of quick sexual intercourse; the expression is first recorded in the Southwest.

whang leather Long narrow strips of leather used to make saddle strings and for other purposes. "I can still see his bedroom . . . with a fancy horsehair bridle and ropes on the wall, and a brown buckskin partly cut away in strips for whang leather." [Conrad Richter, *The Sea of Grass,* 1937]

whar A pronunciation of *where.* "Whar are you going?"

what for (1) What sort of (a), what kind of (a). "What for a day it's going to be?" (2) Hell. "Twenty-odd of us stood off more'n two hundred . . . We gave 'em what-for, we did." [Louis L'Amour, *The Lonesome Gods,* 1983]

what I mean I mean. "Get out of here. In a hurry, what I mean."

whatness Equal size. "They're of a whatness."

what's your hand read? Who employs you, where do you belong, where do you stand; after a hand in cards. "What's your hand read, Lando? You a company man?" [Louis L'Amour, *Showdown at Yellow Butte,* 1953]

wheat ranch A large Western ranch on which wheat is grown.

wheel barrel A folk-etymology of *wheel barrow* heard in northern California, Texas and other places in the West.

wheeler dealer In gaming houses of the 18th-century American West, a big wheeler and dealer was a heavy better at cards and the roulette wheels. Through this tradition and the association of a *big wheel* as the man (or wheel) who makes the vehicle (things) run, the expression came to mean a big-time operator by the early 1940s, usually with an unsavory connotation, the *wheeler dealer* being the type who runs over anything in his path with no regard for rules of the road.

whelp A welt. "He raised whelps on him."

when good Texans die, they go to Colorado An old Colorado saying quoted in James Michener's *Texas* (1985).

when you call me that, smile! A famous Western and now national expression often heard as *Smile when you call me that* (or *say that*). It has its origins in one of the most famous scenes in American literature, in Owen Wister's *The Virginian* (1902), whose eponymous hero became the basis for American heroes like John Wayne. When called a "son-of-a———" by the saddlebum Trampas, "the Virginian's pistol came out, and his hand lay on the table, holding it unaimed. And with a voice as gentle as ever, the voice that sounded almost like a caress, but drawling a little more than usual, so that there was almost a space between each word, he issued his orders to the man Trampas:

" 'When you call me that smile!' And he looked at Trampas across the table.

"Yes the voice was gentle. But in my ears it seemed as if somewhere the bell of death was ringing."

Trampas, of course, backs down, *failing to draw his steel.*

where at's   Where is. " 'Where at's Buck?' "   [Edna Ferber, *Giant,* 1952]

whip   An old name for a stagecoach driver.

Whip of God   See quote. "With the men and the horses and the steers mingling and the ground near shaking with the rush, and the dust rising, a strange thing happened. This was that a red scut of blood like a hell-red rainbow came up from the center, shooting to the sky, then bending over and fanning away south. Some horn had slashed a big artery in a cow or horse. Times later I told a Mex about it, and he rolled his eyes and said it was the Whip of God. Said he had seen similar. It is possible he had."   [Charles O. Locke, *The Hell Bent Kid,* 1957]

white-bellied weasel   A weak, contemptible sneak. "That white-bellied weasel? Tell him when I'm ready for him I'll come an' get him. First I want him done brown by the sun. I don't like that pasty hide in front o'me."   [Louis L'Amour, *Kilkenny,* 1954]

white buffalo   (1) An Indian name adopted by settlers for the Rocky Mountain goat. (2) The rare white buffalo, which many Indian tribes treated as sacred.

white hats and black hats   Early Western silent movies dressed the hero in a white hat and the villain in a black hat to make it easier for the audience to follow the plot. Observed Louis L'Amour in an interview: "They joke about the black hats and the white hats, but there were very few grays in the West . . . There were a few men who shifted from one side of the law to the other, but by and large that was not true, they were just what they seemed to be."   [Appendix to the Bantam Book edition of *Comstock Lode,* 1982]

white person (man)   Used to describe someone better off, with more advantages, even better in general. A term insulting to other races, it is still used today, though much less frequently, and has some currency in other regions as well. The expression was common in the early West. " 'Drink some coffee, Joe,' she said. 'Get a cup. You'll feel like a white person in a minute.' "   [Richard Ford, *Wildlife,* 1990]

white wind   See quote. ". . . by a white wind No Ears meant a particular kind of blizzard, one that brought with it billions of particles of dry snow. The wind might blow for three days, swirling the snow so densely that it became impossible to see. The white wind confused everything. The best scouts refused to move in a white wind." [Larry McMurtry, *Buffalo Girls,* 1990]

who-all Who. "Who-all is going?"

whoa up Stop, wait, hold. "Hey, Charles Jay, whoa up a minute."

whoop-la An old expression for a noisy outburst or exclamation of delight that appears to have originated in the West. It may be of Indian origin as is suggested in its first recorded use by a writer, no friend of Indians or reality, in the *Silver City* (Idaho) *Avalanche,* March 4, 1874: "Whoop-la! There will be three hundred wild, wicked-eyed, scalp-yanking, entrail-eating, long-haired, blanketed Indians camped upon the Continental ground at Philadelphia."

whoop ti do A cowboy cry, as in this old cowboy song quoted by Edna Ferber in *Cimarron* (1930):

Hi rickety whoop ti do,
How I love to sing to you.
Oh, I could sing an' dance with glee,
If I was as young as I used to be.

who put Tabasco sauce in his oatmeal? Said of someone who suddenly becomes animated.

whut A pronunciation of *what.* " 'Whut Senator's wife?' Boog said." [Larry McMurtry, *Cadillac Jack,* 1982]

Wichita The Wichita Indians, and thus Wichita, Kansas, which is named for the tribe, may take their name from the tribe's word *wichita*

(waist-deep). One old story, which I can't verify, says that these Indians pushed their squaws out into rivers to see how deep they were. If a place was safe for crossing, the squaws would cry out "wichita" to the relatively timid braves on shore, who proceeded to ford the river. If they sank, presumably, the river wasn't safe to cross.

wickiup Indians in Colorado and California sometimes lived in crudely constructed huts called *wickiups,* improvised structures made of brush, saplings or both. White settlers often used the word in referring humorously to their own homes.

widder A pronunciation of *widow.* "Since she lost her husband, she was called the Widder Brown."

a wide place in the road A very small settlement that doesn't qualify even as a small town. "Blackwater . . . was little more than a wide place in the road waiting for the railroad to come to make it a town." [Frank O'Rourke, *Blackwater,* 1950]

wild and wooly West First came *wild West,* recorded in 1851 and so called because the American West was relatively lawless compared to the "civilized" East. Some 30 years passed before the more alliterative *wild and wooly West* was invented by some unknown poet, the *wooly* in the phrase perhaps referring to uncurried wild horses or the sheepskin chaps some cowboys wore or perhaps to the bragging of cowboys in a popular song:

I'm a wooly wolf and full of fleas,
I never been curried below the
knees—
And this is my night to howl!

The first use of the expression, in an 1885 book called *Texas Cow Boy,* has *wild and wooly* referring to a herd of steers.

a Wild Bill Hickok Any fabled gun-fighter; after James Butler "Wild Bill" Hickok (1837–76) army scout, gambler and town marshal of Abilene, Kansas. Though a handsome dandy, with long blond hair hanging over his shoulders, Hickok was first called "Duck Bill" after his long nose and protruding lip. He met his violent end at the hands of a paranoid rival who shot him in the back of the head while he was playing poker. See also DEADMAN'S HAND.

wildcat Any wildcat venture, such as a wildcat oil well, is generally a speculative one. The word *wildcat* here comes from the term *wildcat bank,* which originally referred to a bank that went bankrupt in the 1830s and had on its banknotes a prominent picture of a panther or wildcat.

wild Indian This derogatory expression was first applied to roaming Indians, as opposed to those settled in pueblos or villages and then given to Indians in general. The expression is first recorded in 1840 Texas.

wild West See WILD AND WOOLY WEST.

wild west show A circus of cowboys and Indians performing various feats ranging from riding to shooting, the words first applied to William F. (Buffalo Bill) Cody's Wild West Show, which opened at Omaha, Nebraska May 17, 1883.

wild, wooly and full o' fleas An old expression for a bonafide cowboy.

Winchester The cowboy's rifle, its full name the Winchester repeating rifle, developed and manufactured by Oliver Winchester's Winchester Arms Company in 1871.

windy See WINDY-MAKING.

windy-making The telling of tall tales, which were called *windies.* "Sometime, he decided he would like to meet a man whose tale involved [not a bear, but a] wolverine, say . . . Or think how much fun a man could have building one about a horde of enraged ground squirrels. Veach decided that if he ever wanted to go in for windy-making it would be something along those lines." [Frank Roderus, *Hell Creek Cabin,* 1979]

win one's spurs The allusion here is not to cowboys of the American West but to those days four centuries before when knighthood was in flower and young men dubbed knights by their lords were presented with a pair of gilded spurs. Since then the expression *to win one's spurs* has been extended from the idea of a knight performing a valorous act and winning honor to anyone performing any deed and gaining honor among his peers—from a doctor delivering his first baby to an author publishing his first book.

winter Texans Retired people, often from the North, who spend their winters in South Texas because of its mild climate.

wipe A cowboy's neckerchief.

wiser'n a tree full of owls Very wise. "Quimper could hardly be stopped, indulging in such Texas phrases as 'Wiser'n a tree full of owls'." [James A. Michener, *Texas*, 1985]

without Unless. "I wouldn't come along without I had the money."

withouten Without. " 'He does nothin' withouten a plan.' " [James A. Michener, *Texas*, 1985]

wo-haw An Indian expression for cattle that was adopted by cattlemen. The Indians derived the term from the "whoa! haw!" of ox team drivers as they crossed the plains heading West.

wolf See PRAIRIE WOLF.

wolfer A hunter of wolves in the early West.

wolfish An old trapper's term meaning hungry. "I was wolfish after that long ride."

won't stay shot Said of someone hard to kill, with great endurance or resiliency. "Bob is hard to kill. He won't stay shot." [Charles Portis, *True Grit*, 1968]

wooden tongue See LUMPY JAW.

wood house A word used in Central Texas for a woodshed where wood is stored.

wood pussy An old term used in California for a polecat.

woolies (1) See quote. "The broad plain south of the Clear Fork of the Brazos River was once dotted with buffalo. The great woolies were mostly gone now, slaughtered by hide hunters in the preceding decade." [G. Clifton Wisler, *The Return of Caulfield Blake*, 1987] (2) Another name for a sheep. " 'Won't take much to spook them woolies,' Tom Hunt said." [Jack Cummings, *The Rough Rider*, 1988] (3) Chaps made from sheepskin without the fleece (wool) removed. See also BAA-BAA; ANGORAS.

woolsey A cheap woolen hat.

woppering Said in the Northwest for something whopping, huge. "A woppering bear came out of the woods."

worked over with the ugly stick Beat up badly; often said of an ugly person. " 'You are a fine one to talk about looks. You look like somebody has worked you over with the ugly stick.' " [Charles Portis, *True Grit*, 1968]

workup A game of baseball played with only a few players.

worrit A pronunciation of *worried.* " 'I'm worrit about you, Jack,' he said, out of a clear blue eastern Oregon sky." [Larry McMurtry, *Cadillac Jack,* 1982]

wouldn't know him (her) from Adam's off-ox An old Western variation of the centuries-old expression *wouldn't know him (her) from Adam* (that is, wouldn't know or recognize him or her at all). An *off-ox* is the ox in a team on the right side of the driver.

wrangle To round up a herd of horses or cattle, to attend the REMUDA.

wrangler A herder, cowboy; first recorded in 1888.

Wrangler jeans The jeans brand of choice for a cowboy.

wranglings Arguments, fights, turmoil—physical or psychological. ". . . he was ready to start his trek through the wilderness . . . There he would settle into another, last year of life, sinking deeper and deeper into the woods, until the voices of the wind and the rivers cleansed from his mind the sound of human speech, human wranglings." [Max Brand, *Mountain Guns,* 1930]

wrathy Mad, full of wrath. "I made it certain I will not stand for this. That only makes him wrathy and he throws me around some more."

[Richard Matheson, *Journal of the Gun Years,* 1991]

wrinkled his spine Started to buck. "The horse wrinkled his spine and threw her."

wrinkle-horn An old steer. " 'Let's get that wrinkle-horn out first,' Benton said . . . They struggled out . . . toward the older steer with its wrinkled, scaly horns." [Richard Matheson, *The Gun Fight,* 1993]

wrote Written. "It was all wrote up in the paper."

wunst A pronunciation of *once.*

a Wyatt Earp A fabled gunfighter; after Wyatt Barry Stapp Earp (1848–1929), most famous for his part in the 1879 gunfight at the O. K. Corral in Tombstone, Arizona. Considered quick on the draw (from a leather-lined waxed coat pocket), Earp was never bested and died quietly in his sleep, one of the two legendary Western gunfighters who definitely didn't meet a violent end (Bat Masterson was the other one).

Wyoming Wyoming takes its name from an Algonquin Indian name meaning "big flats" that was first given to a valley in Pennsylvania. Because of the popularity of Scottish poet Thomas Campbell's poem "Gertrude of Wyoming" (1809), the name was taken by several Eastern and Southern towns, and finally, in 1868, Ohio representative James M. Ashley of the Committee on Territories gave it to the area we now know as the state of Wyoming. An Eastern Indian name for a Western area may have been inappropriate, but "big flats" seemed right for this plains territory. It became our 44th state in 1890.

X

xat A Haida Indian word for the carved totem pole of many North American Indian tribes.

xerga A saddlecloth placed over a sheepskin on a pack animal's back; from the Spanish *jerga* meaning the same.

XIT A 3 million acre Texas ranch in the Panhandle. It was started by 10 Chicago investors in the 1870s (thus the initials XIT, "Ten in Texas"), but went out of business in 1901. (See KING RANCH.)

Y

ya-hoo! cake A cake made of cherries, chocolate, pecans, sugar and other ingredients that is said to have been invented by a cook on the Chisholm Trail, proving so good that the cowboys who were served it shouted "ya-hoo!" in unison on tasting it. The Original Texas Ya-Hoo Cake Company, which now bakes it commercially, claims that "both the story and recipe were discovered written on a piece of boot sole leather stuffed underneath the floorboards of an old cook wagon."

yakima An Indian pony.

y'all all come! An enthusiastic invitation often heard in Texas. "Y'all all come now."

yaw-ways At an angle, slantways.

year Sometimes heard for *ear,* as in "a mule-yeared rabbit."

yedra An old Southwestern word for poison ivy; from the Spanish word meaning the same.

yeller A pronunciation of *yellow.*

Yellow dog A coward, from the old belief that a yellow dog is cowardly. " 'You're a yellow dawg, Weaver,' Martin said, not moving a muscle."

[Norford Scott, *Big Lonesome,* 1967]

Yellow Dog Republican "From the Civil War on a term applied in Texas to loyal Democrats, so named, the legend goes, because they would vote for a yellow dog before they would vote for any Republican," according to the *New York Times* (June 8, 1993).

yellow janders See JANDERS.

Yellowstone National Park The *Yellowstone* here is an anglicization of the French *roche jaune* (yellow rock), which was probably a translation of the Minnataree Indian name *Mitsia-dazi* meaning the same.

yellow streak (stripe) down the back Descriptive of a cowardly person. "He has a yellow streak an inch wide down his back."

Yerba Buena An old name for San Francisco; so named from the Spanish for "good grass" because the area had excellent pasturage for animals.

yippie-ki-yi-yay A cry of cowboys, perhaps in part suggested by the cry of a coyote. *Yip* for a short high-pitched human cry is first recorded in the West: "They chase 'em, with wild whoops and yips over the undulatin' reservation." [Herbert Quick, *Yellowstone Nights,* 1911] *Yip* for a dog's bark is recorded as early as 1400. See also KI-YI.

yonder Over there. "Is that cafe yonder open?" [Cormac McCarthy, *All the Pretty Horses,* 1992]

Yosemite Yosemite Valley and Yosemite National Park are said to take their name from a distortion of the Miwok Indian *uzumaiti* (grizzly bear), a word the Indians never used for the area.

you-all Though mainly associated with the South, *you-all* is also used in the West for the plural *you,* as in "You-all be sure to come."

you-all's Your. "Can I borrow you-all's car?"

you bet! Of course, for sure, that's right. "Slang was the language of Nevada . . . Such phrases as 'You bet!' . . . and a hundred others, became so common as to fall from the lips of a speaker unconsciously." [Mark Twain, "Buck Fanshaw's Funeral," 1872]

you can bet your bottom dollar Originated out West about 1857, these words, meaning to bet one's last dollar or money, referred originally to the last silver dollar in a stack or hoard of coins and came eventually to mean the last of one's resources.

you can drive a nail on that You can be certain of it. " 'Jeff's a friend of mine and you can drive a nail on that.' " [Jack Schaefer, *The Kean Land,* 1953]

you can play with my dog, you can play with my wife, but you'd better leave my gun alone A humorous Texas saying, possibly of recent vintage.

you caught me speedin' A common saying of Texas politicians caught in a lie.

you dance with them what brung you A classic line used by Texas legislators in explaining why they have to vote for bills sponsored by certain lobbyists or special interest groups.

youngberry A cultivated variety of the Southwestern blackberry *(Rubus ursinus)* named after hybridizer B. M. Young, who developed it in about 1900.

your all's A Texan variation of *you all's.* "I'll get your all's bread," says a waitress in Cormac McCarthy's *All the Pretty Horses* (1992). It is also found in the same author's *Blood Meridian, or, The Evening Redness in the West* (1985): " 'Where's your all's horses?' said Glanton."

you're lookin' for a marble hat A warning to someone that he or she is courting death, the "marble hat" being a tombstone.

yucca Any plant of the genus *Yucca* native to the Southwest. Yucca, the state flower of New Mexico, has pointed sword-shaped leaves and bears clusters of white waxy flowers on tall stalks. See also AGAVE; JOSHUA TREE.

yucca country The Southwest.

Z

zanja   Spanish for a ditch or trench sometimes heard in the Southwest. "I led my horse to the *zanja* for water . . ." [Louis L'Amour, *The Lonesome Gods*, 1983]

zink   Heard in Texas for *sink*. "I cain't fix the kitchen zink."

Subject Index

Topics appear in **bold face**

O

P